Thunder

Over the Reich

Thunder
Over the Reich
Flying the Luftwaffe's He162 Jet Fighter

Wolfgang Wollenweber

This book is dedicated to my children and their descendants. May these lines remind them that we bear responsibility for all that we do. But also for that which we fail to do.

First published in 2012 by Helios Verlags und Buchvertriebsgesellschaft

This edition published in 2014 by Crécy Publishing

ISBN 9781902109398

Printed in China

Crécy Publishing Limited
1a Ringway Trading Estate, Shadowmoss Rd, Manchester M22 5LH
www.crecy.co.uk

Front cover drawing: Yellow 3 Werknummer 120 072. Profile copyright Simon Schatz based on an original drawing by Miroslav Billy and Michal Bradac.

Back cover drawing: Me 110F-2 `LN-TR' flown by Hauptmann Schlossstein. Claes Sundin

Contents

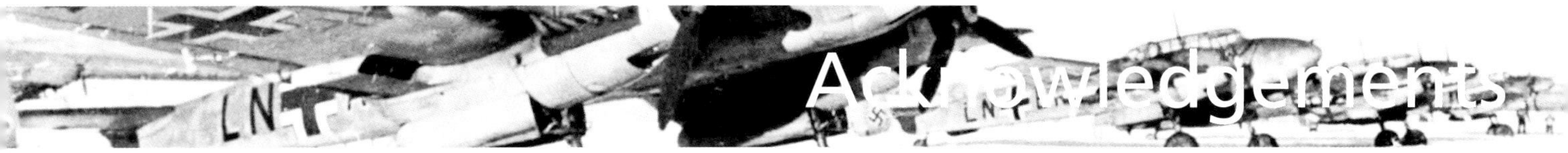

Acknowledgements

My special thanks go to Frau Nortrud de Vries; Frau Kyoko Uike, Switzerland; AK Junkerswerke and Fliegerhorst Bernburg; Messrs. Dave Ails, USA, Dieter Demmer, Michael Fluck; Oberst a.D. Wilhelm Göbel, Gemeinschaft der Flieger; Rudi Kurpiers; Legends Aviation, London; Christian Mayer, Austria; Eric Mombeek, Belgium; Karl Ostwald; Richard L. Reid, USA; Thomas Rübmann; Simon Schatz, Austria; Oberstleutnant a.D. Karl-Fritz Schlossstein; Prof. Dr. Dr. Holger Steinle, Deutsches Technik Museum Berlin; Nicholas Trudgian, England; Traditionsverband der Eismeerjäger; Walter Waiss, Traditionsgemeinschaft Boelcke e.V., and to my biographer, Horst Kube, without whom this book would not have been written.

To all those persons or institutions who have helped me in the writing of this book, but whose names I have neglected to mention, I offer both my humble apologies and my most sincere thanks.

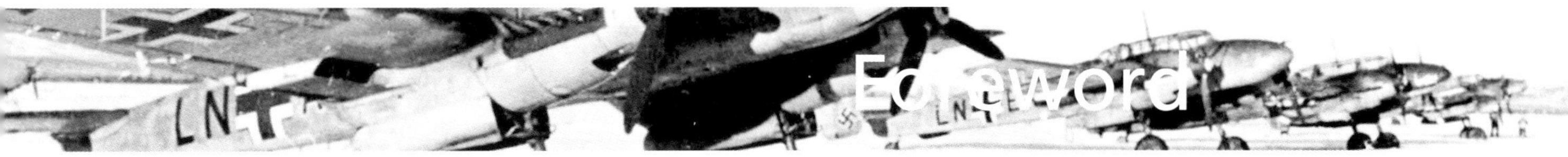

Foreword

It was during a visit to the International Air Meeting in Cologne that I bumped into my old wartime comrade Wolfgang Wollenweber, whom I knew well from my days as a Staffelkapitän with JG 5. Needless to say, we were delighted to see each other again after an interval of very nearly seven decades and, as you might imagine, our conversation revolved almost entirely around our time together on the Arctic Ocean front in northern Norway, in Karelia and in Finland. We were both amazed at how vividly the memory of those operations in the far north had remained in our minds. But we also took the opportunity to find out what the remaining months of the war had held in store for each of us after our respective transfers in 1944.

Wolfgang's accounts of his missions and his air combats, the day-to-day events at the front, life among his fellow pilots – but also the deaths of true comrades – whether above the Arctic Circle or in Defence of the Reich, were so fascinating that I urged him to write them down at all costs. This he has now done, adding a wealth of new anecdotes and details to his experiences to form the book you now hold in your hands.

Every page is both a treat and a revelation. His descriptions of flying the He 162, one of the most unusual and remarkable aircraft of the war, make an invaluable contribution to the written history of aviation. But read between the lines and you will be struck time and again by the ignorance displayed by those in higher command, still clinging to the outdated dogmas of the First World War, whose misjudgements and wrong decisions prevented the latest weapons technology from reaching the hands of the Luftwaffe at the proper time. This incompetence also led to the total breakdown in tactical cooperation between the Luftwaffe and the Navy, a failing that resulted in many tragic losses.

Despite my four years in command of both Zerstörer and single-engined fighter units, I did not get the opportunity to fly the He 162. Wolfgang Wollenweber was granted that privilege, and here brings to life his experiences as one of the few to pilot this revolutionary machine.

I hope you enjoy this unique book. It makes a totally absorbing read and I wish it every success.

Karl-Fritz Schlossstein
Staffelkapitän of 13.(Z)/JG 5

A word from the author

The days I spent in basic and flying training differed little from those described in many other memoirs written by Luftwaffe fighter pilots of World War II. In order not to bore the reader of this book with a similar account of my own experiences while learning to fly, I am therefore cutting to the chase and taking him straight onto operations, which for me began early in 1943.

Everything that appears in the following pages actually happened. Names, dates and details, right down to the exact times of day, have been taken from the flying logbooks, other records and photo albums that are still in my possession.

Even though the events I describe here took place during one of the most tragic eras in Germany's history, I hope I have been able to give a realistic glimpse not only into a chapter in the annals of aviation history that heralded an entirely new form of aerial warfare, the introduction of rocket and jet-powered technology, but also into the final and dying days of the once so proud 'Eagles of the Reich'.

Military career

1940: Volunteered for Luftwaffe service

20.11.1940: Basic training in Kaufbeuren

01.02.1941: Officer Selection Company Kaufbeuren

01.03.1941: Air Warfare School Fürstenfeldbruck, Course 'J'

10.03.1941: Promotion to Fahnenjunker-Gefreiter (Officer-candidate Corporal)

01.06.1941:A/B Flying Training School; Promotion to Fahnenjunker-Unteroffizier (Officer-candidate Sergeant)

01.10.1941: Promotion to Fähnrich (Officer-Cadet)

01.01.1942: Multi-engined training in Zeltweg, Austria; Promotion to Oberfähnrich (Senior Officer-Cadet)

01.02.1942: Promotion to Leutnant (Ing.) (Leutnant (Engineering))

14.04.1942: Instrument training on Ju 86, Do 17, He 111, Ju 88

23.05.1942: Courier flight to Catania, Sicily

27.05.1942: Instrument flight Catania-Rome-Treviso-Zeltweg

05.07.1942: Transfer to Prenzlau Inspection Centre

15.08.1942: Zerstörer school at Nancy, France

25.09.1942: Zerstörer school at Memmingen

20.01.1943: 1./Ergänzungs-Zerstörergruppe at Deblin-Irena, Poland

25.03.1943: Operational with 13.(Z)/JG 5 'Eismeer' at Kirkenes, Norway

15.02.1944: Drafted for studies at the Aviation Academy, Bad Blankenburg satellite school

24.02.1944: Engineering studies; Silver 'C' gliding certificate and authorization as glider-tug pilot

15.07.1944: Volunteered for Defence of the Reich operations

28.07.1944: Posted to Zerbst for preliminary training on Me 163

01.08.1944: Promotion to Oberleutnant

04.08.1944: Gunnery training at Aalborg, Denmark

02.10.1944: Glider training for the Me 163A at Gelnhausen

28.10.1944: Further training on the Me 163 at Berlin-Rangsdorf

09.11.1944: Conversion onto the Fw 190 at Mackfitz in Pomerania

22.12.1944: Posted to the training Staffel of IV./EJG 2 at Sprottau

27.01.1944: Transferred with the rocket-fighter unit to Esperstedt

15.02.1945: Posted to I./JG 1 'Oesau', Garz/Usedom and Parchim

27.02.1945: Instruction on the He 162 at the Heinkel works in Rostock-Marienehe

23.03.1945: Kommando 'Bernburg': ferrying He 162s from the Junkers works

11.04.1945: Appointed Staffelführer 2./JG 1 and transferred to Ludwigslust

15.04.1945: Transferred to Leck. Test, ferry and operational flights on He 162s

23.04.1945: Ferry detachment flying the last He 162s out of Rostock-Marienehe

01.05.1945 until end of war: Operations on the He 162 at Leck.

Operational missions: 46 convoy escort missions flown, 15 bombing missions flown against Murmansk and Russian airfields, two operations as shipboard fighter control officer escorting convoys to Hammerfest. Four aerial victories. Six enemy aircraft damaged. 14 flights on He 162 jet fighter.

Decorations: Iron Cross, Second Class; Iron Cross, First Class; Mission Clasp in Silver; Finnish Mannerheim Cross.

1 The Arctic Ocean not Africa

On Saturday 16 January 1943 Feldwebel Forst, my flying instructor at the Memmingen Zerstörer school, clapped me on the shoulder and said: 'Well, *Herr Leutnant*, my job's done. There's nothing more I can teach you. All that's left for you to do now is to start flying ops and show those boys at the front everything you've learned here. By the way, which unit are you and your wireless-operator Unteroffizier Bengard being sent to, do you know yet?'

With my wireless-operator Unteroffizier Walter Bengard (right).

'No, unfortunately not,' I replied 'Speaking personally, I would very much like to join Zerstörergeschwader 26 in North Africa, but we'll just have to wait and see.'

As a way of passing the time while waiting for our postings to come through, I drove into Munich for the weekend with Forst, who had just completed a reserve officer's course at Memmingen and was likewise waiting to hear where he was being sent next. It had become the custom on all our previous trips to Munich to make first for the district of Schwabing and the Odeon Café, and today was to be no exception.

We had just sat down, but not yet ordered, when a Hauptmann wearing the uniform of the Afrika Korps and with the Knight's Cross around his neck hurried past our table. Just a minute – surely that's … yes, it's my old headmaster Schuldirektor Böckmann from my schooldays in Hamelin! I scrambled to my feet and started to chase after him, but when I saw that he was making towards an attractive young blonde sitting alone at one of the tables, I quickly skidded to a stop.

The young lady clearly wasn't his daughter, whom I remembered well from our time together at dancing school. And when the mysterious blonde beauty proceeded to fling her arms around Böckmann and give him a kiss, I decided it was high time to beat a strategic retreat in order to spare everyone's blushes. Hauptmann Böckmann was killed in Africa not long afterwards and, with hindsight, I regret now that I didn't speak to him that last time in Munich after all.

On 20 January 1943 my wireless-operator Unteroffizier Walter Bengard and I were given orders to report to 1./Ergänzungs-Zerstörergruppe (1st Squadron of the Zerstörer

Operational Training Gruppe) currently based at Deblin-Irena in Poland. To be more precise, our exact destination was the Gruppe's satellite field at nearby Deblin-Ulez. And it was here that we were to spend the next few weeks engaged in a boring succession of training missions. We dropped dummy cement bombs, we carried out gunnery and target practice, and we flew cross-country navigational exercises.

But finally the great day arrived! On 17 March I received my posting to a 'proper' Zerstörergeschwader. Say goodbye to freezing cold Poland, I thought to myself jubilantly – Africa here I come! My transfer orders read: 'Report to 13. Zerstörerstaffel/Jagdgeschwader 5 at Salmijärvi.' Where on earth is this Salmijärvi, I wondered. It doesn't sound very African. There was a large map of the world hanging on the wall of the ops room and I got down on my knees to start searching for what I imagined would be some dead-and-alive little hole in Africa.

The clerk who had handed me the posting could not suppress a grin: 'If you're looking for Jagdgeschwader 5, Herr Leutnant, you'll need a chair to stand on. They're up in the far north – on the Arctic Ocean!'

It's a shame there was nobody around with a camera at that moment, for the expression on my face must have been an absolute picture. The thought alone of the cold and remoteness of the far northern regions was enough to freeze the very blood in my veins. I protested to the Kommodore that I had set my heart on going to Africa, but I got short shrift in reply: 'Africa or Arctic Ocean – our Eagles of the Reich must be ready to fly on all fronts!'

In the event, my transfer to the Arctic Ocean turned out to be a blessing in disguise, for all those of my comrades who were posted to ZG 26 were shot down and remained in Africa.

So it was off to the far north for us, and instead of drawing tropical kit we were issued with winter equipment. In order to reach our new unit my wireless-operator Bengard and I first had to travel by train up to Königsberg in East Prussia. From there we were to make our way, via Libau, Turku and Rovaniemi, to Salmijärvi.

In the meantime the 'longshanks', or knee boots, that Bengard and I had ordered from the Luftwaffe's central clothing stores had turned up. But when we tried them on it was immediately and painfully apparent that they were far too tight and pinched badly across the instep. The Königsberg express paid little heed to its passengers' tight footwear, however. It wasn't about to wait for us, and so we had to continue the battle with our boots during the journey. By the time we arrived in Königsberg we had conceded defeat. The boots had won; we could hardly get them off our feet. There was no question of our being able to travel any further in this state. The services of a shoemaker would have to be called upon to make the boots wider.

This resulted in a two-day 'enforced stopover' and gave us the opportunity to do some sightseeing in this beautiful old city. The world certainly is a small place. One of the first people I bumped into in the street was Fritz Fricke, the brother of Jürgen Fricke, with whom I had done my multi-engined training at Zeltweg in Austria. Fritz confirmed the sad news that I had already heard from others. Jürgen and the entire crew of his He 111 had been reported missing over Russia. It was presumed that he had accidentally collided with another Heinkel while flying through cloud, for a second bomber had also failed to return from the same mission and neither crew had reported making contact with the enemy.

Much later I heard that Fritz Fricke had himself been seriously wounded fighting the Americans in the Battle of the Hürtgen Forest south of Aachen late in 1944. He had subsequently died in a military hospital in Cologne and had been buried there in the city's Cemetery of Remembrance.

Forty-eight hours on a shoemaker's last are enough to break the spirit of the tightest of boots and so, on day three, Bengard and I were finally able to resume our interrupted journey to the far north. Having asked around, we had discovered that the quickest way to get to Finland was to make for Libau in Latvia and from there hitch a lift on one of the navy's patrol trawlers across the Baltic to Turku in southern Finland, which is exactly what we did. In Turku spring had already arrived, the streets were free of snow and ice, and the town's numerous canals reminded me very much of Venice.

At the town Kommandant's office we were given our movement orders for the last leg of the journey. Two days by train would take us as far as Rovaniemi, and from there another five days by car or truck up the so-called *Eismeerstrasse*, or Arctic Ocean road, would finally see us in Kirkenes.

'What, who said anything about Kirkenes?' we asked in some confusion. 'We've got to get to Salmijärvi – that's what it says on our travel orders.' Only then did someone bother to explain to us that JG 5's Zerstörerstaffel was based not in Finland, but in northern Norway.

Through all of Finland to Kirkenes in Norway: our journey to the Far North was some 1,200 kilometres and took us from Turku, via Pori, Vaasa, Kemi and Rovaniemi. Between Kirkenes and Russian Murmansk (top right) lay Petsamo (Pechenga), which at that time belonged to Finland

Our obvious innocence must have stirred some sympathy in the breast of the transport officer, who then explained that there was a much shorter and simpler alternative: take the train, via Tampere, to Pori. The airfield at Pori served as JG 5's rear-area supply depot, and we would have no trouble at all hitching a ride in a transport machine from there up to Kirkenes.

By now it was almost midday and I was told that I would be permitted, indeed welcome, to have lunch in the officers' mess. As the train for Tampere didn't depart until the late afternoon, I decided I had ample time to grab a bite. Although all the tables were laid, there wasn't another soul in the dining room apart from myself. But what's that I see? On one of the far tables I had spotted a tray with an almost untouched bottle of Hennessy and two brandy glasses.

Well, would you look at that, I said to myself – now that's what I call *real* hospitality. After all the trouble I've been through trying to get to my new unit, I reckon I've earned just a small one. I hurriedly poured myself a whole glassful, tipped the amber nectar down my throat in one go and confidently awaited the warm comforting glow that would soon be spreading throughout my whole being. But no sooner had I swallowed the stuff than I was overcome by nausea and racked with the urgent need to be violently sick. Ugh, that wasn't brandy … it was cod-liver oil!

Unfortunately, the dining room now began to fill up, and instead of being able to make my escape and throw up in peace and quiet, I was forced into an agonizing round of small talk as one officer after the other entered the mess and enquired politely where I had come from and where I was heading.

As a guest, I was invited to sit next to the station commander for lunch. Although he gave no apparent sign of noting my discomfort, it was clear to me that he was secretly taking great delight in my obvious predicament and constant fidgeting. Then, just to rub it in, when lunch was over he ordered that the bottle of Hennessy be brought to our table and insisted that we drink a toast together. Knowing full well what the bottle contained, he only pretended to join me in the toast while I was forced to down another glassful. Inwardly, he must have been laughing fit to bust at the knowledge that I – like many others before me, no doubt – had fallen for the sneaky trick of the ownerless bottle of 'brandy'.

I need hardly add that I spent the best part of the train journey to Pori locked in a stinking toilet.

In Pori, known to the troops stationed there as 'Little Paris' on account of its many restaurants, cafés and pretty girls, I was put up at the Hotel Ottawa. Here I discovered to my surprise that I had been detailed to ferry a Me110 up to 13. Staffel in Kirkenes in a couple of days time.

Outside the hotel I was approached by a Luftwaffe female signals auxiliary who asked me if I happened to know a Leutnant Rost. He was a fighter pilot with the Arctic Ocean group

The Arctic Ocean Road was 531 kilometres long and ran from Rovaniemi, via Kirkenes, to Petsamo

and she was his sister, Renate Rost. She had requested a transfer up here to be near him. 'Near?' I thought to myself – it's still another good 1,000 kilometres from here to Petsamo. But I was able to tell her that yes, I *was* in fact a friend of Wolfgang Rost. We had got to know each other during our training at Kaufbeuren and while attending the air warfare school at Fürstenfeldbruck. I wasn't aware at the time of this encounter, however, that I would be meeting Wolfgang Rost up in Petsamo just two weeks later.

The two days that had been needed to get 'my' Me 110 serviceable had now passed and I was naturally anxious to make my way out to the airfield to cast an eye over the machine that I would be ferrying northwards. I found that everything had been thoroughly checked and tested. The armament had been installed and the weapons calibrated. The aircraft was ready to go and the weather was good.

Unfortunately, all that was missing were maps of the areas we would be flying over. I therefore jotted down a few notes and sketches of my intended route, obtained details of the various regional radio beacons from flying control so that my wireless-operator Bengard could keep track of our position, and worked out the course we had to follow to reach our intermediate stop at Kemi some 500 kilometres away.

While I was still busy with these pre-flight preparations, an Oberleutnant by the name of Hans Kirchmeier suddenly turned up, introduced himself to Pori's flying control officer as the deputy Staffelkapitän of 13. Staffel, and baldly announced that *he* would be ferrying the machine to Kirkenes.

Then he turned to me, saying in an off – hand sort of way: 'You can come along with me if you like. I understand you've been posted to our Staffel. Can't on earth imagine why. We've already got five officer pilots in the Staffel as it is, and now you'll make it six. I won't be able to take your luggage though, or that of your wireless-operator; a slight matter of overloading. But there's a Ju 88 out on the field that's flying up to Kemi. Put all your non-essential stuff on board that.'

After a moment's hesitation I came to the conclusion that it would be a waste of time to protest at the high-handed attitude of this experienced 'old hare'. And so, gritting my teeth and resisting the impulse to tell him that I wasn't exactly overjoyed at being sent to the Arctic Ocean either, and would much rather be heading for Africa, I complied with his instructions. Bengard and I carried the bulk of our luggage out to the Ju 88, whose pilot, a cheerful Feldwebel sporting the Knight's Cross, immediately took it on board. Sadly, we never clapped eyes on him or our luggage ever again – either at Kemi, or anywhere else for that matter.

Clutching my hand baggage, I climbed into the Me 110 and settled myself into the seat immediately behind the pilot. Kirchmeier taxied out to the end of the runway, eased both throttles forward and the machine lifted off. During the flight up to our intermediate stop at Kemi I peered round the pilot's back armour and over Kirchmeier's shoulder. I noticed that he seemed to be fiddling about with the throttle of

Kirkenes airfield with the west-east and north-south runways clearly visible

the port engine. When the engine began to splutter and run unevenly, we just happened to be level with the small airfield at Vaasa.

Kirchmeier muttered something over the R/T about an engine malfunction, lowered the undercarriage and landed at Vaasa. There was a solitary car parked alongside the strip and a small barracks hut nearby containing one bed for one airman. Leaving Bengard to guard the Me 110, we drove into town.

Kirchmeier seemed to know his way around extremely well. He made a bee-line for a hotel where, he said, we could spend the night. He then telephoned someone but, curiously, I didn't hear him utter a word about the faulty engine. It was only much later – after we had gone out to meet two ladies in a café, the younger of whom Kirchmeier had greeted particularly warmly, and after we had brought them back to the hotel, and Kirchmeier had disappeared upstairs with the object of his affections – that the penny began to drop: *she* was the reason for our 'engine failure'!

The badge of Jagdgeschwader 5 'Eismeer' ('Arctic Ocean')

I was left with no other option but to invite the older of the two women, who had presumably been brought along to act the part of chaperone, for a drink in the hotel bar. After some little time Kirchmeier and his partner reappeared. The atmosphere seemed to have become a little strained, and not long afterwards the two ladies took their leave.

Even though we never discussed the matter of the 'emergency landing', it was crystal clear to me that Kirchmeier had wanted to take the young lady along with us up to Kirkenes, but that she had turned him down flat. If this had been his intention all along, it would also explain the supposed 'problem of overloading' and Kirchmeier's refusal to take our luggage. I kicked myself now for not having said anything at the time, for I knew full well that the Me 110, even when fully fuelled and armed, could easily carry an extra 500 kilogram payload.

When we drove back out to the airfield the next morning the engine of our machine was running normally again as if by magic. Kirchmeier then pulled another surprise out of the hat by announcing that there was a second Me 110 here at Vaasa that needed to be ferried up to Kirkenes and that I could fly it. Before we took off, however, I made a number of long and fruitless telephone calls in an effort to track down our missing luggage. Nobody knew exactly what had happened to it, although I did learn from flying control at Kemi that the Ju 88 had landed there as scheduled, but that it hadn't unloaded anything before continuing on to Petsamo.

During the flight up to Kirkenes I tried to take in something of the landscape below. This is never easy when flying in formation, as one always has to keep a careful eye on the formation leader – in this case the Me 110 being flown by Kirchmeier. But what little I was able to see didn't do a great deal to dispel my yearnings for Africa: no villages or settlements of any kind, not a single living soul or sign of habitation far and wide; nothing but an endless expanse of white – just frozen lakes and snow-covered forests and hills which, the further north we flew, slowly began to give way to barren and desolate tundra.

After a flight that had been two hours of unbroken boredom, the Arctic Ocean finally appeared over the horizon. Kirchmeier lowered his wheels and prepared to land. So we were approaching the famous Kirkenes – but where the hell was it? I scanned the terrain in front of me, searching in vain for the airfield that I would never have found had Kirchmeier not been with me. At last I saw it. Then I too lowered my flaps and undercarriage, carefully watching the lead aircraft the whole time, before easing my Me 110 down into the whirling flurries of snow thrown up by Kirchmeier's landing only moments before.

2 With the 'Dackelstaffel'

The 'Z' in the Staffel designation of the Kirkenes-based 13.(Z)/JG 5 stood for 'Zerstörer' ('Destroyer', or twin-engined heavy fighter). The unit had originally been formed as the Zerstörerstaffel of JG 77, before then becoming part of Luftflotte 5 (Air Fleet 5) and being redesignated 6.(Z)/JG 5 in November 1941. As Jagdgeschwader 5 gradually expanded from two Gruppen to four, its Zerstörerstaffel perforce underwent further redesignation. In March 1942 it became 10.(Z)/JG 5, before finally emerging as 13.(Z)/JG 5 in July 1942.

JG 5's Zerstörerstaffel was used in a wide variety of roles. It was, in effect, a 'maid of all work'. Its crews flew *freie Jagd* sweeps, escorted the Stukas and Ju 88 bombers during their attacks on the Russian port of Murmansk, mounted bombing raids themselves against Murmansk and the surrounding Soviet fighter airfields, providrd convoy protection for our own ships bringing supplies into Kirkenes and Murmansk, flew low-level sweeps against enemy Flak batteries and lines of supply, on the Murmansk railway and on the Soviet naval base at Polyarnoe. They destroyed enemy field emplacements, locomotives, ships, fuel depots and barracks. They carried out armed-reconnaissance missions over the Arctic Ocean and surrounding waters, and were employed on search and rescue duties whenever one of our own aircraft was reported missing.

The unit's nickname of the 'Dackelstaffel' dated back to the spring of 1941. 'Dackel' is the common German diminutive for dachshund, and it was around that time that Leutnant Dieterichs returned from leave with three dachshunds in tow. The trio were immediately adopted by the crews as mascots and thoroughly spoiled by everyone on the base. After Leutnants Weyergang and Brandis each shot down a Lockheed Hudson, one of the dachshunds was promptly christened *'Lockheed'*.

During the early years of the air war in the east our Me 110s were far superior to, or at the very least the equal of, most of the Russian machines we encountered. One such, for example, was the Soviet I-16 *Rata* fighter, and it was this that gave rise to the Staffel badge – a Dackel with a Rata clamped in its jaws – which was painted on both sides of our Messerschmitts' noses.

In order the better to understand the miserable living conditions endured by the front-line airman serving up here above the Arctic Circle – be he pilot, wireless-operator, gunner, flight mechanic, ground crew or any of the numerous other trades – one only has to picture the hostile environment that he faced throughout the year. In the winter it was pitch dark around the clock for months on end. In this freezing cold, when temperatures often dropped as low as minus 40 degrees, violent snowstorms alternated with icy rain and thick fog. Then, in the short summer months, the sun would shine for 24 hours every day. Proper

The 'Rata-eating Dackel' badge of the Zerstörerstaffel.

sleep became impossible and this, combined with the almost unendurable plagues of midges that could last for weeks on end, led to cases of severe depression and dangerous lapses of concentration.

But the extreme weather conditions, the inadequate rations that came almost entirely out of tins, the distance from the homeland, the remoteness from any kind of civilization and the ever-present danger of losing one's life – either through enemy action or from the failure of some sophisticated but delicate item of equipment that simply wasn't suited to the hash environment – all served as a bond to weld together those sent to this most inhospitable of regions into one single tight-knit community.

It also meant, however, that their behaviour was sometimes very different from that of troops serving on other fronts. It was hardly surprising that an over-abundance of alcohol, coupled with the lack of feminine company, sometimes gave rise to what an outsider might regard as bizarre excesses, but which we ourselves simply dismissed as 'polar madness'.

Staffelkapitän from March 1942: Karl-Fritz Schlossstein.

Whenever one of the short-legged Lapp girls – we called them 'Lapland Dackels' – happened to walk across the airfield, for example, the men would send up a veritable barrage of flares as a sign of their frustration. We didn't stand a chance with the few female Luftwaffe auxiliaries who had somehow or other ended up in Kirkenes. Those who didn't already have steady boy friends back in the Reich or in Finland were far more interested in the dashing young pilots of the Me 109 fighters based at Petsamo. And not even the most dedicated of our womanisers wanted to get involved with what was left; preferring instead to drown their sorrows, if not their desires, in a variety of alcoholic beverages of their own manufacture.

Up in our far-flung corner of the world these concoctions were a popular way of banishing polar madness, if only for a few hours. The cocktail aficionados outdid each other by coming up with ever more weird and lethal combinations. One very popular offering was the 'Airacobra', which consisted of sour milk diluted with a liberal splash of aquavit. Another sure-fire headache-producer was the 'Bear's claw', a toxic mix of vodka and artificial honey spread!

When I reported for duty to Staffelkapitän Hauptmann Karl-Fritz Schlossstein he uttered almost the same words as were still ringing in my ears from my first encounter with Oberleutnant Kirchmeier: 'What are you supposed to do up here with us? We've already got five officer pilots. A Staffel normally only has two, maybe three officers at most.' When I trotted out my usual explanation to the effect that I personally would much rather serve in Africa and that being sent here was not my idea, Hauptmann Schlossstein merely shrugged and said: 'Well, I expect we'll be able to fit you in somehow. Go along to the 'Brandis' barracks. You can share a room there with Leutnant Schwab.'

I made my way across to the barracks hut which, I subsequently learned, had been named in honour of the Staffel's first Kapitän, Oberleutnant Felix Brandis, who had failed to return from a mission on 2 February 1942. My new billet was not exactly palatial. Opposite the door when you entered was a window, beneath which stood an old roll-top desk. The rest of the Spartan furnishings comprised two

Felix Maria Brandis was the first Kapitän of the Zerstörerstaffel.

lockers, two rough wooden beds, each with a straw-filled mattress, a single wash basin and tap that gave forth only cold water, and a somewhat antiquated pot-bellied stove.

A shelf was attached to the wall above my bed. On it stood a 'Volksempfänger', or 'People's Receiver' radio. These sets were common throughout the Reich. Deliberately short-ranged, they could not pick up foreign broadcasts, but were designed solely for listening to the national news and local stations. But up here the only noises that ours could be persuaded to produce were a few occasional squawks, and these only after Gefreiter Neuwirt, who looked after our quarters for us, had lit the stove and got the room temperature above the minus 10 degrees that was the norm for this time of year.

My few items of hand baggage were quickly stowed away into my locker as I introduced myself to Leutnant Georg Schwab. After we had agreed to share the desk, I placed a few papers on it together with a framed photograph of a girl I had met the previous year during my training at Memmingen.

But no sooner had I done so than Leutnant Schwab, whose attitude had suddenly changed and who was now fairly foaming with rage, demanded to know what I thought I was playing at, rummaging among his things. 'What on earth are you talking about,' I said in total bewilderment, 'I wouldn't dream of touching your personal possessions.' 'Oh, yes? So where did *this* come from?' He held up the photograph. In response, I launched into an explanation that would have seemed far-fetched had it not been perfectly true, and which went to show, yet again, just what a small place the world really was.

The 'Haus Brandis' barracks hut. From left: author, war correspondent Antonowitz, Leutnant Georg 'Orge' Schwab, Leutnant Kohlweiss, Hauptmann Schlossstein, and Feldwebel Friedrich.

'It's like this, Schwab,' I said, 'during my off-duty hours in Memmingen I often used to pop into the Friedericus Rex café. On one occasion a girl approached my table and asked if she might sit down, to which I naturally agreed. She wasn't really my type, but when I paid my bill and made to leave, she then asked if I would be kind enough to see her home. She lived with her parents and the house was on the way to the airfield. When we got there she thanked me with a quick kiss, took this picture out of her handbag and signed it "with love, your Gisela".'

Schwab dived into his locker and produced exactly the same photo bearing exactly the same inscription. His eyes went from one picture to the other. 'This can't be happening,' he exploded. 'Just what kind of a girl *is* she – I've been writing to her for a whole year now!' I assured him that I didn't even know the young lady's last name and that I had had no further contact with her since. By the time he had finished apologising to me, we were both laughing so much about our 'faithful' Gisela that the tears were rolling down our cheeks. The upshot of this episode was that we became the best of friends and immediately started to use the familiar *'du'* form of address to each other.

The next day Georg Schwab, whose nickname was 'Orge', showed me around the airfield. In addition to the rather ramshackle building that housed flying control and the ops room, there was an air raid shelter, a sick-bay, a readiness room, the workshops and the enlisted men's quarters. The 'Brandis' barracks, in which Schwab and I shared a room, also contained an officers' mess.

Among the small group of machines standing outside the workshops awaiting repair was an all-white Me 110 bearing the codes 'IB+AX'. When I asked Schwab the reason for the white camouflage, he explained: 'She can't be resprayed any more, she's already got four coats of paint on her. She's one of the old 'E'-series and, besides, nobody wants to fly her as she only brings bad luck. Everyone who's ever flown IB+AX was either shot down or suffered a fatal accident shortly afterwards, like our original Staffelkapitän Brandis.' I resisted the temptation to say that I regarded this as utter rubbish and that I didn't believe in such superstitious nonsense.

From left: author, Hauptmann Schlossstein, war correspondent Jung, and 'Orge' Schwab.

After our tour of the field Schwab and I went into the officers' mess where we bumped into Staffelkapitän Schlossstein. When I asked him how soon I would get to fly, the whole room rocked with laughter. 'I don't think you quite get the picture,' Schlossstein replied with some asperity. 'Now you're here we've got six officers and 24 NCO pilots – and they *all* want to fly. The problem is, we've only got twelve machines – when they're all serviceable, that is. You'll have to wait a good five or six weeks until it's your turn.'

'Couldn't I perhaps fly the white IB+AX then,' I persisted. 'I've heard all about the superstition, but that doesn't worry me. I was born on the thirteenth of the month, and that cancels out all bad luck in later life.'

'Very well, then. Go and see the T.O. (Technical Officer) Oberleutnant Maul and get him to have the bird serviced. That means we'll at least have 13 machines on the books.' 'And only twelve again not long afterwards,' I heard someone behind him mutter ominously.

On 11 April the 'white bird of ill-omen' was declared serviceable and Oberleutnant Kirchmeier arranged for me to accompany him on an escort mission to protect a small convoy of ships bringing up supplies. The vessels had almost reached the port of Kirkenes already, however, and so there wasn't much protection needed. We saw neither hide nor hair of any Russian torpedo-bombers. Perhaps they didn't relish the idea of attacking this close in, given the harbour's strong Flak defences and our airfield nearby.

But this didn't stop Kirchmeier weaving about like a madman. He obviously wanted to see if I could stick close to his tail. Of course I could, and proceeded to follow his every wild manoeuvre just to prove it. The only difficulty I had was when I wanted to make a right-hand turn. Every time I attempted to do so the stick jumped out of my hand and, no matter what I tried, my IB+AX stubbornly insisted on continuing to fly in a straight line.

From left: Oberleutnant Hans Kirchmeier, an unidentified army officer and Oberleutnant Max Franzisket, Staffelkapitän until March 1942.

I reported my problem with the steering over the R/T, but got neither advice nor any kind of acknowledgement whatsoever from Kirchmeier. I therefore radioed back to Kirkenes flying control: 'Am aborting the mission and returning to base'. The moment I landed the *Werkmeister*, or workshops chief, came running up to find out what the trouble was. When I described the machine's odd behaviour whenever I attempted to turn to the right, he got quite shirty, protesting that such a thing was impossible. He had checked everything over himself, he declared, and the aircraft was perfectly in order.

But I was convinced that the problem had something to do with the port aileron, which had to be lowered in order to make a right-hand turn. When I carried out a walk-around inspection of the machine I happened to brush against the auxiliary fuel tank under the left wing – and what do you know: it wobbled. It was only being held in place by one attachment strut. 'Werkmeister,' I called, 'here's our problem. This tank's hanging half loose. It was hitting the mass balance and jamming the aileron every time I tried to turn to the right. Report the fact to Oberleutnant Kirchmeier and get it fixed as quickly as possible.'

Funnily enough, I never heard a word from Kirchmeier about the faulty tank attachment. Perhaps he was still smarting over the fact that I had seen through the little charade of his 'emergency' landing back in Vaasa. Or maybe the whole flight had been a conspiracy; a sort of test designed to prove my flying abilities and aeronautical know-how to the rest of the Staffel and convince them that my official rank of Leutnant (*Ing*) – Lieutenant (Engineer) – was not simply a bureaucratic qualification, but did actually mean that I possessed sufficient technical expertise to recognize an unusual flight characteristic and trace its source back to some defect or other in the aircraft.

As I was now without a machine for a while, I was able to turn my attention back to the matter of Bengard's and my missing luggage. It seemed highly likely that our things were somewhere at Petsamo, which was only about 50 kilometres away from Kirkenes. I rang up the field's ops room and who should be on the other end of the line but my old friend and companion from training days Wolfgang 'Rosti' Rost. After briefly bringing each other up to date on all the latest news, I explained the situation regarding our missing luggage.

'I haven't heard anything about a Ju 88 dropping off any personal kit here,' Rosti replied, 'but I'm hopping over to Kirkenes in the Fieseler Storch tomorrow. Why don't you come back to Petsamo with me and ask around for yourself.'

Rosti was on the dot the following day and gave me the promised lift to Petsamo. Despite all my searching, however, I could find no trace

The attachments of the Me 110's auxiliary underwing tanks are plainly visible.

of our lost luggage there. But at least the trip gave me the opportunity to meet Leutnant Theo Weissenberger, who had previously served with the Zerstörerstaffel at Kirkenes and had been awarded the Knight's Cross for his many successes while flying the Me 110. Now he was at Petsamo carving out an even more illustrious career for himself on the Me 109. Weissenberger welcomed me warmly, for he knew that I had once got his little brother Unteroffizier Otto Weissenberger out of a potentially very nasty situation.

The story goes something like this: Otto Weissenberger had also been a pilot with 13. Staffel at Kirkenes. Because of his small stature, however, he had to strap wooden blocks beneath the soles of his flying boots in order for his feet to be able to reach the rudder pedals and brakes of his machine. On one occasion, while taxiing across the field, the blocks had somehow or other become dislodged. Unable to reach his brakes, he had crashed straight into two parked aircraft. Not even his brother's fame could help him now. Charged with the destruction of Reich property – i.e. the two machines – he was sent back to Germany where he was formally placed under arrest, found guilty and confined to quarters.

Those quarters were at Memmingen, where I happened to be stationed at the time. One day the guard reported to me that Unteroffizier Weissenberger had left base without permission. As Duty Officer it was then my responsibility to draw up the necessary paperwork. But having done so, I decided to tuck the report away in my desk drawer for the time being. When Otto Weissenberger returned a little later, I gave him one hell of a rocket. I then told him that I considered the matter closed, for if I had allowed it to go any higher it would have meant an almost certain spell in a military prison.

It was while Leutnant Rost was flying me back to Kirkenes that I told him of my encounter with his sister Renate down in Pori. 'Families can be an awful burden,' he said, 'especially with the kind of ops we're flying, where something unpleasant could happen at any time.' He didn't seem overly thrilled at the news that his sister was based 'nearby'. I don't know how she took it when Rosti was shot down and captured by the Russians early in 1944. (In fact, Wolfgang Rost survived his time

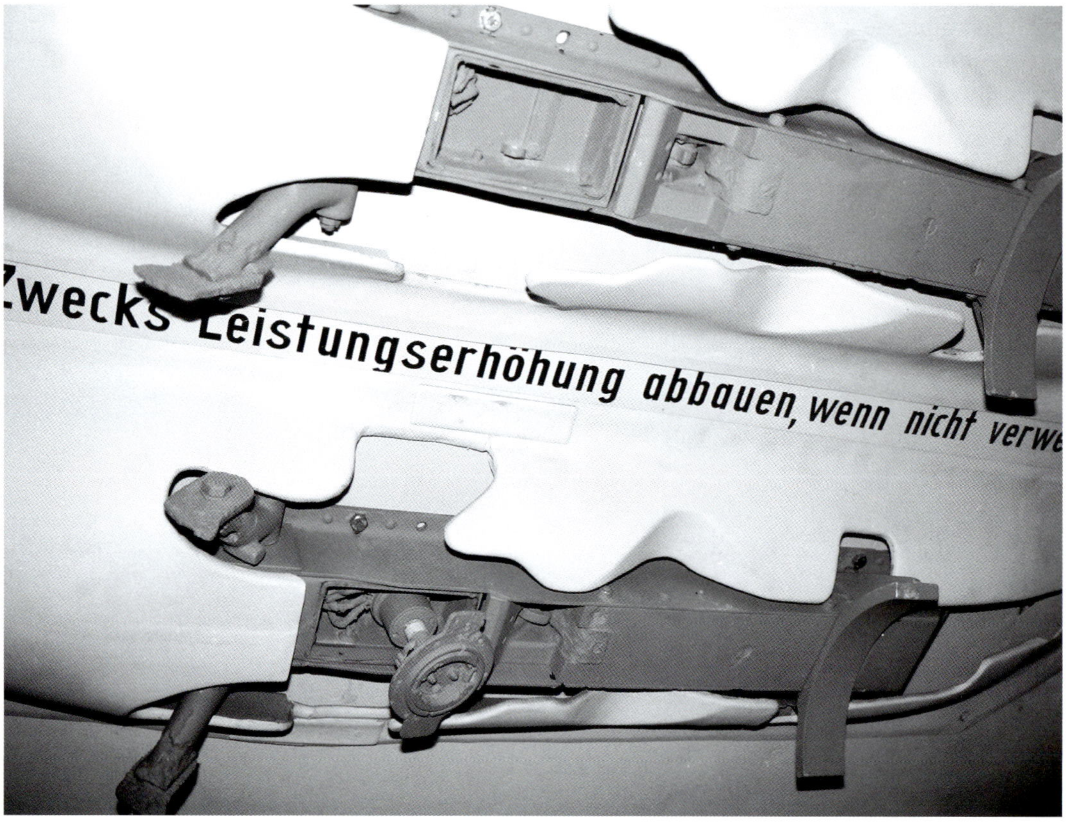

The underwing racks could carry either bombs or auxiliary fuel tanks.

in Soviet captivity and we were to see each other again after the war at one of the meetings of the JG 5 Old Boys' Association.)

Back in Kirkenes I informed Bengard that we'd have to write off any hopes of ever seeing our luggage again. He didn't seem all that concerned as he'd already kitted himself out with new items from the Staffel's clothing stores, something that I hadn't yet got around to.

Although I hadn't done anything special since my arrival in the far north, and couldn't get into the air for the time being because of the shortage of serviceable aircraft, I was nonetheless able to enjoy the 'Startfrühstück' – the 'take-off breakfast', or pre-op meal – in the mess every morning. I was also entitled to draw flight rations, which consisted of 'Studentenfutter' – 'students' fodder', a form of liquorice allsorts – biscuits, and Choco-Cola; the latter being a tin of chocolate concentrate laced with cola-nut oil.

In my youth, but also during my days of training in the Luftwaffe, I had always engaged in a lot of sport. This had kept my physique in fairly good shape, and so I was not unduly surprised when Staffelkapitän Schlossstein found a new job for me: 'Wollenweber, the crews need to burn off their winter fat and give their lungs a thorough airing. I want you to organize some sports sessions. No time like the present, so you may as well start straightaway – say 10-o-clock this morning.'

I realized at once that this was one of those orders that wasn't going to win me any popularity contests. At the same time, it would also demand a certain amount of physical effort on my part. I went across to the aircrews' quarters. Standing in the entrance hall, I yelled at the top of my voice: 'On the orders of the Staffelkapitän everyone is to get ready for sports. Fall in outside the barracks at 10.00 hours sharp!' A furious hubbub of voices came from behind the closed doors. I also heard more than a few choice swear words, but wasn't able to identify the speakers as I didn't know the individual crews all that well yet.

By ten-o-clock they had all fallen in as ordered, but every one of them was wearing full uniform complete with medals and decorations. I proceeded to make it perfectly clear to them that the purpose of the parade was for physical training and that uniform jackets were surplus to requirements. 'We're going for a cross-country run,' I informed them, 'so fall out again and get changed into pullovers, shorts and sturdy shoes. Anyone who keeps up with me, or can overtake me, gets my Marketenderware.

'Marketenderware', or 'canteen items', was Luftwaffe jargon for alcoholic beverages, and this did the trick. The words were hardly out of my mouth before the entire parade disappeared like a flash to get changed into sports kit. After that everything went smoothly. Only when I gave the order 'Right turn!' did one Oberfeldwebel deliberately face left. The culprit was Rudi Kurpiers, who not long before had shot down four Russian aircraft and would later become one of my closest friends.

In the centre, holding *Lockheed* the dachshund, is Oberfeldwebel Rudolf Kurpiers, one of my best friends.

'Your recent successes must have gone to your head,' I observed dryly. 'You seem to have forgotten everything you learned in basic training. Maybe you ought to go back and do it all over again.' At this, Oberfeldwebel Kurpiers immediately executed one of the smartest about-turns that I had ever witnessed!

Now that we had established who was in charge, we set off at the double down the road running alongside the airfield. The closer we got to the shores of the fjord, the more and more of a hurdle race it became as we found ourselves constantly having to jump over 30 to 40 centimetre-high snowdrifts. Totally out of training, my bunch of 'athletes' was beginning to fall ever further behind. But I have to admit that, after more than an hour of leaping up and down like a kangaroo, even I was more than a little glad to get back to the start of the field's east-west runway.

It was another quarter-of-an-hour before the last of the group came in puffing and wheezing. After a ten-minute breather I said: 'Well, you sad specimens, it looks as if I'll be drinking my schnapps myself. So now there's a new set of rules – we'll have a race along the runway back to the barracks and it's the last three to make it who will have to forfeit *their* liquor. Right, get set, ready – go!'

The surface of the runway had been worn smooth and so the going was good. I stayed with the leading runners to check what sort of an effect all this unaccustomed exercise was having on the men. It was shocking to discover just how badly out of condition many of them actually were, especially the ones who had been up here for a year or more. The group was strung out all over the place. Some of those at the back, having resigned themselves to being among the last three, were dawdling along way behind the rest. With only 200 metres to go, I gave the signal for a final spurt and upped my pace to show the men that I was not asking any more of them than I was inflicting upon myself. Some tried to keep up with me, but weren't able to manage it and had to give up just before the end.

For some unaccountable reason no more cross-country runs were ever held – at least during my time at Kirkenes – so I needn't have bothered with my one final act of clemency. For after all the runners had eventually staggered in I had declared: 'You've all done your very best, so I'm excusing the last three the forfeiture of their alcohol. That's all – Dismiss! Now go and recover.'

On 13 April Oberleutnant Kirchmeier and I were ordered to fly a weather-reconnaissance mission to Murmansk. This town was only 150 kilometres from Kirkenes as the crow flies and was of vital importance to the Russians as it was their only ice-free harbour during the winter months up here in the far north. Allied convoys from across the North Atlantic and the Barents Sea delivered a steady stream of supplies and all kinds of military equipment to Murmansk.

In order to help cut off this flow of western aid, one of our many tasks was to carry out reconnaissance and meteorological flights over the Murmansk region. These provided our bombers and Stukas with the information necessary to enable them to mount their raids on Murmansk's town and harbour. We also kept them informed of the convoys' movements in the waters around Murmansk, including the Kola Inlet.

Kirchmeier and I agreed that he would fly the lead and that I would assume the role of *Katschmarek*, or wingman. When we took off from Kirkenes the cloud base was down to 300 metres and it was only after a long climb that we broke out into clear skies at 3,000 metres. After twenty minutes flying in tight formation above the clouds, Kirchmeier plunged back down into the dirty grey-white blanket. When we eventually emerged from thelast few wisps only some 200 metres above the ground, Kola Inlet and the harbour of Murmansk lay spread out in front of us.

Suddenly and without warning, a tremendous barrage of Russian Flak rose up to greet us. Shells exploded all around us like fiery fingers of death intent on clawing us from the skies. Kirchmeier immediately climbed back up into the safety of the clouds and I promptly followed suit, not wanting to lose sight of him. Perhaps I gave him a scare by edging in a bit too close, for he broke sharply away to the left and disappeared behind a thick curtain of cloud. His abrupt move had been totally unexpected, and at almost the same instant my machine fell away to the right. Sensing that the aircraft was on the point of stalling, I quickly switched to instruments.

They were not a pretty sight. The turn-and-bank indicator showed that the machine was almost standing on one wing. Immediately below it, the artificial horizon was upside-down – I was in an inverted spin!

A thousand thoughts went racing through my mind. Bailing out over Russian territory was not an attractive proposition. Besides, the altimeter was waving about so wildly that I didn't have a clue how high I was. Then I remembered the advice my blind-flying instructor had given me for dealing with just such a situation: hands off the throttle levers, let go the stick, and the bird will right itself.

It worked! The ball and needle of the turn-and-bank indicator were back in their proper places and the artificial horizon was behaving normally again. I pushed the throttles forward, set a compass course of 270 degrees and started to climb. At last the sky began to lighten. We were out of the clouds, but where was Kirkenes?

'Bengard, qgo for Kirkenes?' I asked – (qgo was one of the Luftwaffe's three-letter 'Q'-codes and meant 'What course?'). 'I've lost radio contact, Herr Leutnant,' my wireless-operator replied. 'No matter,' I said almost at once, for I had just seen Kirchmeier's machine pop out of the clouds 100 metres away. His wireless-operator would no doubt have already reported our presence. If Kirchmeier thought he had got rid of us, he was sadly mistaken. Convinced that I would again be unable to find the field, I now stuck to him like a leech. I descended through the clouds with him and touched down moments after him on Kirkenes' north-south runway.

Not unnaturally, I enquired what the problem had been and why he had dived away to the left so abruptly. His explanation, that the port fuel valve had shut itself off and his left-hand engine had consequently come to a sudden stop, I took with a large grain of salt. I made no further comment even though, as an engineering officer, I knew full well that the fuel valves on our aircraft's engines were fitted with a safety device designed expressly to prevent such a thing happening.

This rare photo of Knight's Cross-holder Theo Weissenberger shows him shortly before he was presented with the Oak Leaves. Twenty-three of his victories were achieved while flying Me 110s with the Dackelstaffel.

The office of the wireless-operator, who also served as the Me 110's rear gunner.

The airfield's barracks huts were uninviting quarters in an uninviting landscape.

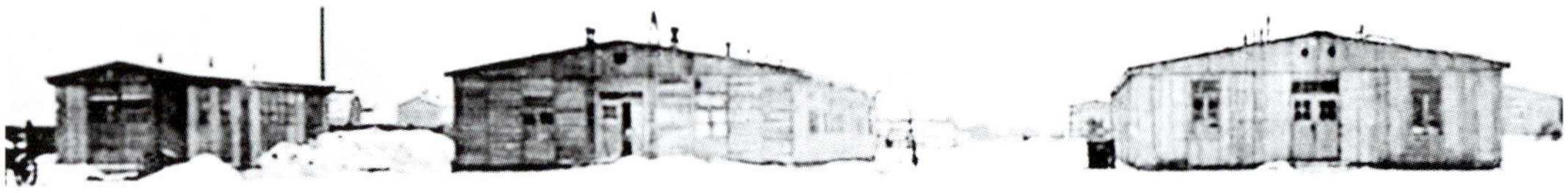

Me 110s of the Dackelstaffel in a Kirkenes winter.

The engines of Hauptmann Schmidt's Me 110 'LN+OR' are warmed up prior to take-off.

Above: Unbelievably, this dismantled wreck of an old bus once served as our operations room.

Left: The Staffel badge on the nose of an Me 110.

Below: The flying control hut. In the foreground are the excavations for an air raid shelter.

One of the guns of Kirkenes' Flak defences.

The view from the airfield out over Hoy Bay.

3 Trouble with Pe-2s

Throughout almost the whole of the following week the weather was so bad that a planned bombing raid on Murmansk had to be postponed time and time again. It wasn't until 19 April that the skies cleared up and I was ordered to carry out a weather-reconnaissance flight over the area to the east of Kirkenes.

When I lifted off in the white bird at 09.30 hours there were still a few lingering veils of low-lying cloud, but above these the sky was a radiant blue and the visibility was excellent. The mission was to be flown at an altitude of 7,000 metres. But as I climbed I really began to notice the inferior performance of my old 'E'-model machine, whose DB 601 engines lacked the high-altitude superchargers fitted to the newer and more powerful 'G'-series. Above 5,500 metres IB+AX began to run seriously out of puff, and it was all I could do to coax her up to the 7,000 metres as ordered.

As I flew over Petsamo the R/T was suddenly alive with an excited chorus of voices from the Arctic Ocean fighter boys stationed below. Only moments earlier, apparently, they had scrambled a Rotte (pair) of Me 109s to investigate the reported approach of a lone intruder. Just to be on the safe side, I informed them of my presence: 'Me 110 of 13. Staffel overhead.' I recognized the voice of Theo Weissenberger: 'That's a load of bull for a start. We've not been notified of any friendlies in the area.' I lost no time in putting him straight: 'This is IB+AX flying a weather-recce at 7,000 metres, course 105 east-southeast – so now clear off!'

After returning to Kirkenes I made my report on the weather conditions and also mentioned the incident with the fighters over Petsamo. I now found out that – 'purely through an oversight,' of course – nobody had thought to inform the Petsamo fighter controller of my flight. Later still I also discovered why all the pilots at Petsamo had been so irritable and on edge on that particular 19 April. It was on this date that one of their leading aces, the 94-victory Knight's Cross-holder Rudolf 'Rudi' Müller had been shot down during a mission to Murmansk. Forced to make an emergency landing on the frozen surface of Lake Bolshoye, he had been captured by the Russians.

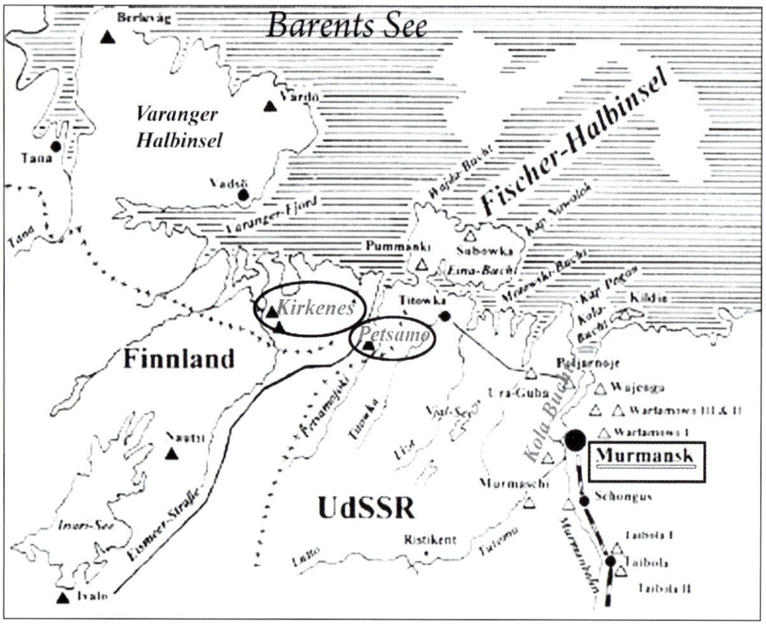

Our bombing raids were directed mainly against the ice-free harbour town of Murmansk, the neighbouring Russian airfields at Varlamovo and Murmaschi, and the Murmansk railway line.

Other important missions were those flown against the Allied convoys carrying supplies across the North Atlantic and the Barents Sea to Murmansk, and in support of our own coastal convoys in the area of the Varanger Peninsula.

Our airfields at Kirkenes (Norway) and Petsamo (Finland) lay only 50 km apart. The distance from Kirkenes to the Russian port of Murmansk was about 150 km.

On 22 April we finally took off on the long delayed mission to bomb Murmansk. Our formation consisted of three Rotten – six machines in all. Leutnant 'Orge' Schwab and I made up the third and last Rotte, fervently hoping against hope that the old German proverb about its being 'the ones at the back who get bitten by the dogs' wouldn't apply today.

With a one-ton bomb load slung beneath each aircraft, the poor performance of my Me 110E was even more noticeable. The other machines maintained a steady rate of climb. But by the time we got to 5,000 metres I was finding it increasingly difficult to keep up with them. I began to fall further and further behind and soon realized that in my old IB+AX I would never be able to reach the operational height of 8,000 metres as instructed. I could of course have upped my engines' output to 110% by ramming the throttles through the stops and employing emergency boost. But this could only be used for a very short period and, as its name implies, was intended for emergencies only – such as when trying to escape from enemy fighters, for example.

All this time good old Schwab, who was flying a 'G'-model and could quite easily have remained with the others, had been sticking faithfully by my side. I signalled for him to rejoin the two leading Rotten, while I plugged along at 6,000 metres, which would just enable me to keep the formation in sight.

Shortly before Murmansk the air really began to fill with lead. The Russian Flak gunners were firing like madmen, sending up a tremendous box barrage. The sky became a dense kaleidoscope of fiery reds and glowing yellows as the shells exploded in front of us, slowly turning darker until they formed a solid curtain of black cloud at 7,000 metres.

Flying through the trajectories of all these shells, I was buffeted by turbulence. My machine was being thrown about so much that I didn't even have to bother with a 'Flak waltz' – this was the expression we used to describe the weaving about we did when flying through enemy anti-aircraft fire ... either that, or a whole flock of guardian angels must have been watching over me to make sure I didn't get hit.

We let go our bombs over the harbour area with what we thought was a fair degree of accuracy. In the inferno of Flak being thrown up at us it was impossible to observe initial results. Things were clearly becoming too hot for my comrades above me as well, for they were now diving steeply away from the target. This meant

Knight's Cross-holder Rudi Müller was shot down near Murmansk on 19 April 1943.

that I was able to resume my position as tail-end Charlie for the flight back to base.

On 25 April we carried out another raid on Murmansk, but this time we took off at night. Approaching the town from a more southerly direction in order to avoid the main Flak defences, we bombed at 01.05 hours. By now, however, I was becoming pretty fed up, for once again my white bird, the only machine not fitted with high-altitude superchargers, was unable to keep station. For a second time I was left gnashing my teeth 2,000 metres below the rest of the formation and could only regain my correct position after the others had completed their bombing runs and dived back down to my level for the flight home.

We had arrived back at Kirkenes at 02.35 hours. After snatching some sleep, Leutnant Schwab and I were then given orders to fly a convoy escort mission. 'Just make sure you bring both machines back in one piece, we've only got four crates serviceable at the moment,' was technical officer Oberleutnant Maul's parting shot as we taxied out to take off at 10.51 hours.

We had been circling 300 metres above the convoy of ships for a good 90 minutes when Orge Schwab called me over the R/T: 'Indianer' – 'Indians', the name we used for enemy aircraft – behind us, 180 degrees. Indianer approaching from behind!' I craned my head around and spotted what at first I took to be six Me 110s closing in fast about 100 metres

Oberleutnant Maul (foreground) was the Technical Officer (T.O.) of the Dackelstaffel.

Maintenance on the propeller mechanism of a DB 605 engine.

Reloading the MG 81Z twin machine guns – note the ring gunsight.

The bomb dump at Kirkenes.

I'm waiting for my machine to be bombed up.

Winging past the icebound fjords.

Hauptmann Schlossstein leads the Staffel out on an escort mission.

The 'black men', or ground crew, take a break in front of my 'AX'. The 'white bird' still bears traces of its winter camouflage.

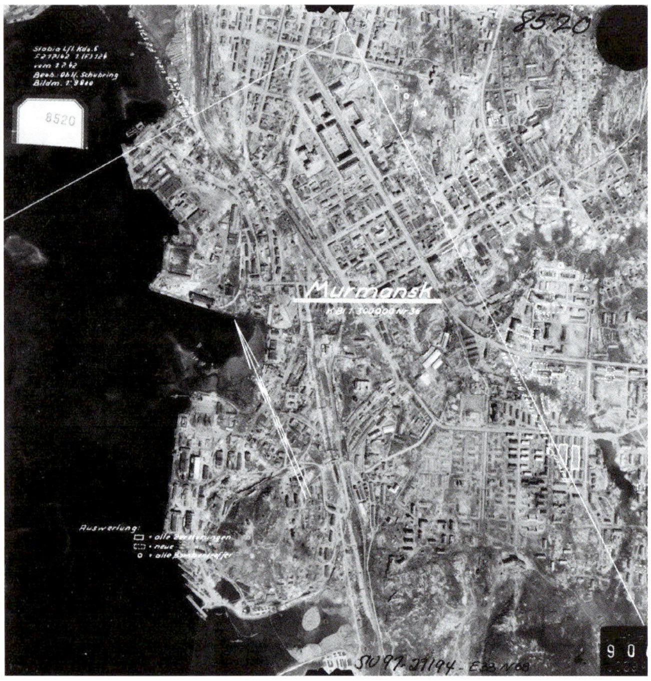

An aerial reconnaissance photo of Murmansk showing the harbour area, one of our principal targets.

Murmansk harbour burning after a bombing raid.

In this photo-reconnaissance oblique of the Murmansk region the waterways leading inland from the Barents Sea, via the Kola Inlet, to Murmansk are clearly visible, as are the fighter airfields at Varlamovo and Murmashi, and the line of the Murmansk railway (far right). Kirkenes lay 150 km to the west of here as the crow flies.

below us. But then I thought to myself: Hang on, they can't be ours, we're only supposed to have four machines serviceable at present – and *we're* flying two of them!

All doubts were dispelled when I saw the red stars the machines were wearing. I pressed the R/T switch: 'Orge, Russians below us to starboard. Break left!' While Schwab curved sharply away to port, I winged over into a steep right-hand turn, arming my guns as I dived down to get behind the enemy.

I must have poured on a bit too much gas, for I suddenly found myself sitting only a bare 50 metres behind the last machine in the Russian formation. The instant I fired my four nose machine guns large pieces began to fly off his cockpit canopy. Because of my excess speed the next Russian was already filling my sights. I hadn't taken my finger off the gun button, but my machine gun bullets didn't seem to be having much of an effect on the enemy. So I let loose at numbers three and four with my cannon as well.

I still had far too much speed on, however, and when number five started to curve away with the possible intention of forming a defensive circle, I had no other option but to zoom straight past beneath him. It was only now that I realized my machine guns were out of ammunition and that my cannon had fallen silent too. 'Don't try firing the cannon, there's a shell jammed in the breech and I haven't managed to get it out yet,' yelled my wireless-operator, whose job it was to reload the two underfloor cannon by hand.

Being temporarily 'unemployed', I closed up on one of the Russian machines that was attempting to escape out to open sea at low level. It was the one whose canopy I had shot to pieces, and I could now see why I had at first mistaken the enemy formation for Me 110s. They were, in fact, twin-engined Petlyakov Pe-2s, a type that was used by the Soviet air force in a variety of roles, including ground-attack and dive-bombing. With their extensively glazed cockpits and twin tail units, it was all too easy to confuse them with our own Messerschmitts.

'Bengard, this one's trying to get away. Have you got those cannon working yet?' I called to my wireless-operator. 'Give me another second – I'm just replacing the ammo drum,' he replied. These last ten minutes, which I had spent sitting right on the tail of the fleeing Pe-2 with my guns out of action, had seemed like an eternity to me. So what must have been going through the minds of the Russian crew

Shot down over the Kola Inlet, 'LN+DR' was put on display by the Russians in bomb-damaged Murmansk.

all this while, I wondered to myself. Did they know my guns were jammed, or did they think I was playing some cruel kind of cat-and-mouse game with them? Every one of them must have had loved ones – parents, perhaps a wife and children, possibly a fiancée – who were anxiously awaiting their return. Were the men praying, hoping for a miracle, or were they gripped by the unspeakable terrors of an imminent and violent death? In this merciless arena that was modern air warfare it didn't pay to dwell too long on how quickly the hunters could themselves become the hunted.

The moment Bengard shouted 'Ready!' I sent a burst of cannon fire into the Pe-2's port engine. The enemy machine immediately snapped over onto its back and smashed into the Arctic Ocean. The violence of the impact sent up a huge column of water, which very nearly brought me down as well. And over there – not far away another fountain of water told me that Orge Schwab had also caught and shot down the Pe-2 that he had been chasing.

We congratulated each other over the R/T and then, after circling one last time over the

The Russian Petlyakov Pe-2 ground-attack aircraft.

wreckage marking the spots where the two enemy machines had gone in, we returned to the convoy. There we found that the relief Rotte had already arrived and had taken up station above the vessels, so Schwab and I set course back to base. We roared low across the field waggling our wings. And because it felt so good, we turned round and did it a second time. We could see the ground crews waving up at us as they came running from all corners of the field – they knew that our victories meant celebratory drinks all round.

After parking our machines and being debriefed, I reported to Staffelkapitän Schlossstein: 'Four Pe-2s attacked, one shot down.' Schwab's report was the same. We saluted and turned about. As we reached the door the Staffelkapitän called us back. Addressing me, he said: 'Come to attention! For the mission just flown I hereby award you the Iron Cross, Second Class. The medal is to be worn for the entire day' – usually the recipient of an Iron Cross, Second Class, wore just the ribbon tucked into a tunic buttonhole. Then he turned to Orge: 'Schwab, I've only got the one Iron Cross, but you'll get yours later. As you've already been waiting over a year for a decoration, I'm sure a day or two longer won't matter. But consider the award effective as of now.'

The Kapitän then presented us with our 'victory prizes': three bottles of champagne apiece, to which the station commander added another two bottles of cognac. As was customary, we first gave some of the bottles to our wireless-operators and ground crews. The rest were earmarked for a 'session' with the other officers in the mess.

My victory had obviously earned me some kudos among my comrades. They were suddenly much more approachable and happy

The Russian Pe-2 and our Me 110 were deceptively similar.

to accept me into their ranks. I was told that no new arrival had ever before claimed a kill within fourteen days of joining the Staffel. Everybody was being extremely pleasant to me. It was left to Oberleutnant Kirchmeier to sound the only sour note: 'If you'd aimed at the engines in the first place you could have been celebrating *four* victories now.'

In our room later that evening Schwab confided to me in a whisper: 'You've got to watch your step with that Kirchmeier, he almost got me sent to gaol once. When I first arrived here twelve months ago I shared this room with Leutnant Hans-Bodo von Rabenau. He was shot down southeast of Murmansk on 13 August last year. His wireless-operator managed to bail out, but von Rabenau didn't make it and was later found dead in his cockpit. Once it was established that he hadn't survived the crash, it was up to me as his room-mate to sort out his personal effects and get them sent to his next-of-kin.

'At that time every pilot was issued with an expensive automatic aerial camera that had to be returned to the Staffel when he was posted away elsewhere, or officially accounted for in the event of his being killed or reported missing. I happened to know, however, that von Rabenau had two of these cameras; one belonging to the Staffel and one that was his private property. I naturally assumed that the camera he had taken with him on his last flight was the one he had been issued with, and that the one I found among his effects was his own.

'But when I put this camera with the things to be sent back to his family, Kirchmeier demanded to see it. He found a number stamped on it proving it to be official issue, which meant that the camera lost in the crash had to be the one owned by von Rabenau. Without discussing the matter with me, and without giving me a chance to explain that von Rabenau possessed *two* cameras, Kirchmeier promptly had me charged with theft. I was later found not guilty due to lack of evidence. But since then Kirchmeier and I have not been exactly the best of friends.'

I described my own experiences with Kirchmeier in the 'Vaasa affair' and his questionable behaviour during our weather-reconnaissance mission together on 13 April. Schwab and I decided there and then that it would be in our best interests to give Kirchmeier an even wider berth in future and agreed to let each other know at once should he ever try to get either one of us into hot water again.

On 29 April we received orders to mount another night raid on Murmansk. This time there would be a whole eight of us lined up at the end of the Kirkenes runway ready for take-off at 01.15 hours. But once again I had to suffer the indignity of plodding along in my 'AX' behind and below the rest of formation, waiting for them to complete their bombing from 8,000 metres before condescending to come down to my altitude for the flight home.

We had touched down at 02.30 hours and, after a short night's sleep – which was more than made up for by a leisurely breakfast – I was briefed for my next op. As of immediate effect I was officially made up to Rottenführer, meaning I would be the leader of the Rotte, or pair, and would have my own wingman. We were to take off at 12.00 hours for a convoy escort mission. It promised to be a routine assignment, but just as we arrived over the vessels a fiery stream of tracer went sizzling past my port wing. I instinctively wrenched my Me 110 over into a dive, noticing out of the corner of my eye as I did so an Airacobra breaking away to the left at a tremendous rate of knots.

It was probably this surplus of speed that had caused the Russian to miss me with his first hurried burst of fire. It had certainly cost him the element of surprise. He was already circling to come in for a second pass. But this time I would be ready for him.

A few days earlier we had been talking shop in the mess. Among the subjects discussed was how best to shoot down, or at least shake off, an enemy fighter attacking from astern. One favoured method was to dive the Me 110 until it had built up sufficient momentum to go into a steep climb. The enemy pilot would presumably be following these manoeuvres but, with his fixed forward-firing guns, he would have to allow for deflection – in other words, aim *ahead* of his quarry – if he wanted to hit it while both aircraft were still climbing.

The Bell P-39 and the Me 109 could also be easily mistaken for each other in the air. These Airacobras are pictured on the Russian fighter airfield at Varlamovo near Murmansk.

This in turn meant that the pursuing fighter would have to climb the more steeply of the two. As the enemy machine approached the vertical and its angle of attack reached 90 degrees, the pilot would no longer be able to hold it. The flow of air over the wing surfaces would be insufficient to keep the aircraft flying. It would then stall and go into a spin. This was the moment the Me 110's wireless-operator – who also doubled as gunner and manned the flexible machine gun in the rear of the cockpit – had been waiting for. Now was his chance to open fire on the pursuing enemy fighter as it fell away beneath him in an uncontrollable spin.

This, at least, was the theory that I was now about to put to the practical test!

I held my machine's nose down in a screaming dive until I thought the rivets were going to start popping out of the wings. Then I yanked her up into a full-throttle climb. My Katschmarek was following my every move, and *he* had a string of five Airacobras on his tail. Perhaps I held the climb for a fraction too long, for not only did the Russian behind me stall and fall away, I felt my own machine becoming mushy. I no longer had enough speed to keep it flying. Tipping almost lazily over onto one wing, it too went into a spin.

On my way down two Airacobras appeared for a fleeting instant in front of my nose. I immediately took pots at both of them, but didn't manage to hit either as my Me 110 was spiralling out of the sky like an autumn leaf. But then, maybe due to lack of fuel – or for some other unknown reason – the Russian fighters suddenly all sheared off. There was no point in our chasing after them as they were much faster than we were.

When I had regained control of my aircraft, I took the opportunity to tear a quick strip off Bengard and the other wireless-operator – why the blazes hadn't they warned us of the enemy fighters closing in on us?

After landing back at Kirkenes at 14.39 hours, I really hauled the pair of them over the coals. And then the truth came out. They admitted somewhat shamefacedly that they had mistaken the approaching Airacobras for Me 109s. But even this should have been reported. I decided to let the matter rest there however, as, apart from a single bullet hole in my Katschmarek's tailwheel, no damage had been done.

After all the excitement I would have welcomed a shot of cognac and an hour or two's rest, but it wasn't to be. I was ordered to take off again almost at once on another convoy escort mission. It seems we had too few machines serviceable, and none of the other gentlemen was willing to go up in my old 'AX'. When I finally returned from this latter op my day's flying time totalled more than six hours. But at least the white bird was now scheduled for a major service, and I had every hope of getting my hands on a supercharged 'G'-model.

On 1 May I flew my tenth operational mission since arriving in the far north. It was yet another convoy escort job. Upon landing back at Kirkenes I was at first more than a little surprised to be congratulated so heartily on this 'anniversary'. Then one of the mechanics filled me in. Up here, apparently, the rule of thumb was: 'If you survive your first ten missions, you'll survive a whole lot more'.

The next seven days saw steadily increasing temperatures and the advent of the spring mists. On 8 May all the buds burst forth and the branches of the stunted birch trees began to display their first tiny green shoots. At long last the snow and frost were being forced to give way to warmer weather. Unfortunately, however, enemy activity allowed us little opportunity to wallow in whatever joys the tundra spring might have to offer.

On 10 May my Katschmarek and I were sent up to cover an inbound convoy. At a height of 300 metres I discovered that we had lost radio contact with ground control. It was not long after this that my wingman pointed upwards, drawing my attention to a dogfight raging some way above our heads. Without radio contact I had no way of telling who was involved in the scrap – was it our own Me 110s, the ones we were supposed to relieve over the convoy, or a bunch of Me 109 fighters up from Petsamo?

I rammed the throttles to the gate and was just about to start climbing to find out for myself when I saw a Pe-2 coming down with its port engine burning like a torch. It was clearly trying to escape out over open water, but its descent was going to take it right across my line of fire. Just before it reached my level, I gave it a little deflection and opened up. As I had anticipated, it flew straight through my fire, which shattered its starboard engine. With one engine already in flames and the other now dead, the enemy machine plunged into the sea.

At that moment another Pe-2 came diving down, also seeking to get away at low level. I immediately set off in pursuit. As I slowly gained on the fleeing Russian, it struck me as odd that its rear gunner hadn't opened fire on me. Maybe he too had been deceived by the similarity between our two machines and had mistaken my Me 110 for one of his own squadron's Pe-2s. If so, it was a fatal error. My opening burst of fire smashed into his port engine and almost sawed the entire wing off. Seconds later he also skidded into the sea, throwing up a huge wall of water in his wake.

At debriefing back in Kirkenes there was some confusion concerning the Staffel's victory claims. Oberleutnant Kirchmeier reported two kills. He had claimed one enemy aircraft destroyed in the high-altitude dogfight and had then set fire to the engine of a second Pe-2 – the one which had subsequently flown in front of my nose in its efforts to escape, and to which I had delivered the *coup de grace*.

Following the traditional old huntsman's adage that "the kill rightfully belongs to he who strikes the first mortal blow," I considered Kirchmeier's claim for the second Pe-2 to be perfectly in order. Later I was told that, had he been able to extinguish the fire, the Russian would have stood every chance of making it home on the one engine if I had not knocked out the other. It also transpired that the log of the naval vessel escorting the convoy, whose commander had witnessed the air action, had credited my low flying Me 110 with two enemy aircraft destroyed.

But I didn't want to start any arguments – and certainly not with Kirchmeier. After all, he'd been up here for a whole year and had only managed to get two confirmed kills under his belt to date. He was welcome to add 'mine' to the list to make it three. I'd been in the north for just four weeks and was quite content with my one uncontested victory.

On 24 May I was ordered to fly the recently serviced IB+AX down to Nautsi, which lay some 100 kilometres to the south of Kirkenes. The airfield at Nautsi housed a Flugwachkommando (Air observer detachment; 'Fluko' for short), whose job was to monitor, coordinate and record all aerial activity – ours as well as the enemy's – in the northern area. This detachment was in constant contact with all local air defence HQs and could, if the need arose, organize appropriate defensive measures and direct air operations.

Apparently, my white bird was to be used for some test measurements or other required by the Fluko, but nobody had bothered to tell me what these were. So I duly flew down to Nautsi, landed, was instructed to take off again and climb to 6,000 metres, land again, and then fly back home at 5,000 metres ... and that was it!

4 Shipboard Fighter Control Officer

When I got back from Nautsi there was no sign of Leutnant Schwab. He had been seconded as fighter control officer to the local naval command HQ down in the port of Kirkenes. His task there was to try to help solve a long standing and extremely irritating problem we had been having with the navy's Flak. Whenever one of our convoys came under attack from Russian aircraft, the Flak gunners aboard the naval escort vessels – and any other ship armed with a weapon – would simply point their guns at the enemy and blaze away. They paid no notice whatsoever to the correct angles of deflection and didn't seem to realize that if you wanted actually to *hit* a moving target, you had to aim ahead of it. Consequently, their fire was being sprayed around all over the place behind the enemy machines and was, if anything, much more likely to bring down any of our fighters that happened to be sitting on the Russians' tails!

We were also attempting to improve communications between ourselves and the convoys so that the presence and course of any approaching enemy aircraft picked up by our ground radar could be reported to the ships' escorts without delay.

But Orge Schwab was back with us that same afternoon. The navy couldn't use him, they said, because he was totally unfamiliar with naval procedures. Staffelkapitän Schlossstein was wandering about the ops room looking worried and seemingly at a loss what to do next. It had been his idea in the first place to try to come to some arrangement with the navy people that would be to our mutual benefit and help make our combined convoy defences more effective.

When I came out with the suggestion that he could perhaps send me in Schwab's place – I had, after all, spent five years in the naval branch of the Hitler Youth and was quite conversant with maritime practices – his face lit up: 'Hell's bells, Wollenweber, why didn't you say so straightaway?' Before I could point out that nobody had asked me, he was already giving me my orders: 'Right, get going! Grab your hand baggage. It's off to the navy for you. Try to explain about angles of deflection to them. When we're chasing Russians around their convoys it'd be nice not to have to worry about being shot at by or own Flak for a change. And tomorrow you'll get the chance to sniff some sea air again. You're escorting a convoy on the long haul around the Varanger Peninsula.'

The town of Kirkenes – the harbour area is off to the left.

The landing stage in the old harbour of Kirkenes.

A convoy leaves Kirkenes at daybreak and heads up towards Varanger Fjord.

The so-called 'long haul' up around the Varanger Peninsula to the north of Kirkenes was just a hop, skip and a jump for us flyers, but shepherding a slow convoy that distance on the surface promised to be a slow and tedious business. I hastily packed a few things together as ordered and within the hour I was standing on the quayside at Kirkenes gazing out over the motley collection of shipping that jam-packed the harbour. There were vessels of every kind: barges, colliers, tugboats and a whole variety of other ships that had been converted into armed escorts to protect the convoys bringing vital supplies, medical equipment and military material up to our troops in the far north.

Many of the ships were moored in trots side-by-side with gangplanks connecting them. Unfortunately, their decks were all at different heights and it was quite a precarious process clambering from one to the other. It was not until I climbed aboard the third vessel, an armed escort ship, that I found the officer in charge, who introduced himself as Leutnant Köchert. I explained that I was the 'new' fighter control officer. His response to this statement lacked a certain amount of enthusiasm. But when I went on to add that I had undergone some naval training he became much more affable.

'Dump your gear here for the time being. We've got to get over to HQ. There's a heap big pow-wow – er, I mean there's a meeting of all the ships' masters – just about to start,' Köchert said with a grin. I had the feeling we were on the same wavelength and that we were going to get on well together.

At the entrance to the HQ building we were met by the officer who was chairing the pre-departure convoy conference. He introduced himself in a somewhat grand manner as Leutnant zur See Schwarzmann. Once he was out of earshot, however, Köchert quietly murmured in my ear: 'We just call him "the black man all at sea"' – a none-too-subtle wordplay on the unfortunate Schwarzmann's name and rank.

The meeting opened with discussions on various nautical matters relating to the coming convoy operation. Then I was given the floor so that I could explain to the assembled naval types the reason for my presence amongst them. I described the problems we were having and the dangers we faced from their sometimes less than accurate anti-aircraft fire. This didn't go down at all well. Some of the real old salts sitting around the table were obviously annoyed at my veiled criticisms. I could tell from the expressions on their faces exactly what was going through their minds – What's this Luftwaffe idiot trying to tell us, the young fool doesn't know what he's talking about.

My comments on their wild shooting had clearly rubbed them up the wrong way. But I didn't want to lose what little good will they may have had left, so I tried to sugar the pill with my next words: 'Gentlemen, I'm here to assure you that, as from today, we will be passing on to you all the information we ourselves receive from our radar stations. This will give you warning whenever Russian aircraft are approaching one of your convoys. It will tell you what distance they are away from you, and from which quarter the attack can be expected.

'Unfortunately, our radar can't give us the altitude. But as most of the enemy formations take off from the airfields around Murmansk, we in Kirkenes – and our single-seaters over in Petsamo – will have plenty of time to scramble, establish the attackers' height and inform you accordingly. Hopefully, we will be able to intercept them before they even reach you. We really will be pulling out all the stops and doing everything we possibly can. I only ask that you judge the results of our efforts for yourselves over the course of the next few convoys!'

When the conference was over I accompanied Leutnant Köchert back aboard his ship, where he allocated me a bunk. I don't know if I was overly tired, or whether it was the vessel's gentle rocking motion, but I slept like a log that night. I finally resurfaced on the morning of 25 May to the ear-piercing howls of ships' sirens and the loud shrilling of bosuns' pipes. Then the ship's engines throbbed coughing and spluttering into life, and the smell of diesel fuel mixed with burning oil slowly began to permeate the already stuffy below-decks atmosphere.

It was not long before the convoy weighed anchor. One by one the vessels filed out of Kirkenes harbour. As we made our way northwards up the 25-kilometre length of Kirkenes Fjord towards the more open waters of Varanger Fjord, the armed escorts took up station to starboard – the side from which any enemy attack was more likely to be launched – while the merchantmen hugged what was considered to be the greater safety of the western shores of the narrow fjord. A deck-chair was set up for me on the port wing of the bridge. If I hadn't known there was a war on, I could almost have convinced myself that I was enjoying a luxury cruise.

We crossed the mouth of Varanger Fjord and set off on the long slog up the coast of the Varanger Peninsula. Near its north-easternmost tip we passed Svartnes. This was the site of a small satellite airfield, although Svartnes itself was perhaps better known for its local Finnmark radio station, which broadcast a non-stop stream of popular hit music. As the convoy negotiated the channel between Svartnes and the offshore island of Vardö I watched the towering cliffs of the peninsula sliding by to port. I was also making a mental note of the various buoys and other navigational aids along our route, little realizing at the time that these would one day prove to be my saviour.

We were about three hours into the voyage when one of the lookouts shouted a warning: 'Floating mine – ahead to starboard!' There was a sudden flurry of activity on the bridge. The report was immediately flashed to the *Mathias Stinnes*, the large merchantman sailing close alongside us. Then Köchert grabbed a couple of rifles from the rack and handed one to me: 'Quick! We've got to render that thing harmless. If we can shoot a few holes in its outer casing it should hopefully sink, then it won't be a danger any more.'

Although it was fun standing next to Köchert taking pot-shots at the mine bobbing about in the water off our bow I must, at the same time, admit to having a nasty feeling in the pit of my stomach. I had a very healthy respect for mines. I think it was their unpredictability and silent air of menace that made my skin creep. At the moment, though, our efforts didn't seem to be having much effect. Every time one of us managed to hit the target there was a loud metallic 'ping' as the bullet ricocheted off its rounded sides. We were never going to sink it at this rate. I motioned towards the twin 20-mm Flak gun mounted on the bow, and at Köchert's affirmative nod the gunner loosed off a short burst that sent the mine disappearing into the depths.

It was less than half-an-hour later that we had our next bit of excitement. This time the lookout's warning yell was even more alarming: 'Torpedo!! Surface runner on the beam ahead!' Köchert immediately called all the crew up on deck, rapidly explaining to me as he did so: 'We've got to stop that eel at all costs. The *Mathias Stinnes* won't be able to take avoiding action in time.' He began to snap out a series of orders: 'Full ahead! Stop! Full astern! Stop!' I realized at once that he was trying to churn up the water and deflect the torpedo from its course, even at the risk of sacrificing his own ship to save the merchantman.

'Hold tight to the railing and stand on tip-toe,' he called to me as he dashed from one side of the bridge to the other. The next couple of minutes stretched our nerves to near breaking-point. Every man on board stood rooted to the spot, not uttering a word – just holding his breath and expecting the big bang at any second. But the big bang didn't come. If the torpedo was going to hit either ourselves or the transport it would have done so by now. The tension relaxed.

Köchert heaved a sigh of relief. 'Our lucky day,' he remarked as he produced a bottle of brandy from its hiding-place in the wheelhouse. He handed me the beaker from a thermos flask: 'I reckon that little fright calls for a toast to cement our friendship. By the way, do you know why I told you to stand on tip-toe just now?' When I shook my head he went on: 'It's a precautionary measure. If you're standing with your feet planted firmly on deck when a torpedo hits, the shock wave from the explosion usually means broken ankles – and broken ankles make it that much harder to swim if you end up in the drink!'

'Dammit, can't a man enjoy a well earned drink in peace and quiet?' Köchert grunted in mock annoyance as the ship's wireless-operator interrupted us with an urgent report: 'Herr Leutnant, message from ground control. Indianer approaching – grid reference just coming through now.' I indicated to Köchert the position of the enemy aircraft on the map and said that, in my opinion, the attack would come in on our starboard side. Then I switched over to our fighter frequency and, after listening in for a few moments, turned back to Köchert: 'Relax and pour yourself another drink. It was just a bunch of Russian fighters. Our own boys were already in the air. They caught them over open water and shot the whole lot down.' As nothing else seemed to be brewing we enjoyed another shot of brandy and, without further incident, were rounding the North Cape by midnight.

'Fancy a drop of midnight soup?' the wireless-operator enquired with a smile, offering me a bowl of chicken broth with a generous amount of meat floating in it. The soup didn't just smell good, it tasted good as well. I could feel its welcome warmth spreading through my stomach. All unsuspecting, I asked if there was any chance of a second helping. At first, I couldn't understand why my innocent request caused everyone on the bridge – who had hardly touched the delicious soup themselves – to burst into fits of laughter.

But it wasn't long before a change in the ship's behaviour revealed the reason for the crew's mirth and seeming lack of appetite. Apparently the stretch of sea to the west of the cape was notorious for its heavy swells. The whole vessel was already beginning to shake and tremble as it pitched viciously up and down. After balancing momentarily on the crest of one huge wave, it would plunge steeply down to the bottom of the intervening trough, where it would then bury its bow deep into the next onrushing roller. Rearing up, the entire foredeck would disappear under a wall of water – which is exactly what it felt as if the chicken soup inside my stomach was doing.

Just hang on in there! These navy types would no doubt love to see a seasick birdman feeding chicken broth to the fishes. But I was used to this queasy feeling in the pit of my stomach. I'd experienced it many times before while flying particularly violent manoeuvres and had learned how to suppress it. A surprising number of the crew, however, had succumbed to the relentless rollercoaster motion of the ship as it butted its way through the mountainous seas. A lot of them were hanging over the railings on the lee side retching fit to bust. There were even a few real old salts among them offering up the contents of their stomachs in tribute to King Neptune.

But the most miserable of the lot was the wireless-operator who had brought me the 'midnight soup'. I now saw his friendly smile for what it really was – an evil grin! He had no doubt been looking forward to the sight of some fool of a Luftwaffe Leutnant 'chucking up his guts'. But now it was he who had his yellowish-green face deep in a bucket as he heaved his insides outside at ever more frequent intervals.

In the grey dawn light of 26 April we finally put into Hammerfest, the most northerly town in Europe. As convoy commander, Leutnant Köchert had to report our arrival to the office of the local Staatssicherheitsdienst (SD, or State Security Service) and he invited me to come along. Since the outbreak of war between England and Germany, the free movement of much of the world's merchant shipping had been blocked. Many Norwegian vessels and their crews, now sailing under the British flag, operated out of Britain's ports. The vast majority of them were unwilling to return to Norway, and those few who did want to go back were prevented from doing so by the sea war being fought in the Atlantic and neighbouring northern waters.

It was perhaps little wonder then, that many Norwegian women whose menfolk were serving the Allied cause, were working for the British secret service and carrying out espionage activities in German-occupied ports such as Hammerfest. I was amazed at the huge apparatus that the SD had built up here to keep watch on and control the local population. Espionage, counter-espionage, surveillance, wireless-monitoring, the laying of false trails, searching for 'dead-letter boxes', infiltrating, supplying false information and shadowing suspects – all these, and more, were part and parcel of daily life.

I was even more astounded when Köchert told me that some of our U-boats based up

Convoy escort commander Leutnant Köchert (right) and the author during the voyage from Kirkenes to Hammerfest.

here in Hammerfest were equipped with 'Bachstelze' ('Wagtail') mini-helicopters. These tiny, one-man machines, designed by Focke Achgelis, were actually unpowered gyro kites. Tethered to the U-boat by a long cable, they could be raised to an altitude of 100 metres and more. From this height the pilot, who was in telephone contact with the U-boat and was acting as its 'eyes', had a range of vision of some 40 kilometres – five times the distance that could be seen from the surfaced boat itself – and was thus able to spot targets that would otherwise have remained invisible.

The following day Köchert departed for Tromsö, where his ship was due to go into the yards for overhaul. This deprived me of my berth on board and meant moving into a hotel ashore until I took passage back to Kirkenes.

I was not to stay in Hammerfest for long. By 28 April a new convoy had been assembled and the game began all over again. It started with my reporting to the naval officer in charge. This time it was the commander of an 'M'-class light cruiser, an elderly Kapitän zur See who, after listening to my little speech of introduction, asked me what on earth a member of the Luftwaffe was supposed to be doing on board his ship.

The captain, obviously a re-tread left over from the days of the Kaiser's navy, left me in no doubt as to his opinion of my supposed duties: 'Radio location, wireless interception, radar – I've got all that on board already. But I don't need any of this new-fangled nonsense.' My response, that the information relayed to me by the fighter control centre would enable me to provide him with advanced warning as to the times and direction of any Russian air attacks, he brushed aside with the words: 'You won't convince me of that in a thousand years, it's all a load of mumbo-jumbo.'

Despite this, the voyage passed without incident until shortly before Vardö. I had been using the time to show the ship's wireless-operators how they could call up information and keep tabs on the situation in the air by referring to the Luftwaffe's gridded maps. But now messages about Russian air activity were beginning to come in thick and fast. Armed with these, I reported to the bridge: 'Herr Kapitän, we're going to have visitors. The enemy will attack us from astern.' 'Never, the Russians always attack from ahead,' he replied dismissively.

Worried that the captain's obduracy could lead to a disaster, I got on to our fighter control centre in Petsamo to voice my concerns: 'Wireless control officer here. Expecting attack by Indianer from astern. Request confirmation. Over.' The response was immediate: 'Message received and understood. Our Alarmstaffel is already in the air. They'll soon be sitting on the Ivans' tails. Out.'

'Herr Kapitän, you're about to see something worth watching,' I said. And hardly were the words out of my mouth before the first columns of water were climbing into the air behind the rearmost ships in the convoy. I counted six Pe-2 bombers, four of which were promptly shot down by our fighters. The remaining pair ditched moments later. Switching to our fighter frequency, I was greeted by the usual wild hubbub of excited voices. 'Two Russian bombers in the drink, send out the air-sea rescue Heinkel,' I yelled above the din. Later I heard that the crew of one of the bombers had been found and picked up.

I refrained from pointing out to the captain that my warning of an attack from astern had been right after all. Apart from this one incident, nothing else of note happened and the convoy duly arrived back in Kirkenes safe and sound.

At the debriefing conference I did, however, have one final proposal to put forward. While the Me 110s of our convoy escort patrols were circling above the ships protecting them from enemy air attack, they were also in an ideal position to spot the approach of enemy submarines and to observe the tracks and course of any torpedoes fired at the convoy. I therefore suggested that all ships should remain tuned to the Finnmark radio station at Svartnes throughout the voyage. Our aircraft's wireless transmitters were powerful enough to interrupt the station's music broadcasts and the ships would thus be able to receive immediate warning of any submarine threat. Knowing from which direction the torpedoes were coming, they would hopefully have sufficient time to turn bows-on towards them and thus greatly reduce the danger of being hit.

My proposal was approved almost unanimously by those present at the conference. Only my 'Captain Stubborn' expressed doubts that the idea would work in practice. And, to be perfectly honest, I wasn't totally sure myself how some of our younger and more inexperienced pilots might react upon seeing a spread of torpedoes for the first time. Would they pass on the warning via the radio station in the correct manner?

As luck would have it, I was ordered to fly another convoy escort mission some three weeks later. Before I took off Staffelkapitän Schlossstein had a word of caution for me: 'The Fliegerführer (local air commander) General Holle has just phoned through to inform me that the Luftwaffe supply ship *Rüdesheimer* will be among the incoming convoy. So make sure you keep an extra careful lookout, Wollenweber!'

We had been monotonously circling the convoy for well over an hour when I suddenly spotted bubbles in the water directly below me. A fan of three torpedoes was heading for the convoy, which was only about a kilometre away. I quickly yelled to my wireless-operator: 'Switch to the Finnmark frequency and transmit the following message to all ships: "Torpedoes heading for convoy, all ships stop engines immediately, alter course to 360 degrees, am indicating direction of approach!".'

I dived to within five metres of the sea's surface and flew along the line of bubbles left by the middle torpedo of the three, hoping that the watching ships' crews would cotton on to what I was trying to show them. And it seemed to be working! All the ships had turned due north as ordered, and the gaps this manoeuvre had opened up between the individual vessels meant there was every chance that the enemy eels would pass harmlessly by.

Did I say *all* the ships? No, there was one merchantmen hugging the coast that seemed to be totally oblivious to my urgent warning. It was sticking to its original course – and naturally it had to be the *Rüdesheimer*! I tried calling the ship directly, warning once more that it was in imminent danger of being hit by a torpedo, but I got no reply. I flew as low as I dared over the vessel, but could detect no signs of life. By now I was certain that whoever was asleep at the wheel was about to get an extremely rude awakening indeed.

When the torpedo struck home it could also make things very uncomfortable for me at my present height. So I turned back and went looking for the Russian submarine. The enemy commander must have been very sure of himself, for the boat was ploughing through the water with its periscope raised. At least I can rob him of the pleasure of watching one of our ships sinking, I said to myself, as I let fly with all guns at the unwinking glass eye.

The Russian Murmansk medallion depicts an air attack on one of our convoys.

By this time the torpedo had hit and I was very glad indeed that I had been nowhere near the *Rüdesheimer* when it did. The explosion sent a colossal fountain of water 50 metres into the air. If I had been caught up in it my machine would have been very severely damaged, if not totally destroyed.

The *Rüdesheimer* turned in towards the coast and beached herself in shallow water. Over the next few weeks her cargo was gradually unloaded. She must also have undergone makeshift repairs, for she disappeared from her temporary resting place and I never saw her again. Unfortunately, I never got to meet her captain either. I would have dearly liked to ask him why he had handled his ship in such an odd manner.

Leutnant Köchert's escort vessel on the high seas.

5 Shocks under the Midnight Sun

Between 30 May and 5 June very little happened in and around Kirkenes. Long periods of boredom spent at readiness alternated with uneventful convoy escort missions each lasting anything from two to three hours. There *were* one or two emergency scrambles during this period, but the reported enemy machines were either nowhere to be seen or were already on their way home. Summer had well and truly arrived, and up here above the Arctic Circle the sun didn't set from mid-May until the end of July. This meant that, throughout these ten weeks, we always flew in daylight – even if our watches were telling us it was midnight.

Such was the case on 6 June, when Leutnant 'Orge' Schwab and I were given orders for an emergency scramble at 00.50 hours. The engines of my white 'AX' sprang into life immediately, but my room-mate was having trouble getting one of his engines started. I waited for him as long as I dared, but then took off on my own and headed for the grid square where the intruders were reported to be.

After climbing to 300 metres I saw a lone enemy fighter flying eastwards along the coastline below me. Then I spotted five of his colleagues some distance away. I identified the enemy machines as Curtiss P-40 Kittyhawks, an American type supplied to the Russians in

The Dackelstaffel played its part in shipping escort operations.

considerable numbers under the so-called 'lend-lease' scheme. When the five other fighters suddenly reversed course and headed back in my direction I presumed the single P-40 had seen me and was calling his comrades for help.

'There's just time to deal with you before your five friends get here,' I thought to myself as I quickly closed in to within 20 metres of the Russian's tail. I couldn't afford to hang around for too long though, so I gave the P-40 a full salvo; thumbing the cannon button and triggering my four machine guns all at the same time. A single stream of tracer shot across the Russian's wings. Out of my formidable battery of six forward-firing weapons, only one machine gun was working!

With the speed I had built up in my dive, I flashed past above my 'victim' and banked towards the five rapidly approaching enemy fighters, my single machine gun still hammering. With just one gun in action I was in a near hopeless situation against five much more manoeuvrable single-seaters. But to break off and try to escape would only have made matters worse. So I decided to risk everything by staying put and mixing it with them.

The outcome was inevitable. Within seconds there was a sudden loud bang in my starboard engine. White smoke began to pour out of it. The loud scream of tortured metal came from under the cowling. It subsided into a dull grinding sound before the engine gave up the ghost altogether. But then, to my utter astonishment, the Russians turned away! Either they thought I was done for, or perhaps they were running low on fuel. Whatever the reason, they reformed into a loose gaggle and headed off eastwards.

I didn't have time to ponder their actions – or even to thank my hard-working guardian angel – there was too much to do: close starboard engine fuel cock, trim the machine to relieve the pressure on the stick, feather starboard propeller. But, like five of my six guns, the feathering mechanism also refused to work. The propeller blades remained at full pitch and were acting like an enormous airbrake. By this time I was only 15 metres above the surface of the water and, despite pushing the port throttle to the gate, I couldn't persuade the machine to climb any higher.

While my faithful Bengard was busy sending out a constant stream of SOS messages relaying our grid position to ground control, Orge Schwab appeared on the scene. He pulled up close alongside me and indicated that he was going to stay with me and cover my tail. That was one worry less, for it was only with the greatest difficulty that I was now able to hold the white bird at 15 metres while at the same time keeping an anxious eye on the oil temperature of my starboard engine.

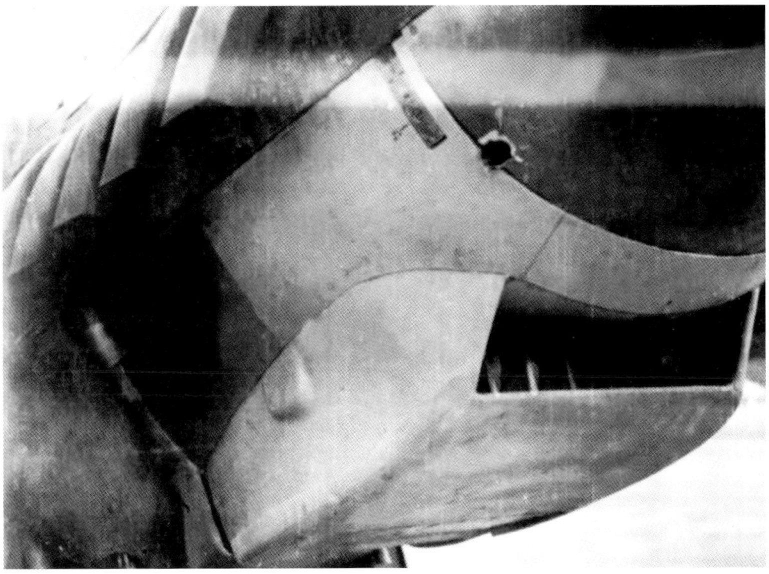

This hit from a P-40 Kittyhawk severed a coolant hose on my Me 110 and forced me to make a one-engined landing.

Although I had my hands more than full adjusting the trim every few seconds in my efforts to stay on an even keel, being careful to handle the stick with kid gloves, and trying not to be too heavy on the rudder pedals, a thousand thoughts were racing through my head: would the port engine hold out, how bad was the damage to my starboard engine, could I possibly get it going again, had the hydraulic or fuel pipes been hit, what would happen if my dead engine caught fire, would I be able to ditch with the sea running this high or would we smash into a wave and sink like a stone, how far was it to Kirkenes and would we be able to make it?

One tiny glimmer of hope: the oil temperature of the starboard engine wasn't rising. Could I possibly coax it back into life and gain a little more altitude? We must be getting close to Kirkenes by now. I decided to risk it: fuel cock on, ignition on, right-hand throttle fully forward and – wonder of wonders – the engine responded. At first just a low unwilling whine, then more of the earlier grinding noise. It spat once or twice, emitted copious amounts of alternating white and black smoke ... but it was working!

This was no time for half-measures. I hauled the stick back into my stomach. The machine started to climb and I started to pray. At 400 metres the game was finally up. The engine burst into flames. So fuel cock and ignition off again, feather propeller – still didn't budge – but at least we'd gained some precious altitude. At last the airfield came into sight. As I eased 'AX' down in a smooth one-engined landing, Orge Schwab roared past low over my head.

And what a reception committee had turned out to meet me! Not just the field's fire section and ambulances, but other knots of men armed with fire-extinguishers, rescue crews, medics, ground crews and mechanics were all lined up to left and right of the runway. Even the station commander came running. By this time it was 01.22 hours, and after the usual congratulations and much slapping of backs it was soon back down to business and the normal daily routine.

For me, still being officially at readiness, this meant making my way out across to the readiness dispersal point again. Here there was a small hut furnished with a table and four easy chairs for the two crews of the 'Alarmrotte', or readiness flight. Each spell of duty at readiness lasted twenty-four hours, from noon on the first day until midday the next. Throughout this time the crews had to remain in full flying gear – overalls, boots and life-jackets – ready to dash at a moment's notice to the two fully fuelled and armed Me 110s standing just outside the door. The crews ate their lunches immediately prior to, and after their period of duty. All other meals, supper, breakfast and the like, were taken out to them at the dispersal hut.

As I settled down into my easy chair again, I got to wondering whether the engine of my white bird was repairable. If it wasn't, the Russian who had hit me might, in fact, have done me a favour. Perhaps I'd be given one of the supercharged 'G'-models in its place?

At 04.44 hours we were ordered up on another scramble. Within five minutes I was back in the air; this time in IB+GX, the reserve machine. But my wingman and I made no contact with the enemy. Their reported position was much too far off. Even if we had managed to get a fix on them, pursuit would have been pointless as they would be long gone before we reached the given area.

So instead we turned back and amused ourselves on the flight home by carrying on with the card game we had been playing in the dispersal hut before being so rudely interrupted by the order to scramble. Only now we did it from memory, calling out our cards to each other over the R/T: 'Queen of hearts.' 'Jack of diamonds.' 'Ace of hearts.' 'Ten of hearts.' 'You lose!' I had to laugh out loud as I pictured the Russians monitoring our wireless transmissions. They must have got quite a headache trying to decipher our new 'secret code'!

From mid-May until the end of July above the Arctic Circle the sun never set.

The hours spent at readiness and circling over convoys were pretty boring as a rule. The only breaks in the monotony were provided by the occasional bombing mission, but these were few and far between during this period. Obstinately refusing to sink into the sea, the midnight sun would continue to shine twenty-four hours a day until the end of July. This meant that we were flying around the clock. Nor did the constant light allow me any proper sleep. It was as if the body was permanently on the go. And the result was total overfatigue.

12 June saw me sent up on another emergency scramble. Once again, I was in the air and climbing hard within five minutes. My wingman on this occasion was Gefreiter Jettkandt. He had lifted off shortly after me and together we began our pursuit of the reported Russian intruder. As we had been given his exact coordinates, we had every hope of cutting him off.

We were flying just below a thin layer of cloud when ground control came on air: 'You must have the target in sight now!' I presumed the Russian must be above the cloud and so ordered Jettkandt: 'Stay down here below the cloud, I'll go up and have a look.' But when I eased up through the thin layer there was not a thing to be seen far or wide. I called to my wingman: 'Jettkandt, where are you?' 'I'm right behind you,' he answered. I turned my head, but couldn't see him. 'Is Jettkandt behind us?' I asked my wireless-operator. 'No,' came the prompt reply. Suddenly the penny dropped: 'Jettkandt,' I yelled over the R/T, 'you're sitting on the Russian's tail – shoot!' 'I can't possibly shoot at you, Herr Leutnant,' he protested. 'It's not *me*, you idiot,' I was practically screaming at him by now, 'It's a Pe-2! Shoot at it, for Christ's sake – I'm still above the clouds!'

It was at this moment that the ground controller came through again: 'Target turning away northwards.' I dived back down through the cloud and saw Jettkandt stooging around in the sky 50 metres in front of me. The Pe-2, which should have been a piece of cake, was already 100 metres further away and diving like mad. He was clearly aiming to make his escape out over the open sea. Burdened with our underwing fuel tanks, we hadn't a hope of catching him and so Jettkandt missed the opportunity to claim his first victory. Unfortunately, he was himself killed only a few weeks later.

There was some more bad news on 22 June. The young crew of Unteroffiziere Karl Herrmann and Alois Hermann had taken off in 'my' white bird – whose engine had apparently been repairable after all – only to lose their lives when they crashed into a fjord south of Kirkenes shortly afterwards. Neither crewman had any blind-flying experience, and it appears that they had got into difficulties and simply fallen out of the clouds. The crash of IB+AX was the final clincher for those who had stuck to the belief that the machine had been nothing but a white bird of ill omen all along.

Shortly before midnight on 10 July a motor-cycle combination screeched to a halt in front of the 'Haus Brandis'. The despatch-rider came dashing into the officers' mess where Orge Schwab and I, dressed in our Sunday best, were in the middle of a game of chess. 'Emergency scramble,' he reported breathlessly. 'Get out to the field immediately. A Russian submarine has surfaced just off the coast. Our coastal artillery has been firing at it, but with no luck so far. Your machines are all ready to go. They've been loaded with special bombs. If you can't find the sub, you're to fly on and bomb the enemy coastal battery on the Rybachiy Peninsula.'

All thoughts of the game forgotten, we rushed outside and jumped on to the motor-cycle combination. A few minutes later we pulled up next to our aircraft. Still wearing our ordinary shoes, without our flying overalls and with no life-jackets, we quickly clambered aboard. After taking off we climbed to 2,000 metres in order to gain as wide a view as possible of the surrounding waters. Although we searched along the whole length of the coastline and then continued on up to the northernmost tip of the Rybachy, or Fisherman's, Peninsula – where we combed an additional 50 square kilometres of choppy open sea – the submarine was nowhere to be seen.

So we retraced our steps and flew back down the western side of the peninsula to our alternative target. This was a known Russian coastal battery set into the mouth of a rocky cave or tunnel. We had already discussed our tactics. Orge would carry out the first attack, dropping the special HE bombs originally intended for the submarine on the gun emplacement, while I remained at 2,000 metres to guard against the Russian fighters based on the peninsula. Orge commenced his dive. He released his bombs individually, placing them neatly on the rocky terrace. When he had climbed back up to me, we exchanged places and I tipped over onto one wing intending to complete the job.

But on the way down a stream of shells from a heavy Flak gun suddenly came hurtling

A contemporary drawing of an Me 110 of the Dackelstaffel carrying out a low-level attack.

up to meet me. The first of them exploded only five metres or so in front of my windscreen. To avoid flying straight into the rest of them I immediately eased off the gas and forced the Me 110 into an even steeper dive.

With the sea rushing towards me and lines of tracer whizzing past the roof of my cockpit, I could only hope that the Russian gunner would soon run out of ammunition. Taking hurried aim at the rocky nest, I jettisoned rather than released my bombs, and prayed that I would be able to pull out of the dive before hitting the water.

One last fiery 'tomato' detonated like a New Year's Eve firecracker just above my head, and then I was hauling my machine into a 90 degree pull-out. I heaved back on the stick with all my strength and after a few interminable seconds found myself in level flight ten metres above the wavetops.

Behind me I saw the Flak gun and lots of other unidentifiable bits and pieces go flying into the air as my bombs exploded. But on the way home I couldn't shake off the thought of what would have happened if that Russian gunner had held his fire and not opened up at me until a second or two later. Fully committed to the dive, with no time and not enough height to take the avoiding action I did, I would have been a certain goner.

At one hour past midnight on 11 July we landed back at Kirkenes. Later that same day we put in over another three hours in the air, escorting an outbound convoy in a mission that lasted from 20.04 hours until 23.14 hours.

6 Trials and Tribulations

The following stories really belong in the realms of the fairy tale. But as they are all true and so typical of the more absurd inanities of those times, I feel I have simply got to tell them.

Every officer in the Staffel had to carry out 'additional duties'. And one day Oberleutnant Kirchmeier ordered me to take over a couple of jobs for which he had been responsible in the past. These were counter-espionage and the looking after of all the secret teleprinter messages – the so-called 'GKdos' (geheime Kommandosachen, or top-secret communications) – that we received. Kirchmeier also instructed me to go through the files and destroy all teleprints that were more than two years old and didn't directly concern us.

Recruiting my wireless-operator to give me a hand, Bengard and I set to work. We were soon coming across all sorts of 'important messages' such as, for example, the fact that the east-west runway of Catania airfield on Sicily was closed due to construction work, or that General Stumpff, the AOC Air Fleet 5, had left his slippers behind after visiting unit 'XY'!

All the teleprints carried consecutive reference numbers. And while sorting them out I discovered that several were missing, without there being any record as to the reason for, or the date of, their removal from the files. A little voice inside me told me to make a careful note of the missing items, and also to record the reference numbers of those we were ourselves weeding out and destroying.

It wasn't long before Kirchmeier came to see me to ask, with seeming innocence, whether the two teleprinter messages with reference numbers 'so and so' had been destroyed. Thanks to the notes I had made, I saw through his little ruse and was able to inform him that those particular messages had already been removed, but that neither the name of the person responsible, nor the date of the occurrence, had been entered in the files.

I'm quite certain in my own mind that he was planning to put me on a charge for destroying documents that didn't actually exist any more. And as nobody other than Kirchmeier could have known about the two messages that had mysteriously 'disappeared', it could only be he himself who had taken the items without counter-signing for them. This put me in the position of being able to level charges against *him*, but I refrained from doing so.

Another even more unwelcome – not to say hated – duty that had landed in my lap back at the end of April was the overseeing of dead comrades' personal effects. If any member of the Staffel was killed it would be my job to go through his things, make a list of all the personal items, pack them together and send them – along with an account of the events surrounding his loss and a letter of condolence – to his next-of-kin.

I had hoped that I wouldn't be called upon to perform this unenviable task too often, but the first losses occurred within a couple of days. On 1May my room-mate Leutnant Schwab and his wingman, Oberfeldwebel Renke, had taken off on a convoy-escort mission. Between 13.00 hours and 15.00 hours the convoy came under sustained attack from Russian bombers, during the course of which Schwab managed to bring down a Pe-2 and Renke a Handley-Page Hampden. But then Renke's own machine was hit and crashed into the sea. Both crew members, Oberfeldwebel Renke and his wireless-operator Unteroffizier Reiher, were killed instantly.

Orge Schwab was able to provide me with all the details as he had witnessed the event at first hand. But I can't imagine that it was much of a consolation for the two men's families to be told that they had shot down an enemy bomber shortly before their own deaths. To make matters even worse, I learned from Renke's room-mates that he had, on this very day, received a letter from his wife informing him of the birth of their son. What on earth did one write to a young woman who had just become a mother and a widow at one and the same time? I was only just 21 years old myself and it was totally beyond my powers to find the right words.

As already mentioned earlier, the crew of the almost identically and rather confusingly named Karl Herrmann and Alois Hermann had crashed into a fjord south of Kirkenes on 22 June. After I had sent their effects to their next-of-kin, one of the families wrote back to complain that the coffee, which their son was intending to bring home with him on his next leave, had not been in the package. This was not as frivolous as it might now appear. Real coffee was an almost unheard-of luxury and practically unobtainable in wartime Germany.

I therefore looked into the matter and discovered that the deceased had kept the coffee in his gas mask container, believing that the tightly-sealed cylindrical metal canister would help retain its freshness and aroma. The gas mask was official issue, of course, and had to be returned to stores upon the owner's demise. Before it was handed in however, the dead crewman's room-mates, who knew all bout it, had emptied the canister of its unofficial contents which, they assured me, they had thoroughly enjoyed!

I can no longer remember how I replied to the disgruntled heirs regarding their 'rights to compensation', but at least the matter didn't come to court – which is more than can be said of the next incident:

It was towards the end of July when Staffelkapitän Schlossstein instructed me to drive down to the courthouse in Kirkenes, where I was to act as an assessor to the judge in a military hearing. Two other members of the airfield's personnel, an Unteroffizier and a Gefreiter, had also been nominated as jurors in the same case.

The judge – I've long forgotten his name – received us wearing his full black robes, and when the Unteroffizier politely requested: 'Herr Amtsrichter, may I use the toilet, please?' the judge regarded him haughtily. 'Just come down out of the trees, have we? 'Amtsrichter', indeed! I'll have you know I'm not some little county court magistrate. I am a military judge advocate and you will address me accordingly as 'Herr Kriegsgerichtsrat'! What we are dealing with here is a criminal act, not some petty civil misdemeanour!'

Before the proceedings began we were taken into a small side room where the 'Herr Kriegsgerichtsrat' outlined the case. He informed us that the accused, an Austrian and a member of our station staff, already had a previous conviction to his name. His latest crime: He had stolen a bottle of champagne from the supply bunker and had shared it with his barracks comrades.

'What is the world coming to when common soldiers start drinking champagne? huffed the judge indignantly. 'We are in a state of war, and theft in wartime is a particularly serious crime. The man has to be severely punished as a warning and deterrent to others. I consider a two-year prison sentence appropriate. Now let us go into the courtroom.'

When we entered the chamber we found six spectators, a female court secretary and two Feldjäger, or military policemen, already present. The MPs – commonly known as 'Kettenhunde' ('chained dogs', on account of the gorget worn on a metal chain round their necks) – sprang to attention the moment they saw us. 'The court is in session, all rise!' yelled one at the top of his voice. The other then brought in the miscreant, who was looking thoroughly cowed and bewildered.

After giving his name, rank, date and place of birth, and marital status, the prisoner was questioned about the circumstances of the crime he was charged with, and asked to give details of his previous conviction. We already knew all about his present 'crime'. As to his previous conviction, it turned out that as a boy he had been caught stealing an apple from a tree and eating it!

At the end of his account, and by now very nearly in tears, he pleaded in a broad, almost unintelligible Austrian accent: 'I'll never ever do it again, please have mercy, Herr Obergeheimrat.' I thought that was laying it on a bit thick, calling the judge a 'supreme privy councillor'. I didn't know whether to laugh or cry – yes I did, in actual fact I was seething with rage at the whole ridiculous charade that was keeping me away from other more important duties.

We retired into the side room to consider the verdict. 'Well, there you are, gentlemen,' the judge was almost gloating, 'You heard it with your own ears. The man is nothing but an inveterate thief who belongs behind bars!'

I made no attempt to conceal my distaste when I replied: 'Herr Kriegsgerichtsrat', firstly, as to that previous conviction; we were all young once and I'm sure we've all stolen a few cherries or the odd apple or two from a neighbour's garden – but perhaps not you? I would call that pilfering at the very most and hardly worth bothering about, if indeed at all. But that's neither here nor there. Furthermore, I cannot share your view that a Gefreiter ought not to be allowed to drink champagne. Only recently I was presented with three bottles of champagne for shooting down an enemy aircraft. I shared these out among the ground crews, and this included several Gefreiter. So perhaps it's not in fact all that unusual for other ranks to enjoy a taste of champagne.'

'Which is why,' I continued, barely able to keep my anger in check, 'I consider your proposed sentence far too draconian. In my opinion, the theft of a bottle of champagne is not a matter for this court. I would therefore suggest that it be dealt with at unit level, and that the sentence be determined by the Gefreiter's own disciplinary superiors. Any other course would be both inappropriate and excessive.' I turned to the two other jurors: 'What do you think?'

As they both agreed with me, the black-robed 'hangman' was left with no alternative but to stalk back into the courtroom and announce through gritted teeth: 'The accused is to be referred back to his unit for the necessary disciplinary action.' I never saw or heard anything of this bloodhound again, but from the surreptitious grins I got when I returned to the airfield it was clear that word of my speaking up in the poor wretch's defence had already spread.

With the midnight summer nearing its end, our operations would soon have to be adapted to suit the changing weather conditions. No longer would be called upon to fly around the clock. During the summer the ground crews and mechanics had also been working ceaselessly to keep the machines in the air. Now they too could look forward to quieter times.

On one occasion during this period I was detailed to take a newly repaired aircraft up on a test flight. Somewhat to my surprise, the flight mechanic insisted on accompanying me, saying that certain checks still need to be carried out. I was to fly perfectly straight and level, and follow his instructions to the letter. Once we were aloft he started to issue a string of most peculiar commands, such as: 'Port engine to half revs, OK, now starboard engine to half revs.' He continued in a similar vein, spouting a load of nonsense that had nothing whatsoever to do with the testing of the machine's airworthiness. I was puzzled at first, but then the light slowly dawned: he had only come along with me in order to get his hands on the pre-flight rations!

So that's your little game, is it? Well, in that case, you'd better start earning them then. At 2,000 metres I flew into a large cloud. Once enveloped in the murky white blanket I suddenly, and without warning, flicked the Me 110 onto its back and went into an inverted spin. I heard a startled yell behind me as my passenger landed on the canopy roof, and when I emerged from the cloud, still in a steep dive, there was a distinctly sour smell coming from the rear of the cockpit.

I righted the aircraft. But I don't think he was entirely convinced when I reassured him: 'Stability test completed, nothing wrong with this crate.' After we landed he still seemed to be having some difficulty in swallowing, and he disappeared as fast as his rubbery legs would carry him.

One of the most tragic incidents, however, occurred on 25 July. That morning a Feldwebel came to see me. He was Oberleutnant Kohlweiss' wireless-operator and he explained in a shaky voice that he had just had the most awful dream – that he was going to die this very day! Pale as a ghost, his whole body trembling, he asked whether Bengard, my wireless-operator, could possibly fly today's scheduled convoy escort mission in his place.

I tried to calm him down by saying that the Russians had never yet attacked one of our convoys as close to harbour as this one would be and, besides, a bad dream was just that; it was a far cry from being reality. In addition, I explained that Bengard and I were due to relieve one of the present readiness crews at noon and that, under the circumstances, I simply couldn't spare my wireless-operator.

I thought that I had managed to allay his fears, but then the unthinkable happened: a formation of Russian bombers attacked the convoy just off the coast. Four of them were shot down without loss to ourselves. Oberleutnant Kohlweiss claimed one of them. But he returned to base with a dead man on board. There was a 20-mm shell hole in the rear canopy of his machine, and the wireless-operator was slumped in his seat shot through the head.

This incident really got to me and I seriously began to wonder whether there actually *was* such a thing as being able to foresee one's own death in a dream. It was following this tragedy that I went to see the Staffelkapitän and asked to be relieved of the harrowing task of handling my fallen comrades' effects, a request to which he kindly agreed.

7 An Operational Miscellany

At midday on 6 August eight of us, under the command of the Staffelkapitän, took off from Kirkenes to bomb the Russian fighter airfield at Varlamovo 1 to the northeast of Murmansk. Hauptmann Schlossstein particularly wanted to lead this mission as he had been told that he was soon to be posted to a desk job on the staff of Luftflotte Nord (Air Fleet North) HQ in Oslo.

I had been flying my 'own' supercharged-equipped Me 110G-2 since 1 August. So I was now perfectly capable of accompanying the others up to altitudes of 7,000 to 8,000 metres and no longer had to swan around by myself a couple of floors lower down. The 'older' crews were flying at the head of the formation, but by this time I had grown quite accustomed to bringing up the rear. As leader of the last Rotte, the only aircraft behind me was the machine flown by my wingman, who today was Leutnant Müller, a relative newcomer to the Staffel.

It wasn't long before things started to get uncomfortable. Shortly before Murmansk the Russians' massed Flak defences opened up with everything they had. I'd heard somewhere that Murmansk had the greatest concentration of anti-aircraft defences and more fire power than any other town or city in any war zone – greater even than London. Judging by today's performance, I could well believe it.

As the formation was echeloned to starboard, I was fully expecting the Staffelkapitän to go over onto his left wing at the start of his dive. This was standard practice, for it allowed each pilot then to release his bombs without endangering the aircraft in front of him. But on this occasion, for some reason, Hauptmann Schlossstein chose to stand his aircraft on its *right* wing before diving away almost directly beneath us. This meant that all the other machines had to corkscrew in order to follow him. And this in turn resulted in every pilot having another machine right in front of his nose on the way down. We all had to wait until the boss had dropped his bombs and pulled away to port before we could let go our loads one after the other in quick succession.

Did I say we *all* had to wait? Not so my wingman, the new boy still sticking faithfully to my tail. His bombs came whistling past above my head, missing my canopy by a hair's breadth. Fortunately, my wireless-operator Bengard had seen the danger. His lightning-fast yell of warning gave me just enough time to stand the machine even more steeply on its head and get out of the way of the falling missiles.

Me 110F-2 'LN+TR', flown by Hauptmann Schlossstein.
(Profile drawing by Claes Sundin)

Staffelkapitän Schlosssstein's 'LN+TR' over the Kola Inlet. An Me 109 up from Petsamo flies escort (top right). *(Artwork by Dave Ails)*

Due to my involuntary imitation of a Stuka, I didn't pull out of my dive until very close to the ground. From this low down I could plainly see a number of Russian fighters attempting to take off. Some ran straight into the fountains of earth thrown up by our exploding bombs. Others somersaulted onto their backs as they careered into the fresh bomb craters. They certainly aren't going to pose any danger to us, I thought. And I was right. We all returned home safely and without loss, landing back at Kirkenes at 15.44 hours.

On 6 September Hauptmann Schlosssstein summoned me to his offices to brief me on my next mission. I was to lead a Schwarm of four machines to provide aerial cover for the minelayer *Roland*. The vessel was currently some 100 kilometres north of the Varanger Peninsula laying a mine barrier to protect our Norwegian coastal supply route. Prior to her conversion into a naval minelayer shortly before the outbreak of war, the *Roland* had been a small peacetime pleasure steamer shuttling between the port of Bremerhaven and the North Sea holiday islands of Heligoland and Norderney.

Oberleutnant Franzisket (left) with Oberleutnant Koch next to him; Staffelkapitän Schlosssstein is in the right foreground.

The minelayer *Roland*.

'Take the two new crews with you,' the Staffelkapitän added. 'It will give them a chance to get some idea of the featureless landscape and the fjords up here.' I duly gathered the 'new boys' together to explain the coming mission. I told them that after take-off they were to form up and follow me in loose formation, keeping a distance of 20 to 30 metres between each machine.

We lifted off and climbed to an altitude of 1,000 metres as we headed northwards. As the crow flies, the southernmost point of the Varanger Peninsula is only about 60 kilometres away from Kirkenes and we soon had it in sight. We passed the little coastal township of Vadsö where we altered course slightly to port before flying across the entire width of the peninsula to our next navigation point, the settlement of Berlevag situated at its northern tip. From here it should only be another 100 kilometres or so to the position where the *Roland* was going about its business out on the wide expanse of the Barents Sea.

Actually, I was fully expecting to be able to spot the *Roland* out to sea ahead of us as we overflew Berlevag. But there was no sign of the vessel. Instead, we were confronted by a meteorological phenomenon that none of us had ever seen before. A perfectly straight, almost tubular bank of thick fog – some 100 metres wide and 50 metres high – stretched northwards from the coast to the distant horizon like some spectral line of longitude drawn across the sea's surface. We flew out along the western edge of this peculiar fog bank but when, after a good 30 minutes, there was still no sign of the minelayer, I decided to turn round and return to Varanger.

Once the coast of the peninsula had reappeared out of the sea in front of us, I next decided that it would be a good idea to fly through the wall of fog and have a look at the other side. It should take less than a minute and, if we kept in tight formation, even the new boys ought to be able to make it without difficulty. I gave my instructions over the R/T, ordering my wingman to close up on my right and the other pair to take station on my left. Once they had done so, we descended almost to sea level. Here, between the surface of the water and the base of the fog bank, forward visibility was about 50 metres.

Five minutes dragged by. We should have been back out into clear air long before now, but we were still swimming through the whitish-grey soup. I was just beginning to wonder how I could have miscalculated so badly, when the ground radio station suddenly came on air: 'Achtung, Achtung*!* Fog descending, fog descending. No landings possible at Kirkenes, Petsamo or Banak. Out.'

In reality, of course, the station's message closed not with 'Out', but in the German manner with the word 'Ende', or 'End'. 'End?' I thought to myself, but not for us if I can help it! From my frequent visits to steam baths in the past I knew that there was always a layer of slightly clearer air between the steam and the tiled floor of the baths – which is exactly what we were experiencing now between the base of the fog bank and the surface of the sea. But even here the fog was growing thicker by the minute, and I desperately needed to find some kind of landmark or reference point to get us out of this mess.

I knew that we had to approach Varanger's northern coastline at an angle. If we headed straight towards it in this appalling visibility there was every chance that we would either smash into the peninsula's towering cliffs or find ourselves unwittingly flying into one of the region's many narrow, ravine-like fjords from which there would be no escape.

It was here that my recent stint as fighter controller on board Köchert's convoy escort vessel came to my rescue. The hours I had spent sitting in my deck-chair on the ship's bridge making mental notes of the Varanger Peninsula's rugged coastal features, the many inshore buoys and other navigational aids – even the wave patterns in certain areas – now proved their worth. For suddenly, and much to my relief, I spotted jutting out of the sea a rocky outcrop that I instantly recognized.

It was the first sign that we were nearing the coast. We turned southeast and flew down the right-hand side of the peninsula. This particular stretch was studded by numerous capes, headlands and fjords, so we reduced speed to 300 kph. Hopefully, this would give us enough time to take avoiding action should any obstacles loom up unexpectedly in front of us. But in this fog it was going to be a problem to identify the south-easternmost tip of the peninsula – which lay some way beyond the small offshore island of

The search for the minelayer *Roland* (outward flight in red, return flight in blue).

Vardö – and then make the turn to the southwest that would get us back on to the correct course for Kirkenes and home.

Just as Vardö was sliding past on our port side, however, I caught a glimpse of what I at first took to be a mirage: there, clamped to the top of an enormous wall of rock on the mainland facing the island, was a 200 metre layer of slightly clearer air. And through it, wraith-like, I could make out the small fighter airfield at Svartnes. Its untidy collection of huts were blanketed by fog, but the outline of the runway was still dimly visible.

There's our one and only chance, I thought to myself, quickly deciding to land first by myself and then talk the other three down over my machine's R/T from the ground. But just as I was preparing for final approach I realized that the machine on my left was still keeping station on me and was also clearly intending to land … the only trouble was, he had forgotten to lower his undercarriage!

I immediately aborted the landing. 'Resume close formation again,' I ordered as I climbed away. That was all I needed; to have Svartnes' single runway blocked by an aircraft that had accidentally belly landed and was preventing the two machines still in the air from putting down safely. In the meantime the deteriorating weather conditions had scotched my hopes of talking down the other three from the ground, for by now the entire field was covered in a thick layer of fog.

We had had no other option but to press on, keeping the shadowy mass of the Varanger coastline just in sight to our right. It wasn't long before we got our next scare. In the water ahead of us was a German convoy. At first the ships were just vague shapes. But as we drew closer we could see the Flak gunners of the naval escort vessel rushing to their action stations. They had evidently mistaken us for Russians and were preparing to give us a hot reception. It was only thanks to our true enemy – the accursed fog – that we were able to escape the 'friendly' welcome thrown up at us by our seafaring comrades.

We finally rounded the south-easternmost tip of the Varanger Peninsula and altered course southwest. In front of us lay Varanger Fjord, the 30-kilometre-wide stretch of water that separated the southern coast of the peninsula from the mainland. But now we were faced with a new problem. There were no navigational markers of any kind on the far side to indicate which of the numerous mainland fjords was the right one that would lead us down into Hoy Bay and thence to the airfield at Kirkenes.

We had already been in the air for the best part of three-and-a-half hours and our fuel would soon be getting dangerously low. If I had only had my own skin to worry about, I would have put my machine down on a likely looking spot and made my way back to base somehow or other. But as Schwarmführer I was also responsible for the safety of the three other crews and had to take them into consideration too. My wingman was doing a good enough job sticking closely to my starboard side. But he was offering no practical assistance; simply following every move I made. Nor could I expect any kind of help from the two new crews behind us.

In short, I was – almost literally – between a rock and a hard place: if I couldn't locate the entrance to the fjord that opened out into Hoy Bay, all four machines would be forced to ditch offshore. If I *did* manage to find Hoy Bay and spot the wrecked ship in the water just short of the airfield I might, with a lot of luck, still be able to reach the north-south runway. But even then, assuming that I chose to ignore the ground controller's earlier warning of 'no landings possible at Kirkenes', there was every likelihood that our four aircraft would end up as four piles of wreckage scattered across the field.

It was at that moment that my hard-working guardian angel emerged out of the fog in the guise of another patch of clear air along the very stretch of coast that led down into Hoy Bay. We flew along the short length of fjord and I soon saw the distinctive shipwreck that was as good, if not better than any marker buoy pointing the way to Kirkenes.

Now there wasn't a moment to lose. It was only another 500 metres or so to the end of the airfield and I hoped that all three crews would respond at once to the orders I rapped out over the R/T: 'Lower undercarriages, flaps down, wingman remain in place just off to my right, numbers 3 and 4 tuck in behind us.'

I started a careful descent. At a height of 60 metres the fog was so dense that we had nil visibility. It wasn't until we were down to 30 metres that I could just make out the vague outlines of the north-south runway. I put the machine down as if on eggs and hoped to God that I had landed close to the midway point of the runway – if I had overshot and was too near to the end there was going to be one hell of a bang any second now!

Out of the corner of my eye I saw that my wingman was also down cleanly and safely.

But then came the next shock: some complete idiot was strolling across the runway right in front of us! As our two machines emerged out of the mist he threw himself flat on the ground and disappeared beneath our wings. We later learned that the jaywalker had been a member of the station fire section. Fortunately he survived his ordeal with nothing more than a few minor bruises.

All four machines had got down in one piece. Now all we had to do was to find our dispersal area in the all-pervading mist. Soaked in sweat, but happy to have brought my three charges home safe and sound, I flipped the R/T switch to give my last orders of this eventful day: 'Follow me in single file to the east-west runway, taxi down to far end, park machines in a row and – Well done!'

Our Staffel comrades and members of the ground staff came running across to us from all corners of the field, yelling out congratulations at the tops of their voices. The boisterous welcome they gave us could not have been warmer or more sincere. Because of the fog and the length of time we had been in the air, everybody here on the base had long given us up for lost. Our unexpected reappearance called for a 'birthday party' to celebrate our making it back – and what a party it turned out to be!

But first I had to report to Staffelkapitän Schlossstein: 'Leutnant Wollenweber returned from mining support mission. Search continued for 200 kilometres north of the Varanger Peninsula but still unable to find the *Roland*. All crews and four machines returned intact.' 'How the devil did you manage it, Wollenweber?' the Staffelkapitän asked. 'We already feared the worst. Nobody's ever got back safely in such conditions before. In a fog like todays, other crews have either crashed or simply disappeared into the sea. My congratulations and admiration for pulling it off!'

After a complete change of my sweat-soaked clothes, from flying overalls down to my underwear, I joined the crews and other officers in our small mess for some serious drinking to celebrate our collective 'birthday' and escape from the fog. I don't remember much about the rest of that evening, but it must have been quite a session. The next morning dawned fine and clear – the only fog still around was all inside our heads!

Actually, this was meant to be a rest day for us and for lunch my wireless-operator Unteroffizier Bengard and I were planning to demolish a 15-pound sea salmon that we had caught in the fjord. But then, without warning, an order came through. I was to find a wingman and fly up to Svartnes at once. The AOC of Air Fleet 5, Generaloberst Stumpff, had been stranded there by yesterday's fog. We were to provide fighter cover for the General's return flight to Banak. And so, instead of being able to savour our salmon at leisure, we had to swallow it down almost whole before hurriedly taking off for the little airfield at Svartnes, where yesterday's brief break in the fog had played such a dirty trick on us. Today, we flew up there beneath a sky so radiantly blue that it was hard to imagine that it had been such a lethal murky grey just twenty-four hours earlier.

Hoy Bay on the approach to Kirkenes airfield, with a shipwreck marker left of centre.

After touching down at Svartnes we reported to the Generaloberst. He immediately invited us to lunch: 'Get some food inside you. As my fighter escort, I'll be expecting you to take good care of my machine later on! We're having asparagus with ham.' 'Our apologies, Herr General – it's a great pity, but we had a salmon just before take-off and, with the best will in the world, we couldn't eat another thing at the moment.' Stumpff shook his head in disbelief: 'Well, I must say, you seem to be living in the lap of luxury up here.'

While Stumpff was enjoying his asparagus, I took the opportunity to discuss the coming escort mission with my wingman. As we landed I had noticed that Svartnes' sandy surface had thrown up an enormous cloud of dust which had taken ages to settle. I had already been informed that the General's He 111 would take off from the hutted, or western end of the field and climb away eastwards out over the sea before reversing course and heading for Banak. We therefore decided to take off in the opposite direction; in other words, from the seaward perimeter. This meant that we would not have to make the change of course from east to west, and could utilize the time thus saved sitting on the ground waiting for the dust storm created by the General's departing machine to clear.

Everything seemed to be going to plan. The AOC's Heinkel lifted off and we taxied out to our take-off positions. But it was at this point that my wingman signalled to me that his port engine was not developing full revs. I indicated in return that I couldn't afford to wait for him. I would take off immediately and he would have to follow on as quickly as possible.

I got into the air just in time to formate on the Heinkel, which had completed its turn out to sea and was now roaring back across the field at low level waggling its wings in farewell. As I climbed I looked back over my shoulder and saw a lot of feverish activity going on around my wingman's machine. Then I took up station slightly off to one side and some 20 metres above the General's machine. As its pilot wasn't flying 'with all the stops out', I hoped the Svartnes mechanics could get my wingman's engine to run properly and that he would soon be able to catch up with us.

For reasons of safety, the Heinkel pilot had opted to fly the overland route to Banak. Our more usual operational missions along the coastal areas were regularly menaced by the threat of attack from Russian aircraft searching for our supply convoys. But suddenly there was an urgent warning from the local radar station: 'Unidentified aircraft approaching you from the seaward side!' The Heinkel pilot promptly poured on the gas, while I curved away to confront the oncoming 'enemy' who, as I had already guessed, proved to be my wingman chasing after us at maximum speed. Together, we then shepherded the General's machine safely to Banak. Once it had touched down, we flew a lap of honour around the field before setting off back to Kirkenes, our 90-minute mission successfully accomplished.

Not long afterwards a teleprint message was sent to Kirkenes with words of commendation from the General to the effect that: '... by our prompt action we had forced an enemy aircraft to turn away.' My wingman and I were somewhat bewildered when we read this – it seems the General had been completely unaware of the problems we had had in delivering him to Banak! (Some time after the war I saw Hans-Jürgen Stumpff again at a meeting of the Arctic Fighters' Old Boys' Association in Oberauroff near Wiesbaden. There I told him the 'true' story of our escort mission. He remembered both the flight, and the 'dangerous encounter with the enemy machine' well – but now we could both have a good laugh about it.)

In August there occurred a phenomenon that I have since learned is repeated every year in the Arctic Ocean region but which, at that time, I had not yet experienced. One day I decided to go hunting for ptarmigan. Many of these grouse-like birds were to be found among the shrubs and stunted birches that ringed our bomb dump. I selected a shotgun from the cupboard where the Staffel kept a small stock of captured weapons. The moment she saw the weapon in my hand, Herdla – a dachshund

General Stumpff (left) in front of his He 111 personal transport.

bitch and another of the unit's menagerie of mascots – came rushing up to me. I presume she must have been trained as a gun dog. She certainly seemed to know what a shotgun was for, and refused to budge from my side.

I set out with Herdla trotting at my heels. As we neared a bush that I suspected might be concealing a ptarmigan or two, I began to wonder why the surrounding copse was such a peculiar grey colour. The mystery deepened when Herdla suddenly started howling and shot off home like a rocket. Then the entire 'copse' rose into the air in a slow circular motion, emitting a shrill penetrating whine as it did so. I had heard that noise before. It was when a single gnat had been pestering me – but this was a thousand times worse. Now I understood why our room orderly Gefreiter Neuwirt had insisted that I take a camouflaged mosquito net along with me on my hunting expedition: up here at this time of year the air is filled with millions of midges just waiting to pounce on any living creature with blood in its veins.

Hastily throwing the green veil over my head, I raced off after Herdla as fast as my legs would carry me. But the huge swarm of insects had already beaten me back to the barracks. When I got there everyone was rushing around in their camouflage nets like a bunch of green whirling dervishes, cursing loudly and flapping their arms about wildly.

The nightmare lasted a full three days, during which time even the reindeer and all the other local fauna took to the mountains. Our constant swatting of the invading hordes soon left the walls and ceilings of our quarters looking like some blood-spattered slaughterhouse. And those unlucky enough to fall prey to the tormenting bloodsuckers came out in such enormous lumps and bumps that they looked for a while as if they were suffering from bubonic plague.

Shortly before this our dachshund bitch Herdla must have been covered by one or other of the numerous stray dogs that roamed around the airfield, for a few weeks later she produced a litter of six cute little mongrel puppies in the corner of the clerks' office that was her 'home'. At first, none of us was allowed to approach her and her small brood. If anyone got too close she would immediately bare her fangs in a threatening snarl, protecting her pups as any perfect canine mother would.

Then one day, when the pups had grown a little bigger and were able to walk, Herdla proudly led them outside – only to be caught in a sudden heavy downpour of rain. The pups were completely drenched. As a boy I had grown up with dogs and so knew that young puppies had to be rubbed down as quickly as possible to prevent them from catching distemper. I called to my friend Orge Schwab to help me round them up and bring them into the dry. But first we had to convince a very suspicious Herdla that we meant no harm to her youngsters. This was no easy task, but eventually we got the bedraggled pups indoors, dried off, and wrapped in a warm blanket. The whole bundle, with the pups tucked snugly inside, was then placed carefully on Schwab's bed.

It was while Orge and I were still swapping stories about the various dogs we had owned that Leutnant Ziegenhagen burst into the room gesticulating theatrically. Ziegenhagen had something of a reputation as a ladies' man and had consequently been nicknamed 'Bel Ami' by the rest of the Staffel. He was brandishing a letter from Fee, his girlfriend back home, which informed him that she had met and fallen in love with an older man and that there was no point in their writing to each other any more.

Before we could stop him, the distraught Ziegenhagen had dramatically hurled himself full length onto the bed where the puppies were snuggled up inside their blanket. At our belated yells of warning Ziegenhagen immediately leapt to his feet again, but it was too late: four of Herdla's pups were dead, only two had survived the sudden crushing weight. I don't mind admitting that, even today, I am still moved when I think back on that little canine tragedy in the middle of a world at war.

Upon returning from yet another 'naval operation', or convoy escort mission, on 25 September I found the whole Staffel in a state

The trio who gave the Dackelstaffel its name: Lockheed, Bamse and Herdla

of high excitement. Every available machine was to take off to provide cover for the heavy cruiser *Lützow*, which was preparing to leave the protection of the Alta Fjord on the northwest coast of Norway for a sortie out into the open ocean. I desperately wanted to be part of this mission but, wouldn't you know it, my own aircraft was currently in the workshops stripped down for a major overhaul. I tried to find a spare machine, but everywhere I asked it was the same story: I hadn't a hope – everything with wings already had a crew assigned to fly it.

Then I heard that there was an aircraft in the shops that had just undergone inspection and was being readied for a check flight. I got our despatch rider to run me across to the maintenance hangar on his motor-cycle and there, sure enough, was an Me 110 having a final once-over before being taken up on a test flight. Needless to say, I immediately 'confiscated' the machine for my own nefarious purposes. After dashing back to my quarters to get my flying gear, I lost no time in clambering aboard the Me 110 and taxiing out for my 'test flight'. The rest of the Staffel was still lined up alongside the runway. They had not yet received permission to take off as all the fjords in the Alta region were still shrouded in fog.

I had only just lifted off and retracted my undercarriage, however, when there was an almighty bang and, at the same moment, a thick stream of white smoke began to pour out of my starboard engine. I knew at once that a coolant pipe had burst. Either that, or one of the connecting clamps had worked loose. Below me I could see the Staffel starting to take off. But any hopes I may have had of accompanying them on the *Lützow* mission had gone up in smoke along with my starboard engine.

Instead, I now had problems of my own to worry about. With just my port engine working, I could only climb very slowly. And to make matters worse, off to my left was the start of the chain of high mountains that led away southwards from Kirkenes. During flying training we had been expressly forbidden ever to turn in the direction of a 'dead' engine. In my present predicament this meant to my right, for then my port engine – of necessity now at full throttle – would automatically try to flip the machine onto its back; a position from which it would be impossible to recover.

But with the mountains rearing high into the sky on my left, I had no other option. Using the rudder with the utmost caution, I commenced the gentlest of sliding turns to my right, taking great care to keep the machine on an even keel throughout the entire manoeuvre. I had to repeat this process two more times as I slowly circled above the field, gradually gaining sufficient height to come in for a smooth one-engined landing. Startlingly white against the blue sky above me was a perfect little smoke ring, the last traces of the cloud of coolant spat out by my starboard engine. Although I was safely down on the ground again, my nerves were still taut. I only really relaxed when the chief mechanic climbed up onto the wing to enquire innocently: 'Since when has the Herr Leutnant been flying a steam-engine?'

I gazed wistfully after the departing Staffel; eight machines led by Hauptmann Schlossstein on their way to a rendezvous with the *Lützow*. Three days later they were back and I heard that they had been given a very 'fiery' welcome by the cruiser and her attendant destroyers. Although our aircraft had fired off the correct recognition flares as they approached the flotilla, every single vessel had opened fire on them! It was yet one more example of the complete breakdown in communications between naval high command and our air fleet HQ. We could only assume that the ships had either not been informed of where and when to expect our machines' arrival, or that details of the plan to provide them with an aerial umbrella had got lost somewhere in 'official channels'.

With the Flak showing no signs of letting up, and with one of his formation having already been hit, Staffelkapitän Schlossstein had finally had enough. He ordered his pilots to make for the alternative landing field at Herdla, while he stayed with the damaged aircraft. Once all had arrived at Herdla the Staffel waited until the latter had been repaired. Then, after a brief stopover at Stavanger, all crews flew back up to Kirkenes safe and sound.

The following weeks brought a wearying and repetitive round of duties: escorting

The heavy cruiser *Lützow*.

An armourer reloads the machine guns in the nose of an Me 110.

convoys, emergency scrambles, bombing missions, long periods at readiness, and back to escorting convoys again. Then, at the beginning of October, we were given orders to mount an attack on Murmansk using C-500 Flammbomben, the large incendiary bombs that were commonly known as 'Flambos'. Our four Rotten – eight machines in all; each carrying a single half-ton 'Flambo' with its mixture of oil and an HE detonating charge – took off in darkness in order to arrive over the target area at dawn.

But once again I missed the party. When I got to 4,000 metres my port engine began to run unevenly and emit a series of unhealthy grinding noises. I looked across at it to see if I could spot what was wrong. A steady stream of oil was escaping from the engine nacelle and flowing in rivulets across the wing's upper surface before being whisked away in a fine spray from the trailing edge to be left eddying ribbon-like in my wake. I quickly shut the engine down before the pistons seized. So far, so good. But what was I to do about my bomb?

To continue on to the target, let alone take part in the attack, was clearly out of the question. I therefore reported my problem over the R/T, broke away from the formation and turned to make my way back to base. And then? There was still the little matter of the bomb. If I didn't manage to pull off a perfect one-engined landing – if a wingtip accidentally brushed the ground, for example – my 'Flambo' could very well explode and cause an absolute firestorm. Worse still, the field's bomb dump, which was not all *that* distant from the runway, held another 20 of these devilish devices and I dreaded to think what would happen if they went up too!

So instead I altered course northwards, having decided that the safest thing to do was to drop the 'Flambo' into Varanger Fjord. I had hardly got rid of the damned thing when the pre-dawn darkness was rent by a tremendous flash. Below me it was suddenly as light as day. At least 200 square metres of the fjord's surface was burning fiercely as the oil spread across the water. Then I heard the normally unflurried voice of the ground controller shouting in agitation: 'Aircraft crash, aircraft crash!' Although we had been ordered to observe radio silence, I needed to put him straight before he alerted the rescue services: 'No crash – 'Flambo' jettisoned!'

Now I had to concentrate on getting my machine down in the dark on just the one engine. The damage sustained by the port engine meant that the hydraulic pump which actuated the undercarriage and flaps was out of action. I would have to use the emergency compressed air bottles to lower my wheels and flaps.

But when I did so – at an altitude of 2,000 metres and with the starboard engine throttled back – the aircraft went down like an express elevator! I still couldn't see the runway and the starboard engine, now at full power again, was doing its best to push me back out over Hoy Bay. I could hardly keep the machine under control. There was nothing else for it. When I judged the east-west runway to be beneath me, I closed the starboard throttle, dumped my remaining height by side-slipping to port, and felt the wheels rumble as they touched down on the ridged surface marking the start of the runway. I'd made it!

After taxiing to dispersal I summoned the workshops superintendent. He listened to my story, pulled a face and said: 'You must be mistaken, Herr Leutnant. That engine's in perfect working order.' Before I could stop him, he had swung himself into the cockpit, switched on the port engine and rammed the throttle forward. There was one ear-splitting bang – and then silence. The pistons had seized and the ends of the connecting rods were poking through the cowling. The expression on the superintendent's face was a sight to behold, and my next words did little to ease his obvious discomfiture: 'That was a clear case of deliberate damage to Wehrmacht property. If that engine hasn't been replaced by tomorrow, I'll be submitting an official report on the matter. You can no doubt imagine the sort of punishment you'll get. You're looking at a reduction in rank, at the very least.' By noon the following day my 'Anton' had a brand new engine.

On 13 October 1943 we were sent out on yet another convoy protection mission. The weather was rather foggy and we hoped we would be in for a quiet day. But as we circled the ships six Il-2 Sturmovik aircraft suddenly flashed past in front of my nose as they dived towards the convoy. What an opportunity, I thought to myself as I banked hard to get on the tail of the last of the six Russians. When he was filling my gunsight, I triggered my weapons – and absolutely nothing happened! The machine guns refused to fire.

Almost incoherent with rage, I could have cheerfully strangled the armourer responsible with my bare hands. Here I was, sitting only five metres behind the Il-2; the perfect set-up for a certain kill. Was I going to be robbed of a victory yet again? I could have howled. 'Bengard, I'm going to ram,' I called to my wireless-operator. 'No, Herr Leutnant, please don't do that, we're going on leave in two days' time!' Bengard implored me.

There was a crackling in my earphones and then another voice broke in: 'Shoot, you bloody cretin!' it roared. I looked over my shoulder and saw a Schwarm of our Petsamo Me 109s coming up fast behind me. 'Can't,' I replied, 'my guns aren't working.' 'Then get out of the way,' the voice ordered. I broke away to the right to give the 109s a clear field of fire. They immediately waded in, shooting down the Il-2s one after the other while I turned for home in frustration. There the reason for my bad luck was soon found: the plug connecting the gun firing cable to the control column had come adrift!

The Russians' all-purpose Ilyushin Il-2 'Sturmovik'.

8 Bombs for 'Herr Meier'

On 15 October 1943 leave passes were made out for Orge Schwab, myself, and our two wireless-operators. For me it was to be a half-private, half-official trip, for after visiting my parents I was scheduled to attend a course at the gas defence school in Berlin-Gatow. A Ju 52 transport took us as far as Reval, the capital of Estonia; today better known as Tallinn. On board the tri-motor with us was Oberstleutnant Richter, our Kirkenes station commander. On the flight down he told us that he knew Reval well. This was no idle boast, as he proved by taking us on a tour of the ancient city and showing us the sights. After this we visited a number of coffee houses, before rounding off the evening back in our quarters, where we helped the Oberstleutnant finish the cognac he was intending to take home on leave with him!

After spending the night in Reval, we made our way to the main railway station the next morning. Here we boarded a special leave train that would take us – together with a vast throng of troops from the Leningrad front – back home to the Reich. The soldiers certainly seemed to know the ropes when it came to bartering with the locals during the many stops the train made as it journeyed through the Baltic States. They were already rummaging through their kit sorting out the items they could use for trading: underclothes, blankets and all sorts of other odds and ends.

An army paymaster sitting in our compartment proudly showed us his wristwatch. Although it wasn't working, he was proposing to exchange it for foodstuffs with some unfortunate Estonian at the next stop. It was not long before the train drew to a halt at a small country station. A horde of civilians, both men and women, appeared as if from nowhere to offer live geese, ducks and chickens, as well as eggs, vegetables and other produce to the troops hanging out of the carriage windows.

The paymaster was swinging his watch enticingly to and fro. It soon caught the attention of a young lad who was carrying a large parcel wrapped up in newspaper under his arm. He expressed interest in swapping his packet of fresh butter for the watch, and opened one corner of the newspaper so that the paymaster could see for himself the quality of the wares on offer. But the deal wasn't done that easily. The lad kept asking to be allowed to hold the watch to his ear, which the paymaster deftly managed to avoid. It wasn't until the train began to move off that the items were finally and hurriedly exchanged.

While we leaned out of the window watching the irate young Estonian chasing after the train, the paymaster had a contented grin on his face as he unwrapped his parcel and prepared to make himself a nice, thickly buttered slice of bread. But then he let out a howl of rage – the package was a fake. Only the opened corner the lad had showed to him consisted of a tiny pat of butter. The rest was a slab of rotting, congealed curd. The swindler had been well and truly swindled! But the paymaster didn't take kindly to our helpless peals of laughter. He packed his things together and left the compartment swearing loudly.

Before reaching Tilsit on the Reich's border with Lithuania the train stopped several more times, either at yet another small country station, or – for no apparent reason – in the middle of open country. But wherever we came to a halt it wasn't long before a crowd of locals were flocking around the carriages and bartering was in full swing. At Tilsit we changed on to a German train for the last leg of the journey to Berlin. During this stage through the Reich's eastern provinces those on board who were fortunate enough to possess ration coupons were permitted to exchange them for so-called 'survival parcels' containing sausage, butter and bread. Unfortunately, our little group did not number among the lucky ones.

Upon our arrival in Berlin's Stettiner Station there was total bedlam as the Feldjäger, or military police, insisted on checking all leave passes. Hundreds of soldiers milled about on the tracks or formed untidy queues at the exits complaining vociferously as they waited impatiently to be let through. Most of them carried bartered live fowls, either in their rucksacks or in some sort of makeshift cage, and the birds' frantic cackling and quacking only added to the general din.

A soldier just ahead of me in the queue had a goose tucked securely under one arm, which posed something of a problem when he was asked for his papers. These were in his breast pocket, and in order to get at them he had to clamp the bird between his knees. The goose objected strongly to this ignominious treatment and pecked the soldier so painfully in the thigh that he involuntarily opened his knees. The goose saw its chance. Squawking angrily, it wriggled from between the legs of its temporary owner, fluttered across the platform, spread its wings and disappeared in the direction of a subway tunnel. It was closely followed by two more of its kind, their triumphant screeches suggesting that they had made their escape in a similar fashion.

After visiting my parents in rural Eimbeckhausen near Hamelin, I returned by train to Berlin to attend the gas defence course. Every Luftwaffe Geschwader had to have an officer trained in gas defence procedures, and before leaving Kirkenes I had been 'volunteered' for this privileged post as I was going to be on leave in the Reich in any case.

When I arrived at the gas defence school in Berlin-Gatow that afternoon I found ten fellow sufferers who had also been nominated by their units to experience this rare treat. We were welcomed by a Major of the Flak arm. He assigned us quarters in the nearby Kant Hotel and told us to reappear on time for the start of the course the next day.

We duly turned up at 09.00 hours the following morning. Everyone was carrying his gas mask – except me. This got me off on the wrong foot with the 'Gas Major' from the word go. 'That's totally irresponsible of you,' he snapped. 'The gas mask must be carried at all times. What would you do if you returned from a mission to find your airfield under gas attack?' 'I'd call up ground control and get them to tell me the nearest airfield that wasn't affected,' I replied breezily,

'They're *all* affected,' he persisted. 'In that case, I'd land on my own airfield and my wireless-operator and I would switch our oxygen masks to pure oxygen. Then I'd instruct one of the ground crew to go and fetch our gas masks. But I'd warn him not to open the containers, because that's where we store our coffee beans to keep them nice and fresh,' I retorted with a grin, recalling the incident of our fallen comrade and his aggrieved coffee 'heirs'. The burst of laughter from the other course members didn't go down at all well with the gas major. So, in order to defuse the situation and make amends for my admittedly facetious remarks, I politely requested a replacement mask.

The course kicked off with details of the various poison gases – mustard gas, nerve gas, and the like – all of which I already knew from my earlier training. On the second day we were given the afternoon off. This suited me down to the ground as my girl friend Uschi from the Prenzlauer Berg district of Berlin was coming to visit me. I had phoned to tell her that I would be in town and we had arranged to meet at around 7-o-clock that evening outside the Zoo Station of the S-Bahn, the capital's elevated metropolitan railway system.

As I had plenty of time to spare before Uschi's arrival, I decided to drop in to the Café Berlin, which was on the 'Kudamm' or Kurfürstendamm, one of the city's major thoroughfares, next to the Ufa-Palast cinema. The café was famous for its two bands, one of which played on the ground floor, the other on the floor above. The two bands had just struck up with a simultaneous rendition of 'Tiger Rag', a tune that was officially frowned upon by the authorities in the Third Reich as being decadent Negro music, when the lively opening bars of jazz were drowned out by the wail of sirens – an air raid alarm!

All the customers immediately grabbed their things together and rushed off to the nearest air raid shelters. In order not to miss Uschi, I hurried instead to the S-Bahn station, which was only about 100 metres away, hoping that it was a false alarm and that the all-clear would soon sound.

But it was not to be. I had just reached the entrance to the U-Bahn, the underground station whose concrete roof canopy supported the tracks of the elevated S-Bahn situated immediately above it, when the air was filled with the roar of what sounded to me like several hundred four-engined heavy bombers. I didn't dare risk leaving the protection of the underground station entrance to find out, but it seemed as if the enemy bombers were directly overhead; in other words, over the very heart of Berlin. And they were!

The shrill penetrating whistle of falling incendiary bombs was punctuated by the dull thumping of the capital's heavy Flak batteries to form an unholy crescendo of noise. The scattered incendiaries rained down all over the city, starting fires wherever they fell. I had been joined in the station entrance by an Unteroffizier of the Luftwaffe and together we dashed to a nearby building site to gather up as many sacks of sand and cement as we could carry. With these we were just able to smother the closest incendiaries that were already threatening to engulf the entrance to the station.

It was hard work, and touch and go for a while. When our supply of sand began to run out, I threw a sack of cement onto one of the last remaining bombs… and was almost knocked flat by the resultant explosion! It must have been one of the newer type of incendiaries that also contained a small charge of explosive and a delay fuse. These were specifically designed to keep the fire and rescue crews at a distance and thus prevent the bomb from being extinguished before the fire could take hold. I was not aware of it at the time, but during the Second World War England alone produced 100 million incendiary bombs, over 80 million of which were dropped on Germany.

The apocalyptic scenes all around us could not have been more horrific had they been orchestrated by the devil himself. I don't know how long the terror and the chaos lasted, but certain incidents have stuck in my mind. The almost ludicrously eerie sounds emanating from a blazing car parked outside the now shattered ruins of the Ufa-Palast cinema, for example. At first hooting loudly, the noises it was making slowly subsided into a kind of long drawn-out mechanized death rattle before eventually tailing off into silence for ever.

When the Flak ceased fire a deceptive quiet descended on the tortured city. The only background noise for a while was the crackling of burning houses. But then a new and even more terrible sound assailed our ears as crowds of panic-stricken people began to run screaming through the blazing streets. The tower of Berlin's famous Kaiser Wilhelm memorial church was a huge flaming torch pointing accusingly into the sky. The ghastly shrieks from the injured animals in the nearby zoo were almost too much to bear. Individual shots rang out at intervals as the wounded beasts were put out of their agony.

I just wished that our 'Reichsmeier' could be forced to watch over and over again the dreadful scenes I was witnessing now; 'Reichsmeier' – or, to give him his proper title, Reichsmarschall Hermann Göring – who, with typical bombast, had announced at the start of the war that, so great was the Luftwaffe's air superiority over the Reich: 'If ever a single bomb should fall on Germany, you can call me Meier.'

Although the Zoo station had not been hit, I was convinced that the S-Bahn would no longer be running and that Uschi would not be able to make her way the seven kilometres from Prenzlauer Berg into the burning city centre. I therefore offered the Unteroffizier the use of the second bed in my hotel room; the one which I had hoped Uschi would be occupying. The offer depended, of course, on the hotel's still standing, and so we fought our way across to Kantstrasse to check. The building itself was relatively intact, although all the windows facing the street had been shattered by the pressure wave from a heavy bomb exploding nearby. But many of the surrounding apartment blocks were burning fiercely, and so I gathered together the five other course members who had managed to get back to the hotel to help me in fighting the fires.

The huge tongues of flame that were leaping from the glassless windows of those buildings already blazing were threatening the neighbouring properties. As many of their owners had not yet ventured out of the safety of the air raid shelters, we often had to break down the doors to get into the flats. We pulled down burning curtains and moved furniture away from the walls. The heat was so ferocious inside the apartments that even in rooms where the fires had not yet penetrated, the carpets were already beginning to smoulder.

Using the pitifully few buckets of water and sand that every householder was obliged by law to keep ready in case of emergencies, we continued our hopeless struggle against the all-consuming flames. But it was no use. The conflagration was growing larger by the minute, constantly and greedily seeking out – and finding – fresh sustenance among the maze of narrow alleyways and cramped courtyards behind many of the old apartment blocks.

Exhausted and disheartened, we returned to our hotel. When I looked at myself in the mirror I got one hell of a fright. Staring back at me was an apparition caked in dirt and grime. My face and clothes ranged in colour from pitch black, via ash grey, to a ghostly white; the latter presumably from the cement sack that had exploded at the entrance to the U-Bahn. I was just about to have a good wash when I was called down to reception – and there, to my utter astonishment, stood Uschi from Prenzlauer Berg! We stared at each other in silence for a moment, and then burst into helpless laughter. She was just as dishevelled and soot-stained from flying sparks and embers as I was!

While we cleaned ourselves up, Uschi described her recent odyssey; the four hours it had taken her on foot – between salvos of falling bombs, along burning streets, and over mountains of fresh rubble – to cover the four or five final kilometres from the Stettiner Station to the Kant Hotel. As we were both parched from the heat, I went back down to the hotel's kitchen to find us something to drink. But what I in fact found was the proprietress very much the worse for wear. Slurring her words and almost paralytically drunk, she was being 'squired' by two Feldwebeln. It was they who immediately provided me with a large pot of coffee liberally laced with rum. They even threw in a couple of slices of bread as well. I thanked them for their generosity. But whether they were genuinely concerned for my well-being, or simply wanted to get rid of me as quickly as possible so that I didn't have the chance to enquire too closely into the exact nature of the 'assistance' they were offering the lady of the house, I wouldn't like to say.

My next concern was to organize a bed for the night for the Unteroffizier who had earlier been helping me to fight the fires. This was no problem, as several of the course members had not managed to find their way back to the hotel amidst all the turmoil and there was plenty of space in the other rooms. But the night was short. The air raid sirens began to wail again at four in the morning.

Uschi and I set off for the nearest shelter. Sitting dog-tired on carpets spread out on the bare concrete floor, we witnessed at first-hand the terror and misery of the people bombed out of their homes. At every explosion the children trembled and cried. The reproachful stares of the women and old men were hard for me to bear. I could hear in my own mind the question they must have been asking themselves – why is this young Luftwaffe officer just sitting around down here in the shelter with his girl friend when by rights he should be up there protecting us?

It was a great relief when the attack ended after only two hours and I was able to escape the confines of the shelter. I said goodbye to Uschi, who had to start making her way back across town to Prenzlauer Berg. Unfortunately, but perhaps not surprisingly, I never saw or heard from her again.

Bomb damage on the corner of Berlin's Kantstrasse and Joachimstalerstrasse.

When my colleagues and I turned up at the gas course in Gatow a couple of hours later, the Flak Major showered us with praise for our 'heroic actions' during the air raid. I've no idea how he had got to hear of our fire-fighting efforts. His initial animosity towards me had disappeared completely. Not that it mattered very much, for he then went on to inform us that, due to the damage inflicted upon the capital, the gas defence course had been cancelled and we were all free to return to our units. While I had been in Berlin my Staffel had telephoned through to me with instructions to collect an Me 110 from Anklam in Pomerania on 24 November and ferry it across the Baltic to Pori in southwest Finland. As the premature ending of the gas course had given me three extra days of freedom, I decided to return home again to kit myself out with clean linen.

Everyone was surprised at my unexpectedly turning up again. My parents had imagined me to be well on my way back to the Arctic front. My family home was the forestry lodge at Hemschehausen. It was idyllically situated on the edge of the woods not far from the equally picturesque little town of Eimbeckhausen. There could hardly have been a greater contrast between the hectic throb and bustle of the big city – now descending into chaos under the constant rain of enemy bombs – and the rural seclusion and tranquillity of my home surroundings. Here, where nature ruled, it was a world where time had stood still. The people were friendly and contented with their lot. Nobody complained. Nobody was envious of another's good fortune. It was as if there had never been a war – nor ever could be.

After three days of complete relaxation it was time to bid farewell to this quiet little haven of peace and return to the brutal reality of a world at war. In order to have at least one small, but tangible reminder of home, however, I decided to take my one-year-old fox terrier Strupps back to the Arctic with me. Strupps was just about the most affectionate, mischievous and adorable little dog you could imagine; but talk to any dog owner and they would probably describe their own pet in similar terms.

As a puppy Strupps had commandeered my battered old suitcase as his bed. He loved to be carried around in it. This was to prove a great advantage in the days ahead. For on the journey north by rail I would no doubt have to change trains several times. This would be difficult enough with the amount of baggage I had, but it would have been even harder if I had had a dog on a lead to contend with as well.

I did not arrive at Anklam airfield until the evening of 24 November. After being assigned a room, I was told that the Me 110 I was to ferry to Finland would not be ready until 27 November. I spent the intervening days catching up on some paperwork and paying regular visits to the maintenance hangar to see how work on the Me 110 was progressing.

At last all was ready. Take-off from Anklam went without a hitch. I'd thought of everything. Baggage and dog were safely aboard, that was the main thing. Thought of everything? Damn, I'd forgotten to bring along any maps! Should I quickly turn back? No, it wasn't worth the trouble and, besides, I could do without the unmerciful ribbing I'd be sure to get from the ground crews and the personnel on duty in flying control.

I was familiar with the route from Anklam, via Reval and Helsinki, to Pori – so what could possibly go wrong? Quite a lot, as it turned out. My plan to follow the Baltic coast north-eastwards, via Königsberg, to Reval in Estonia was already beginning to fall apart over the island of Usedom, only some 30 kilometres from my starting point. Bad weather was rapidly closing in. The cloud base was down to 300 metres, visibility was steadily worsening, and I could no longer see the coastline. There was water beneath me, but it wasn't the open Baltic. After some time it dawned on me that I had flown a complete circle.

Land appeared out of the gloom ahead. I could see a fair-sized town and so followed the railway line leading towards it. This should bring me to a station where, with any luck, I ought to be able to make out the name of the place. Descending almost to ground level, I spotted a large sign on the station platform. I even managed to read what it said as I flew past – it was an advertisement for a local timber merchant! After circling the station three times in all, I finally gave up my attempts to discover its name and opted instead to continue following the set of tracks that now led off eastwards. Flying at a height of just 50 metres I 'bought a train ticket'. In the Luftwaffe jargon of the time this referred to the practice of a lost pilot's following a railway line until he came to some known point of reference point where he could get his bearings again.

Conditions were deteriorating all the while. I was now flying through heavy storm showers and torrential rain was drumming against the cabin windows. Danzig was just a blur as I passed low overhead. I was beginning to get a queasy feeling in the pit of my stomach. It grew darker and darker. I was just preparing to put down on the next suitable patch of grass – *any* patch of grass – when a bolt of lightning struck the ground, turning night into day for a split second and illuminating a large airfield directly in my path. I recognized it instantly as Königsberg.

At that very same moment the runway lights were switched on. These fellows are really on their toes, I thought to myself. I hadn't expected such care and consideration to help me down. After landing safely, Strupps and I made a dash for it through the pouring rain to the flying control office. There my welcome was less than cordial. Apparently, the airfield lighting hadn't been switched on for me at all, but for a Ju 52 passenger airliner of Lufthansa that was on final approach. The field's D/F operator had radioed the Ju 52 that it was nearing its destination, and it was he who had illuminated the runway when he heard the noise of engines above the storm. In actual fact, the Ju 52 was still a good five kilometres away when I touched down.

Eventually tempers cooled and everyone was simply relieved that there hadn't been a mid-air collision above the field. The following morning I first obtained clearance from flying control for the next leg of my journey to Reval. Then, after dropping in on the 'weather frog' for the latest reports, and topping up my tanks, I taxied out to the take-off point with Strupps and baggage all stowed securely on board.

But at Reval my onward flight to Helsinki was delayed and I had to wait a full seven days for conditions to improve. It snowed continuously throughout that time and regulations stipulated that the Gulf of Finland could only be crossed in good weather. 6 December dawned fine and clear. I took off for Helsinki under blue skies, made an overnight stop there, and finally handed the Me 110 over to the Pori workshops superintendent on 7 December. He in turn informed me that the Fieseler Storch, which our Staffel had been eagerly awaiting for ages, was also in the Pori workshops undergoing a final check. It would be ready for me to fly up to Kirkenes on 9 December.

The last lap of my journey northwards in the slow, short-ranged Storch had to be made in a series of hops, broken by numerous landings for refuelling, plus a succession of nightly stopovers *en route*. After three weeks living the life of a nomad, I was more than glad finally to be back with my Staffel on 15 December.

9 Wartime Christmas 1943

While I was away our popular Staffelkapitän Karl-Fritz Schlossstein had been transferred to Oslo. His successor, Hauptmann Herbert Treppe, would remain at the head of the Staffel until June 1944. When I got back to Kirkenes the new Kapitän, together with Oberleutnant Kirchmeier and most of the other officers, had all departed on Christmas leave. It therefore fell to Leutnants Müller, Schwab and myself to make the necessary arrangements to receive an 'important guest'.

We had been sent a teleprinter message giving notice of the imminent arrival of the Reich's Minister of Construction and Armaments Albert Speer, who was intending to spend Christmas with our 13. Staffel. The whole base was absolutely buzzing with excitement and activity. Steps had to be taken to ensure the minister's safety, the best quarters had to be furnished and made ready for him and his staff, food had to be prepared, everything had to be cleaned and polished, and the mess had to be suitably decorated for the Christmas celebrations.

One major problem was our total lack of festive greenery. The only things that grew on the rocky ground up here were mosses, sparse little bushes and stunted birches. The nearest proper fir trees were to be found around Lake Inari in northern Finnish Lapland, which was some 150 kilometres away. Fortunately, there were several Gefreiter in the Staffel who owed me favours. I collared two of them and packed

Hauptmann Treppe (right) with his wireless-operator/gunner Feldwebel Brüggenthies (left).

them off to Ivalo on the lake's southern shore with orders to select and bring back a really splendid Christmas tree.

Our cook was faced with an even greater headache: where on earth was he going to find a Christmas roast to set before our honoured guest? Rising to the occasion, I suspect he made a secret deal with one of the sentries, for on the morning of 24 December a delicious aroma of roasting meat began wafting across to us from the direction of the cookhouse. It was now that we learned the true story behind the single shot that we had heard fired somewhere out on the perimeter of the field the night before.

The sentry on duty explained that he had seen a shadowy figure lurking in the bushes. He had challenged the intruder, repeatedly ordering him to halt and give the password. When the third and final challenge produced no response, he had fired. It was only then that he realized he had 'accidentally' shot a grazing reindeer. Not wanting to let such a large amount of fresh meat go to waste, 'it seemed only natural to offer it to the cook'. It should perhaps be pointed out here that reindeer represented a vital source of food for the indigenous Lapp population and we were strictly prohibited from taking any of the animals for our own purposes.

But the biggest problem of all was the cleaning of the toilet facilities – if our primitive thunderbox could be dignified by such a title. It was located in a small hut about 50 metres away from our living quarters. It consisted of a wooden framework base with a long plank attached to the top of it. This served as a communal seat, and the eight individual holes evenly spaced along its length gave the construction its name. In Luftwaffe parlance it was an 'eight-cylinder' job.

At this time of year, with temperatures often falling to 30 degrees or more below zero, the 50 metres out to the hut were best covered at a smart gallop, and the ensuing business performed at the double. Toilet paper was an unheard-of luxury and so we used Soviet rouble notes in its stead, and sometimes even the paper money from our own basic pay – after all, there was very little else we could do with it up her above the Arctic Circle. Our ground crews were perhaps the worst off in such a situation. They had to decide whether to wash their oil-stained hands *before* paying a visit to the 'eight-cylinder', or to put up with returning from it with a backside as black as their overalls. But my real sympathies lay with the unfortunates whose job it was periodically to remove the huge, and ever-growing pyramid of frozen excrement before it reached the level of the plank!

During the night of 24 December the thermometer dropped to 40 below. Only the shimmering green-blue-orange curtains of the northern lights compensated somewhat for the biting cold. At midday I was sent up on an emergency scramble, but all was quiet and I saw no sign of the enemy.

By the time I landed again the Minister for Armaments had arrived and was being looked after in a manner befitting his exalted status. Our 'chiefy', Hauptfeldwebel Ros, had managed to lay his hands on a red coat and hood from somewhere or other. With a long white beard glued to his chin, he was playing the part of Father Christmas to perfection. There was only one minor slip-up. During his speech of welcome he referred to the Armaments Minister as the 'Procurer of Ammunition and Supplies'. His face was nearly as red as his costume when he realized what he had said. But Speer was laughing uproariously and neatly covered the Hauptfeldwebel's obvious embarrassment by quipping: 'And they're not the only things I'm good at procuring!'

After the obligatory singing of carols and reading out of Christmas messages from home, Speer and his party retired to their quarters, whose exact location hadn't been made known to us for reasons of security. Once they had departed the atmosphere became much more relaxed and the increased intake of alcohol by all present loosened tongues, manners and behaviour. Some of the men had put together a so-called 'Bierzeitung', or 'beer newspaper', filled with entertaining snippets of information – most, if not all of them witty and good-natured – describing the various faults and foibles of the unit's members. It was while leafing through it that I first discovered my nickname among the Staffel. Apparently I had been dubbed 'Strammsack', or 'Sturdy sack'. This harked back to an occasion when I had lifted the rear wheels of a Kübelwagen – the Wehrmacht's equivalent to the jeep – clear off the ground, leaving its puzzled driver revving hard and wondering why he wasn't moving.

After a while Orge Schwab and I decided to make a start on our Christmas presents, a basketful of apples, oranges, some chocolate, a bottle of wine and a bottle of egg liqueur. But some thoughtless halfwit of an orderly had left the basket outside. Most of its contents were frozen solid and the bottle of wine had burst. All that we were able to rescue was the bottle of egg liqueur, which went down a treat after it had been thawed out. Some of the other revellers were more adventurous; filling a coffee pot with red wine and heating it on the stove. They then added cloves to taste, and 'refined' the resulting brew with an entire bottle of rum – mulled wine with a punch!

On 26 December 1943, some 160 kilometres north of the North Cape – practically on our doorstep, in other words – there occurred one of the greatest tragedies ever suffered by our navy. Its last operational battle-cruiser, the *Scharnhorst*, had set out with five destroyers to intercept an Allied convoy on its way to Murmansk, only to be sunk after a ferocious engagement against two battle groups of the Royal Navy.

Up here in the far north at this time of year it was virtually pitch black all day long except for a brief hour of twilight around noon. And our naval command's mistake had been to let the *Scharnhorst* put to sea with her radar switched off. They were aware that the British could get a fix on our ships' radar emissions, and so assumed that our vessels would remain invisible under the protective cloak of darkness if they did not betray their position by using their radar. The High Command suspected that the British had some new kind of radio-location device, but didn't realize that the Royal Navy's cruisers and destroyers were equipped with radar of a type so advanced that it could pinpoint the enemy even in total darkness and the most adverse of weather.

Destined to fight her final battle under just such conditions, the mighty but 'blind' *Scharnhorst* was at a hopeless disadvantage against her radar-equipped opponents. After an engagement lasting several hours, during which it is estimated that she was hit by over 2,000 shells and struck by 14 torpedoes, the *Scharnhorst* was finally battered beneath the waves. Over 1,900 members of her crew perished. Just 36 were rescued.

Such a humiliating defeat had to be avenged, and our Zerstörerstaffel was to do the avenging. We were expected to find, attack and sink the British warships by any and every means at our disposal. But our retaliatory strike planned for 27 December had to be postponed until the next day because of bad weather and thick fog. Nobody was able to tell us where the two battle groups and the convoy now were. Even our highly experienced reconnaissance crews were pinned to the ground by the atrocious conditions.

Staffelkapitän Treppe was firmly of the opinion that the enemy ships were somewhere off the Russian occupied Rybachiy, or Fisherman's Peninsula. He outlined his plan to find them: two Schwärme of four machines each would carry out a fan-shaped search, one along the western coast of the peninsula, the other along the eastern coast. He would lead the Schwarm combing the eastern side, with me and my wingman forming the second Rotte of his group. We would fly northwards parallel to the coastline for 100 kilometres, alter course to the southeast for 50 kilometres, then turn and head due north again, before repeating the whole procedure a second and third time if necessary. Meanwhile, Oberleutnant Maul and his Schwarm would be employing similar tactics to search the sea area to the west of the peninsula; flying a north, southwest, north pattern.

Take-off was set for 09.10 hours on 28 December. But because of the cold – the thermometer was registering 20 degrees below – I started my engines and let them warm up for 30 minutes before the scheduled time. We had only been in the air for 15 minutes when the red warning light on my fuel gauge began to glow. I suspected that the fuel transfer pump was

The battle-cruiser *Scharnhorst* was sunk by the British on 26 December 1943.

Searching for the Royal Navy.

iced-up and started rocking my wings in an attempt to thaw it out. Ten interminable minutes passed until the red light went out. I was mightily relieved that my guess had been correct. If the problem had been a leak in the injection feed, my wireless-operator and I would have ended up in the drink and been frozen to death in the icy waters in no time at all.

Treppe had made a number of turns during the flight and this had played havoc with my orientation. Concentrating of resolving the problem with my fuel warning light, I had not been taking note of our various changes in course. But by my rough reckoning we should now be somewhere in the vicinity of the Kola Inlet to the north of Murmansk. As we turned north after completing another south-easterly leg, I spotted four aircraft heading towards us. The British convoy was reportedly being protected by an aircraft carrier, so my first thought was that these must be enemy fighters. Despite having been ordered to keep radio silence, I warned the other pilots. Hauptmann Treppe banked to the right to meet the oncoming unidentified aircraft head on.

As we got closer we saw that they were twin-engined machines. This ruled out their being carrier-borne enemy fighters. Then I recognized them as Oberleutnant Maul's four Me 110s which, according to the original plan, should by rights be searching the *west* coast of the peninsula. What a cock-up! The two Schwärme circled each other and, after some initial confusion, it was decided by hand signal that all eight machines should join forces and carry out a combined search to the west of the Rybachi Peninsula.

We had been in the air for a full two hours by now and still hadn't found the enemy ships. After a further 15 minutes a strip of coastline appeared below us. Hauptmann Treppe seemed to assume that this was part of the Rybachiy Peninsula but, despite the poor visibility and a cloud base of only 100 metres, I was convinced that we had unwittingly flown too far to the west and that the land we could see was the northern tip of the Varanger Peninsula close to the township of Berlevag!

I knew that we would soon be running low on fuel and that the only thing to do was to reverse course immediately and head for home. If we continued to follow Hauptmann Treppe like a load of sheep we'd soon end up in the water, and the prospect of going for a swim off the North Cape didn't tempt me at all. Throwing caution to the winds, I broke radio silence for a second time: 'Anyone who wants to get back to Kirkenes in one piece, follow me!'

I pushed forward the throttles, climbed up over the rocky coastline and set compass course 170 degrees. Five machines trailed in my wake. Only Hauptmann Treppe and his wingman hesitated momentarily, then they too turned to follow the rest of us. It wasn't long before my fuel warning light began to glow red again. This meant I had only about ten minutes' flying time left. If I didn't find Kirkenes within those ten minutes I would have to crash-land. I was now paying the price for starting my engines early and letting them

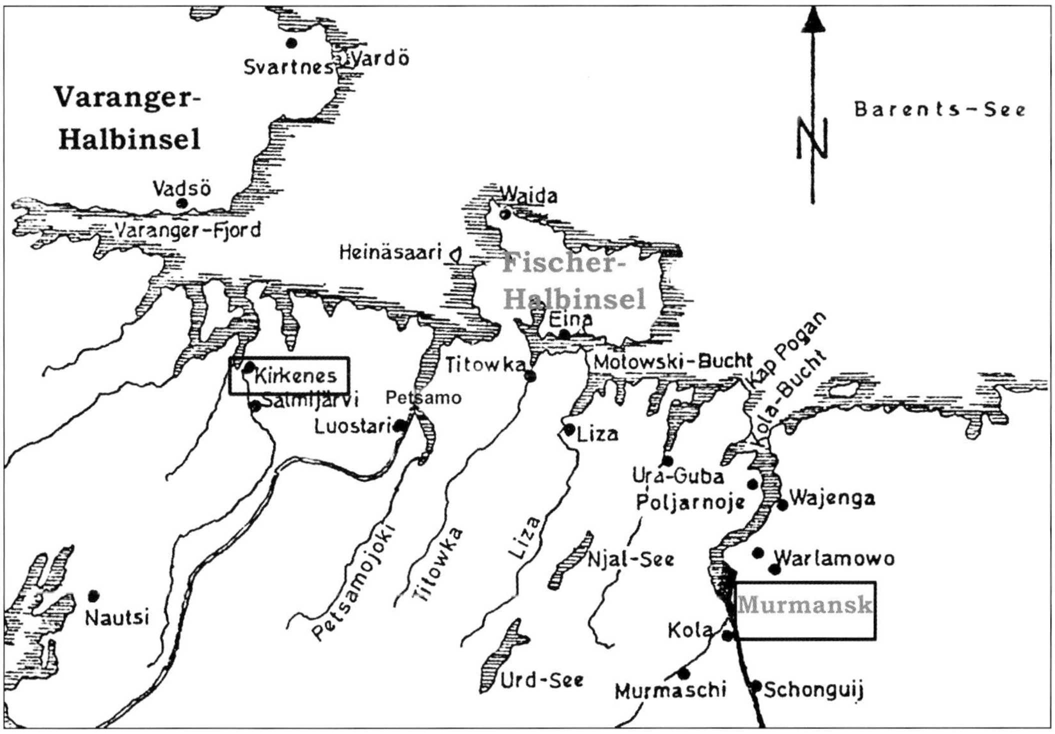

The Varanger Peninsula was controlled by the Germans, the Fisherman's (or Rybachiy) Peninsula by the Russians.

warm up for 30 minutes before take-off.

Eventually the mountains to the south of the airfield hove into view, and then the runway itself. Let's get this bird down on the ground. Fully aware that I must be on my last few drops of fuel, I kept to the far right-hand side of the runway to give the machines behind me enough room to land safely. It was just as well I did, for my propellers windmilled to a stop only about 12 metres after I had touched down.

I was furious that the mission had been such a total failure – not to say fiasco – but at least we had all got back safe and sound. I was also surprised that nothing was ever said about my arbitrarily breaking the imposed radio-silence. It wasn't long after this episode that Hauptmann Treppe appointed me as his adjutant. Did my guiding the two Schwärme back home to Kirkenes play some part in helping him to arrive at this decision, I wondered.

Coming in to land at Kirkenes.

On the morning of 30 December an emergency scramble was aborted almost immediately after take-off because of bad weather. That same afternoon Hauptmann Treppe came to see me to ask if I could possibly help him to sit an oral examination: 'You've mentioned to me in the past that you grew up in a forestry lodge, that you have a hunting licence and intend to be a forester after the war. I'd like to take the exam to get my hunting licence too, but I simply haven't had the time to learn all the theoretical stuff,' he explained. 'This evening three naval types and an official examiner are coming up from Kirkenes and I'd like your support. The navy fellows also want to sit the exam and I hear they're bringing a load of beer and two bottles of brandy with them. Apparently the examiner is an alcoholic, and if we get him tanked up enough, perhaps he won't notice you whispering the answers to me,' Treppe finished hopefully.

That evening the examiner, accompanied by a Kapitänleutnant and two naval Oberleutnants, duly turned up. We ushered them into the officers' mess and, after introductions had been made and the usual pleasantries exchanged, all took their places at a long table; the examiner on one side and the four candidates on the other. In the absence of proper brandy glasses, a water tumbler had been set before each and, as adjutant to the Staffelkapitän, I took on the role of an attentive and conscientious waiter, making sure that the examiner's tumbler was kept full to the brim at all times.

The first questions of the examination were relatively easy. They dealt with the general rules and regulations of the hunting laws and none of the examinees had any trouble in answering them. As the questions grew progressively harder, however, only Hauptmann Treppe was able to come up with the right answers – which I was whispering over his shoulder! At the same time I was keeping the examiner well topped up with beer and brandy, and soon noticed that the alcohol was beginning to have its effect.

The examiner started to slur his words and spout drivel. He rummaged around confusedly in his briefcase looking for documents, and mixed up the candidates' names with increasing frequency. After a few more glasses of schnaps the time had come to test the tester. I slid unobtrusively into the Staffelkapitän's seat and, pretending to be Hauptmann Treppe, launched into a learned discussion of the current hunting laws with the befuddled examiner. He noticed nothing and fell for the trick hook, line and sinker. As the naval officers couldn't answer any more of his questions, he spent the rest of the examination chatting amiably, if drunkenly to 'Hauptmann Treppe' – in other words, to me.

Although by now well in his cups, his brain must have registered the fact that he was talking gibberish, for he suddenly brought the whole painful episode to an abrupt halt by announcing: 'Hauptmann Treppe has passed the examination, all the others have failed. They can apply to sit it again later.' The navy trio weren't at all happy. They protested loudly, saying if that was the case, they weren't going to take the examiner back to town with them. This didn't seem to bother him one little bit. He brushed all protests aside, saying to me: 'Hauptmann Treppe, I will be sending you your certified hunting licence in due course.'

Still playing the part of the Staffelkapitän, I thanked him and summoned an orderly: 'Get hold of my car and driver and have him take the Herr District Chief Forestry Ranger back to Kirkenes.'

10 Going with a Bang

The year 1944 began in the same way as the old year had ended – bitingly cold, with everyone frozen to the marrow and the machines covered in a thick layer of ice. Dense fog alternated with heavy snow showers. Emergency scrambles were constantly being aborted due to the weather conditions, and operations were hardly possible at all.

On 9 January Petsamo requested an Me 110 and crew to guide three Me 109s down to Pori in southern Finland, with a stop for refuelling at Rovaniemi on the way. My room-mate Orge Schwab was given the job. But two hours after he had left we heard from Petsamo that his machine had somersaulted on landing and both crew members were in hospital.

The following day I was despatched to Petsamo in Orge's place. I took off in a snowstorm that grew steadily worse during the short 50-kilometre flight but which, fortunately, eased off just as I was preparing to land. I was on final approach when Petsamo control sent up a cluster of red flares, indicating that the runway had not yet been cleared. But I was already committed and so put the Me 110 down on an open stretch of ground alongside the runway. I created an enormous snowstorm of my own as the nose of the machine slid like a bobsleigh across the virgin white surface and the propellers chewed their way through the nearly two-metre deep snow.

When I finally came to a halt and switched the engines off I saw that a good quarter of each propeller blade from the tip inwards had been bent slightly forward. I reported to flying control and explained why I hadn't been able to abort my landing. They promised to get a tracked vehicle to come and drag my aircraft out of the snow. While in the control office I took the opportunity to ask after Theo Weissenberger and Heinrich Ehrler, only to be told that they were both away on leave.

Across the room a captured Russian fighter pilot who had just shot down one of our Me 109s, only to be brought down himself shortly afterwards, was being questioned by a Hauptmann. Apparently, while still descening by parachute the Russian had opened fire with his pistol at the air-sea rescue Heinkel seaplane that was attempting to fish the German pilot out of the water. The latter had not survived the shock of landing in the icy sea, but the Russian was pulled up onto one of the seaplane's floats by the lines of his parachute and dragged aboard. During questioning, however, he remained stubbornly silent and showed not the least sign of gratitude at being rescued.

When the Hauptmann failed to get anything out of him, the Russian was taken to Kirkenes for further interrogation. The funny thing is, when he saw our Staffel scoreboard on the wall of the mess, I was told that he became quite voluble and immediately began to dispute our claims. He brushed aside all the carefully recorded and incontestable details regarding the time, date and type of Russian aircraft destroyed by claiming that the machines in question weren't in action on that particular day, had been transferred elsewhere – or simply didn't exist! He spent only the one night as our guest at Kirkenes before being collected by the military police the following morning.

By 14 January the weather conditions had at last improved sufficiently to allow me to get on with the job of leading the three Me 109s from Petsamo down to Pori. I flew at an altitude of 500 metres with the Kette of three single-seaters trailing faithfully along behind me. Shortly before our intermediate stop for refuelling at Rovaniemi, one of the Me 109 pilots came up on the R/T to report that he was losing a lot of oil and that he wanted to bail out because he could no longer see through his windscreen.

'There's nothing in front of you,' I said encouragingly, 'Waggle your wings and slide the window on the right side of your canopy open so that you'll be able to see me. I'll close up on your starboard side and will guide you in. It's not far to Rovaniemi now.' He followed my instructions to the letter while the other two Me 109s sheered off a little to give us plenty of room for our landing.

I started to talk him down: 'Lower flaps and undercarriage, ease off the gas a little, watch your turn-and-bank indicator and keep those revs steady, hold her nice and straight, height 20 metres, 10 metres – less gas – 5 metres, round-out, chop throttle – you're on the landing point.'

During this whole time I had been flying slightly echeloned to his right. He had responded quickly and calmly to each of my instructions and had pulled off a nice clean landing. Once he was safely down I pushed my throttles forward and climbed away to go round again. It had been a tense ten minutes, but now I could relax. My decision not to let him bail out had been the correct one. A great weight was lifted from my shoulders, but I dreaded to think of the consequences had he made a botch of the landing, possibly blocking the runway with his wreckage and injuring, perhaps even killing himself.

After the other two Me 109s had put down, it was my turn to land. Our 'blind-flyer' would have to remain at Rovaniemi for a while until his machine was put right. We three refuelled and continued on to Pori without further incident. There my Me 110 caused quite a stir with its six propeller blades all bent evenly forwards. It was taken into the shops for repair, but while waiting for the work to be carried out I received fresh orders: on 23 January I was to ferry a brand new Me 110 back up to Kirkenes, this time with a stop for refuelling at Kemi.

This far south it was at least light for three hours a day already, which meant that my wireless-operator Bengard and I could leave Pori and still reach Kemi before darkness fell. After an overnight stop at Kemi, we touched down back at Kirkenes at midday on 24 January.

There we found the Staffel in the throes of packing up ready to move. When I reported to Hauptmann Treppe he informed me that we were being transferred to Herdla in southern Norway. As we were not familiar with that area, he had requested the services of a Ju 88 to guide us down there. We were to meet up with it at Banak, our first refuelling stop. From there the Junkers would lead us south, via another stop at Bardufoss, all the way to Herdla. Given Treppe's navigational skills this was a wise move, I thought quietly to myself.

Before taking off for Banak I noticed that my engine revs were a little too high at idle; but not high enough to cause concern, I decided. And so it proved. This first leg of the transfer flight was uneventful and we duly put down at Banak to refuel and rendezvous with our Ju 88 guide. Leaving Banak, our Me 110s took up station in a wide echelon to port of the Junkers and we settled down to follow it to Bardufoss. Visibility was adequate, although thick clouds capped the peaks of the mountains and the cloud base was down to as little as 100 metres in places. Nevertheless everything went well at first.

But then, presumably forgetting the width of the formation behind him, the Ju pilot led us into a steep-sided fjord that grew progressively narrower and ended in a wall of high mountains. If we stayed in echelon we'd never get through this bottleneck without colliding with each other! Without hesitation I dived under the machine diagonally ahead of me and pulled a tight 180 degree turn. Luckily his prop wash didn't drive me against the sheer cliffs flanking the fjord. My wingman and four other pilots also recognized the danger in time and performed the same manoeuvre. This left just enough space for the remaining machines to get into line astern of the Junkers and follow it up and over the peaks at the end of the fjord without mishap.

After briefly flying in the opposite direction, we six reversed course again and hurried after the others. Climbing out of the fjord, we slipped back into formation, with the crew of the Ju 88 still seemingly blissfully unaware of the perilous situation they had put us in. Hopefully there wouldn't be any more such incidents.

Another hour passed before the Ju started to let down. It lowered its undercarriage in preparation for the landing at Bardufoss. By this time it was quite dark and only a thin glittering strip betrayed the presence of the runway in the vast expanse of white landscape beneath our wings. We circled the field, each waiting for the man ahead of him to put down safely before going in to land himself.

When it came to my turn, I noticed upon touch-down that the machine in front of me had not cleared the runway, but had come to a halt about two-thirds of the way along its length. The aircraft ahead of *him* were either dawdling about, or had not yet turned off towards the dispersal area, and this was causing a queue to back up along the runway. If I wanted to avoid ramming the man in front, I was either going to have to brake hard or quickly pour on the power and go round again.

The moment I trod on the brakes it immediately became clear to me why the field had glittered so prettily from the air – there had obviously been a recent shower of rain that had frozen and turned the runway into one enormous, mirror-smooth sheet of ice! So now I was left with no other option but to go round again. I rammed the throttles forward, intending to squeeze past to the left of the stationary machine still standing in my path. But what I couldn't see in the darkness were the two-metre high banks of snow that the runway clearance teams had earlier thrown up to either side of it.

At full power my port wingtip grazed the wall of snow. The machine began to drift to the left. I immediately gave full right rudder and hauled back on the stick – but it was too late, I didn't have enough speed to lift off. The port engine buried itself deep into the wall of snow, wrenching the machine around with such violence that the fuselage behind my seat buckled at right-angles. This resulted in the starboard engine now also boring its way into the pile of frozen solid snow. When the rattling, grating and crunching noises finally stopped, I was amazed to see my wireless-operator seated in the back of the cabin alongside me! If the situation hadn't been so serious, I could have died laughing at the stupefied expression on his face. Fortunately neither of us was hurt, but the new machine's operational career had been a short one; broken almost completely in half, it was now nothing but a pile of scrap.

We climbed shakily from the wreckage and were still standing on top of the wall of snow when a Mercedes 540K staff car with a metal command pennant on its mudguard came speeding down the runway towards us. The driver tried to brake, but lost control as the car skidded and slammedd into the snow below us. From it sprang the local air commander, Fliegerführer General Ernst-August Roth, who promptly lost his footing and fell flat on his back on the icy surface.

I slid the two metres down from my lofty 'perch' and helped the General to his feet: 'Herr General, I trust you haven't hurt yourself. Perhaps the Herr General remembers me? You once visited our Zerstörerstaffel up in Kirkenes and congratulated me on a Pe-2 that I had just shot down.' He seemed to recognize me: 'Wollenweber, isn't it? Thank you for your concern; no bones broken, just a few bruises. But how did all this happen? Ah, now I see – the ground here is completely iced over. The important thing is, nobody was hurt. You and your crewman seem to be uninjured.'

General Roth, the Fliegerführer Lofoten.

At dinner in the mess that evening I sat next to a Hauptmann who kept asking me stupid and inane questions. To make matters worse, he struck me as being somewhat neurotic, beginning nearly every sentence with a 'So, so,' and ending it with a long drawn out 'mmm?': 'So, so, you haven't been flying on the Arctic front for long, mmm? So just how familiar are you with the Me 110, mmm? So, so, what sort of flying training have you had then, mmm?'

My nerves were still very much on edge from the crash landing and I'm afraid I answered him rather rudely: 'Perhaps you'd be better off asking the station commander why the runway hadn't been cleared, or at least gritted. The news that a large formation was scheduled to land here today must have filtered through – even to him.' This brought the conversation to an abrupt close, but after the meal I asked one of the mess stewards who my neighbour at table had been. 'That was the station commander, Herr Leutnant,' came the reply.

Under the circumstances I was not altogether surprised to be told the next morning that I was to face a judicial enquiry regarding the accident. I knew that a number of pilots had already been given stiff sentences after being court-martialled for damaging or destroying 'the people's property' – which was another way of saying military arms or equipment. I couldn't count on any of the Bardufoss personnel to speak up in my defence. They were all too scared of possible repercussions or subsequent retaliation on the part of their station commander. The only help that I could hope for would have to come from General Roth, whom I saw among those present when I was led into the courtroom.

Proceedings opened with the charge being read out and the prosecutor's repeating the same damnfool questions that the Hauptmann had asked me the evening before. The prosecutor then launched into a lurid account of the crash landing, making it sound as if it had been all my fault entirely. I had been guilty of gross negligence at the very least, he claimed – perhaps I had even deliberately engineered the whole incident.

I was then ordered to leave the room while my wireless-operator was called to the witness stand. But, so loud were the voices, that even outside in the corridor I could still hear every word spoken inside the chamber. When the prosecutor asked Bengard how long he had been my wireless-operator and whether he was afraid of flying with me, things got quite heated: 'What sort of monstrous question is that,' Bengard replied indignantly. 'I'm sometimes frightened when flying with other pilots, but never with the chief. He's always brought us both home safely. Even here in Bardufoss. If anybody deserves to be up in the dock here it's the people who neglected to grit the runway after yesterday's icy rain!'

I was then called back into the courtroom, where it was put to me that I had told my wireless-operator what to say. I was able to refute this by stating that I had only learned of the charges this very morning and that we two had been escorted to the courtroom almost immediately thereafter. There had certainly been no time to agree on a story, even had we wanted to.

It was at this point that General Roth threw his hat into the ring. 'What exactly is this farce all about,' he thundered. 'I know this officer, he is an experienced pilot. By his actions yesterday he saved his wireless-operator and himself from injury or worse. He is to be released at once. I expect to see the station commander charged with dereliction of duty and a special hearing arranged to establish the true facts!' With that I was off the hook. But it looked as if the station commander was in for trouble.

'Wasser-Ju', the Junkers Ju 52 transport fitted with floats.

On the drive back from the courthouse to the airfield the commander was suddenly all sweetness and light. He had clearly never reckoned with a General jumping to my defence, and was probably now hoping that I could be persuaded to put in a good word on his behalf. At any rate, he was now most friendly and accommodating, saying how much he regretted that my wireless-operator and I had not been able to fly on to Herdla with the other crews due to this morning's 'little misunderstanding.' To make amends, he was putting his own car – a six-seater American limousine; no doubt requisitioned from some unfortunate Norwegian – at our disposal. His driver would take us the 250 kilometres to Bodö, from where we could get a lift in a 'Wasser-Ju', a 'Water Ju', or Ju 52 transport floatplane, down into southern Norway. We would then be able to take a train to Bergen, and from Bergen it was only a short boat ride out to the offshore island of Herdla.

When Bengard and I finally reached Herdla airfield after a five-day journey, it was to find that Oberleutnants Kirchmeier and Maul and Leutnant Orge Schwab were no longer with the Staffel. I was told that our former Kapitän, Hauptmann Schlossstein, had asked for them and that they were now serving with other units.

It was not long after our arrival at Herdla that Staffelkapitän Treppe took me up on a familiarization flight so that I could get to know the various prominent features of the land and sea areas surrounding our new island home. But when the Kapitän blithely flew between two of the smaller outlying islands, I was once again forcibly reminded of his questionable navigational abilities. These islands formed part of our outer defences and Flak batteries were stationed on both of them. Hauptmann Treppe was seemingly unaware of this fact and we only just escaped the lines of tracer hosed up at us by the skin of our teeth.

It was after landing from this flight that Treppe handed me a communication from the aviation academy in Berlin. It contained orders for my immediate transfer, instructing me to report to the academy's satellite school at Bad Blankenburg in Thuringia to commence my studies forthwith. When I showed this missive to Hauptmann Treppe he wanted to know how on earth I had managed to wangle such a posting. I explained to him that when I initially applied to join the Luftwaffe back in 1940, my first preference was to be trained as an Ingenieur-Offizier. This had been duly noted, but I was informed that, after completing my flying training, I would first have to put in a year with an operational unit at the front to prove my suitability for further specialist training as an officer-engineer. That year was now all but up and my original request was being granted: I could begin my studies.

'I can't let you go,' Treppe declared flatly, 'We're being made up to a Gruppe and you're in line to command one of the new Staffeln.' I assured him that I personally would find it extremely hard to take my leave of the Zerstörerstaffel; I got on very well with everybody in the unit, felt really at home and enjoyed flying the Me 110. On top of that, I'd grown very close to my faithful wireless-operator Bengard. We had developed into a well-knit team, and I was not looking forward to breaking the news of my departure to the poor fellow.

A Dornier Do 24 air-sea rescue flying boat moored off Herdla.

Turning into the approach at Herdla, near Bergen.

A Focke-Wulf Fw 58 Weihe comes in to land on the island airfield of Herdla.

The runway at Herdla.

Nor was I ever to see my good friend Orge Schwab again. It had always been his ambition to be transferred to an Me 210 unit, and this he finally achieved. But in 1944 he was to suffer the fate that befell so many who crewed this elegant but lethal machine: a flat spin, a crash and a funeral pyre to mark his end. In Orge I lost not just a friend, but a companion, a comrade and a dedicated pilot who, despite his many previous crash landings, never lost his enthusiasm for flying. Every time I think of him, one of the more spectacular 'crash landings' that he suffered in his private life always springs unbidden into my mind and then my sorrow at his passing invariably gives way:to a fond smile of recollection

While travelling on the Berlin S-Bahn, Orge had once got to know a beautiful girl (after more than a year up on the Arctic front almost *every* girl was beautiful!) who, after much persuasion, finally allowed him to accompany her home. She lived with her parents on the fourth floor of an old apartment block, but on this particular evening those stout guardians of her morals had gone out to the theatre. And both Orge and the young lady were eager to take their blossoming friendship that one all-important step further before her parents returned home.

While the girl was freshening herself up in the bathroom, Orge took the precaution of locking the front door of the flat, not wanting to be caught by surprise should her parents come back early. What he didn't know, however, was that the young lady had already locked the door. Thinking the key must be just a bit stiff, he forced it so hard that it broke off in the lock. Orge called through the bathroom door, explaining the problem and asking where he might find a spare key. This prompted the girl to burst into floods of tears. There *wasn't* any spare key, she howled, nor could he escape over the balcony – they were trapped in the flat together and would have to await the return of her very strict parents. Naturally, all thoughts of romance had disappeared. The distraught young lady now had other things to worry about.

When the parents finally arrived home the girl began stammering out a story about how long she and Orge had known one another, that he had simply asked to see where she lived – and then this stupid business with the key had happened. The father eyed them both suspiciously. But the girl's mother dismissed the matter, clearly captivated by the dashing young Luftwaffe officer. Before he was allowed to leave the apartment, she made him promise to call again for coffee the following afternoon; she *so* wanted to introduce him to all her friends.

At that particular moment Orge would have promised anything just to be able to make his escape. But, being the gentleman he

The Me 210 was a further development of our Me 110. It was while flying a machine of this type that my friend 'Orge' Schwab was killed in a crash in 1944. *Peter Petrick*

was, the next morning saw him out searching for a bunch of flowers to present to the lady of the house as a small token of appreciation for the invitation to coffee. However, as there were no fresh flowers to be found anywhere in bombed-out Berlin, he decided instead that a tasteful little book of literary verse would do the job just as well. He asked at the nearest bookshop for the current best-selling book of poetry, bought the volume recommended by the bookseller and had it gift-wrapped without looking at it too closely.

Arriving for the coffee afternoon, he gallantly proffered his little gift to the girl's mother with the words: 'Dear lady, I have searched long and hard for something suitable for you, and I believe I have found just the thing.' The mother proudly showed the beautifully wrapped little package to all her friends. 'That really wasn't necessary, Herr Leutnant,' she simpered, reddening slightly. 'Do open it, we want to see what good taste the Leutnant has,' the assembled ladies urged. The mother unpacked the slim volume and was obviously delighted when her friends implored her to read a passage out loud.

Orge glanced briefly at the book and saw to his horror that it was entitled 'The Erotic Adventures of the Landlady from the River Lahn'. He waited for the explosion. Without looking at the cover, the mother opened the book at random and began innocently to read aloud – only to let it fall from her nerveless fingers a moment later. She must have stumbled upon a particularly lurid and offensive little ode. A deathly silence descended on the room before she managed to gasp weakly: 'That – really Herr Leutnant, that was absolutely outrageous of you!' Her daughter immediately began to howl again while the assembled matrons, depending upon their moral outlook, appeared either to be close to fainting, or were sniggering fit to bust. All in all, it had not been Orge's finest hour!

Since being informed of my posting I had flown two further missions, both of which passed without incident. Then, on 19 February 1944, there finally came the day to bid adieu to the Zerstörerstaffel. Throughout the journey south from Herdla, via Trondheim, Copenhagen and Berlin, my thoughts kept returning to my moist-eyed wireless-operator Walter Bengard – a true friend and a loyal comrade-in-arms.

11 Back to School instead of onto the 'Komet'

Following a short detour to Eimbeckhausen to visit my parents and change into civvies, I arrived at Bad Blankenburg to commence my studies at the school of engineering on 24 February. After very nearly a year on the Arctic Ocean front living for the most part in very Spartan quarters and sleeping freezing cold on straw-filled mattresses, my new billet in what had previously been a sanatorium seemed to like a luxury hotel. I was assigned a room which I was to share with a Leutnant Vogell.

The head of the school was a certain Oberst Weimann, his adjutant was a Major Lux. But it was the Oberst's wife, Frau Weimann, who looked after the social side of the school's activities and who, as I was soon to find out, had the final 'say' in most things.

Together with about 20 fellow students, ranging from a Hauptmann sporting the Knight's Cross down to a Leutnant with the Iron Cross, First Class, I embarked upon the practical part of the course. Our instructors were Feldwebeln who had all been workshops foremen in civilian life. They were expecting us to cover in a week what a normal apprentice would be given a month to master: forging, milling, welding, woodworking, the dismantling and reassembling of an aircraft engine, the purpose of every component, the function of every instrument, the installation of electrics and much, much more. We also had lessons in theory. These were taken by retired grammar school teachers who helped us brush up on our mathematics, physics, chemistry and philosophy.

In addition to our technical and theoretical studies, Frau Weimann organized social evenings, dance events and sporting activities. At one of the dance evenings my room-mate Leutnant Vogell and I made the mistake of requesting the pleasure of a waltz with our hostess, Frau Weimann. This resulted in our being invited to the family home for coffee the following Sunday afternoon.

No sooner had we arrived than Frau Weimann produced her two daughters. One was 18 years old and the other 20 but, to be brutally honest, neither was a terribly attractive proposition in our eyes. After a few liqueurs, however, Frau Weimann became quite talkative and launched into a non-stop paean of praise as to her daughters' beauty, cleanliness, intelligence and modesty. It was only then – with the two rather plain young ladies already crimson-cheeked with embarrassment – that we recognized the trap we had walked into: she clearly regarded us as potential suitors for her daughters! And if we failed to show sufficient interest in these two perfect pillars of maidenly virtue that were on offer, it could have very nasty consequences for us. Oberst Weimann was head of the school, after all, and we couldn't afford to be in his bad books with final examinations looming.

In the hope of deflecting Frau Weimann from her intentions, we began to describe the highly dangerous lives we led as front-line fighter pilots. Death flew with us on every mission, we said, and honour forbade us from taking a young wife and possibly making her a widow at almost one and the same time. We did our best to comfort Frau Weimann by promising to come to see them all again soon and by assuring her that, should we survive the war, we would be very happy to pay court to her two charming daughters.

Not sure that our waffle was having the desired effect, I laid it on even thicker by mentioning in passing that I had volunteered for Defence of the Reich duties and wanted to train as a rocket-fighter pilot. Frau Weimann must have felt her prey slipping through her fingers, but she put a brave face on it. Her parting words to us were: 'Well then, just make sure you survive the war, you pair of heroes.'

Between the practical course and the final exams, what little free time I had was spent at the glider school based on the airfield at Schwarza, which was only about six kilometres away from Bad Blankenburg. The school's complement of gliders included a DFS Kranich, a fully aerobatic Habicht, three Grunau-Baby IIb's and a couple of powered aircraft that served as tugs. Six other gliding enthusiasts from the engineering course came along to Schwarza with me and we were all keen to get our 'C-Class' certificates, the highest glider qualification there was.

In order not to fritter away valuable time arguing about who was to pilot the tug machine, we devised a system whereby we each took it in turn to tow all the others into the air one after the other. The glider pilot who came back down to earth first would then take over towing duties. This was meant to ensure that every tug pilot got his fair share of gliding time in. But on some occasions the thermals would be so good that all six of the pilots to be towed aloft at the start of the day's flying would still be in the air at dusk. This left the unfortunate tug pilot fuming on the ground as his chances of gliding faded as slowly and surely as the light in the evening sky above.

By the end of the engineering course I was thus able to gain the 'Silver-C', First Class, for gliding and had also been authorized to fly glider-towing machines.

What with my studies and my gliding, the time literally flew by. I had been suffering quite severe pangs of conscience over these past few months for busying myself with what were essentially peacetime activities, rather than fighting alongside my comrades at the front. But I told myself that the training I was currently undergoing was a necessary prerequisite if I was to join either the staff of the new Technical Staff that was being planned, or the Defence of the Reich organization, where I could usefully combine my flying and engineering abilities to work on the revolutionary new aircraft designs that were even now under development.

But then, on 20 July 1944, came the attempt to assassinate Hitler. This raised a huge question in our minds. Given the suffering of Germany's civil population, the wholesale bombing of her towns and cities, the precarious supply situation and the Allies' overwhelming strength, would it not be better to try to negotiate an honourable peace settlement?

Some of the students at Bad Blankenburg seemed to possess a better political understanding of the facts than the rest of us. They maintained that resistance circles opposed to the Hitler regime had already made contact with the Allies on a number of previous occasions, but that the latter were not prepared to enter into discussions. They continued to insist on nothing less than Germany's unconditional surrender. Therefore, we had no alternative – particularly now after the failed assassination attempt – than to defend ourselves as best we could against the inevitability of defeat; knowing all the while that, when the time came, there would be no hope for us anyway.

This led to violent arguments as to whether the war was already lost, or could still be won, as well as to heated discussions about the fatal mistakes made by Hitler and his generals, about the senseless sacrificing of German troops; the bloodletting visited upon the entire nation, and the futility of still clinging to the belief that the so-called 'wonder weapons' – the V1s and V2s, the jet and rocket-fighters, for example – could yet bring about a change in our fortunes.

In mid-July several of the students applied to join what was already being titled the new Technical General Staff. This august body – which would comprise just ten members – had yet to see the light of day, however. And seven others of us on the course, myself included, were not convinced that this was likely to happen any time soon. So, not wanting to spend any more time sitting around doing nothing, we all decided to request a transfer to Defence of the Reich duties instead.

On 27 July I was duly posted to Zerbst, near Magdeburg, to join a rocket-fighter training course that was scheduled to commence at the beginning of August. That gave me just enough time to go home, get out of my civvies and back into uniform, and pack a few small items of hand baggage. I could already see myself as a dashing young rocket-fighter pilot and was therefore more than a little disappointed to discover that, before I could get my hands on an Me 163, I would have to put in yet more hours stooging around in such tame birds as Arado trainers, and even practising aerobatics in various types of glider.

At Zerbst I bumped into my old friend Oberleutnant Haardt, whom I knew from basic training days. It was from him that I learned that I had also been made up to Oberleutnant recently, but that the official confirmation of my promotion had not yet caught up with me

An Arado Ar 66 trainer of the type that Oberleutnant Haardt and I ferried up to Aalborg in Denmark.

due to my many moves over the past few weeks. On 4 August Haardt and I were detailed to fly an Arado Ar 66 biplane trainer up to Aalborg in Denmark, where we were to report for further training.

Oberleutnant Haardt flew the first leg from Zerbst to Neumünster in Schleswig-Holstein. After refuelling there, I took over as pilot for the last lap up to Aalborg-West. As I entered final approach it struck me as odd that there wasn't an aircraft to be seen on the ground; it was as if the field had been swept clean. Everywhere was as quiet as the grave. After taxiing to a stop we had a good look round. We got the impression that we had landed in some ghost town out in the old wild west. Paint was already peeling off the walls of the buildings. The wind was blowing dust, sand and odd scraps of paper about all over the place. Doors and windows that hadn't been fastened properly creaked eerily as they swung to and fro.

Then we came across what looked like a small mess hut. When we went in we found three young Danish women sitting idly around a table. They informed us that the field had been closed down some little while ago. All training had now been moved to Aalborg-East, but somehow or other they had got left behind. Absolutely typical, I thought to myself, some fool in the Zerbst flying control office falls asleep on the job and forgets to tell us that we are meant to land at Aalborg-*East*, not Aalborg-West!

Before we took off again the Three Graces gave us their telephone number and made us promise to let the new mess-secretary at Aalborg-East know of their plight. Ten minutes later we put down on the 'right' field, handed over our machine, and reported to the chief instructor, a certain Hauptmann Haugk. We were both assigned a room in one of the barracks blocks and, after unpacking our gear, made our way over to the mess in search of something to eat.

It was at this point that the fact of actually being in Denmark finally began to sink in. Nobody was eating the standard rations. Here, for very little money, you could get whatever your heart – or, more accurately, your stomach – desired. Haardt and I stared in wonder at plates piled high with ham, sausage, all kinds of cheese and butter. Our mouths watered at the sight but, as we hadn't yet exchanged any of our Reichsmarks for Danish Krone, all we could do was watch as the others dined off the fat of the land. Our rumbling bellies would have to do with basic Luftwaffe fare: one slice of bread, a bit of cheese and 20 grams of butter.

But it seemed even this was to be denied us. We had to wait absolutely ages to be served. And the longer we waited, the less enchanted we became with this new-found 'life of luxury'. Nor were we the only ones. Many of the 'private payers' hadn't been given their meals yet either. All around people were complaining that nothing worked properly any more and that the lazy-arsed orderlies could do with a spell at the front to wake their ideas up.

After half-an-hour of waiting, and still with no sign of our food, we protested to the mess secretary. This harassed-looking individual was nearly at the end of his tether, bemoaning the fact that he couldn't find any proper waiters and that he couldn't stand the constant complaints another minute longer. 'Help is at hand,' I

Further training was done on the Arado Ar 96B-7. This photo shows an earlier 'A' variant.

consoled him. 'Just call this number. Three very chic waitresses are sitting around there waiting for work. Get them over here as quickly as you can and all your troubles will be over!'

Sure enough, the very next morning the three 'orphans' were hard at work and everyone was happy – especially us, for the ladies clearly believed in the old maxim that one good turn deserves another. Haardt and I were particularly well looked after. We didn't need to exchange any more Danish Krone, our glasses were invariably filled to the brim, and when it came time to settle the bill there would always be one or two Aquavits missing from the tab.

On 7 August tuition began on the Arado Ar 96B-7, an advanced trainer powered by a single 465 hp engine and featuring a retractable undercarriage and enclosed cockpit. I was already familiar with the Ar 96 from my time at both the air warfare academy and the Zerstörer school, and so had no problems at all in getting the feel of it again. After the usual briefing about safety, I was let loose to carry out circuits and controlled approaches. I also practised touching down as close as possible to the landing cross and going round again after dummy 'botched' landings. But the main emphasis was on precision approaches and landings, which I was required to perform over and over again.

A few days later I was allowed to take up a Bücker Bü 131 Jungmann to demonstrate my aerobatic abilities. After the strictly supervised practice flights on the Ar 96, it was an absolute joy to really let myself go as I ran the gamut of spins, rolls, loops, half rolls, vertical turns, Immelmanns and the like.

One evening I joined a group of fellow students who wanted to see what kind of night life Aalborg had to offer. We took a bus from the airfield into the centre of town and soon found a promising looking café-cum-dancehall. Sitting at one of the tables just inside the door was an Oberst together with several other high-ranking Luftwaffe officers. Eager to get on with the important business of enjoying ourselves, we saluted our superiors as regulations dictated and then tried to edge past the table as quickly as possible. But the Oberst motioned for me to stop. He murmured his name, which sounded to me like Butler-something-or-other, and asked which unit we were from.

While my comrades lost no time in making themselves scarce, I came to attention and reported: 'Oberleutnant Wollenweber of the Aalborg Fighter Conversion Staffel, Herr Oberst. Forgive me, but may I be permitted to enquire whether the Herr Oberst is by any

The Bücker Bü 131 Jungmann was an outstanding machine for aerobatics.

chance related to Freiherr von Buttlar-Brandenfels, the author of the book 'Zeppelins over England'? As a twelve-year old boy I read – perhaps it would be truer to say devoured – that book and was totally captivated by it.'

'Actually, I *am* that very author,' the Oberst admitted, clearly flattered as he glanced at his colleagues. 'Won't you join us for a little while. I'd be interested to hear what it was that you particularly liked about the book.' I sensed from his tone that the Oberst's 'invitation' brooked no argument. My hopes of rejoining my comrades, who were already showing off their skills on the dance floor, were fading fast. So I took a seat next to the Oberst and told the assembled officers the story of the airship's landing on the Binnenalster, the smaller of the two lakes in the heart of Hamburg. A bevy of female aviation enthusiasts, of whom there were many in those early days, had come to witness the event. But the elegantly dressed ladies had unfortunately chosen a spot on the banks of the lake too close to where the airship intended to land. And when it discharged its water ballast they got a thorough soaking.

'Donnerwetter, you still remember that?' the Oberst exclaimed delightedly. 'Yes, but what I enjoyed even more was your description of how the ladies were dried out afterwards!' I added. My tale had the whole table rocking with laughter. But, aware of the success my comrades appeared to be having with their dance partners, I was less than happy at the officers' invitation to stay longer and have a few cognacs with them.

After several hours and more than 'a few' cognacs, I was relieved to see that my friends were preparing to call it an evening. We would just have time to catch the last bus back to camp. But when we got to the stop some unpleasant news awaited us: a member of the Danish resistance had slashed the tyres of the bus, which meant that we would have to make our way the six kilometres back out to the airfield on foot.

In order to avoid any more such enforced hikes in the future, and to make it a little easier to visit the mess, which was situated on high ground a good kilometre-and-half away from our quarters, I invested in a second-hand bicycle. Although it had no brakes and no lights, it performed sterling service – until the day, that is, when the chain broke as I was racing downhill on my way back from the mess. I started weaving about as my descent became ever more erratic. I tried braking with my feet, only to go flying head over heels into the ditch alongside the road.

The bicycle was a write-off. The pedals, frame and handlebars were all bent. The front wheel was twisted into a figure of eight. And I didn't look much better either. My right leg had borne the brunt of the damage. The end results were: a lot of heavy bruising, my lower leg in plaster and – not surprisingly – a ban on any further flying for the time being. So while my comrades carried on happily with their training, I was forced to sit inactive on the terrace of the mess watching the flying.

The field's take-off and landing strips were neatly tucked between the surrounding meadows, pastureland and cornfields. It was harvest time and the farmers were busy gathering in the crops, oblivious to all the aerial activity going on around them. But what struck me time and again as I sat watching my fellow trainees was that it was the ex-bomber pilots amongst them who, although convinced in their own minds that they could fly anything that had wings, seemed to suffer the most accidents.

Despite the instructors' constantly warning them that the Me 109 could prove extremely tricky to handle at take-off, they kept making the same mistakes. They seemed unable to grasp the fact that the Me 109, with its narrow-track undercarriage and powerful engine, had to be kept on the ground until sufficient speed had been built up for the airflow over the control surfaces to become effective.

Put simply, the stick had to be pushed firmly forward throughout the take-off run. If it was held in the normal position, or if the pilot pulled it back into his stomach too early – before the machine had attained the required speed, that is – the huge engine would develop reverse torque and the aircraft would begin to drift uncontrollably to port. More often than not, the wingtip would then dig in and the machine would be flipped over onto its back, often with fatal consequences for the pilot.

In the first accident of this kind that I witnessed, an Me 109 that tried to lift off before gaining sufficient speed spun around on its longitudinal axis and performed a complete ground loop before it went hopping off across the field, bouncing and leaping about on its spindly legs like a bucking bronco. Inevitably, one wing touched the ground, somersaulting the machine onto its back. The aircraft immediately caught fire and within seconds was engulfed in a sea of flames. Miraculously the pilot, a small slightly built figure, was able to wriggle free through the shattered side panel of the canopy. He staggered away from the inferno and slumped down next to me, still in a complete state of shock.

After the station's fire section had tried but failed to extinguish the flames in the cockpit area, the crew chief came across to me, saying sadly: 'I'm sorry, there was nothing we could do for your comrade, he was burned in the wreckage of his machine.' 'No I wasn't – I'm here!' the little fellow beside me piped up. He even managed the semblance of a grin.

It was only a few days later that the next accident occurred. An Me 109 swerved wildly to the left while taking off, skittered off the runway into a field of stubble and began to somersault end over end. The first time it smashed back down onto the ground one of the wings was torn off. The next somersault wrenched the engine from its mountings. After that, what remained of the machine was just a mass of bent and battered metal. The fuel pouring from the ruptured tanks had left a blazing trail through the stubble and now set light to many of the sheaves of corn still standing in the field waiting to be gathered in.

While watching a large section of the tail unit flying through the air, I caught a movement out of the corner of my eye. I could hardly believe what I saw. A smouldering figure was crawling out from under one of the burning sheaves of corn! It was the pilot, whose guardian angel had catapulted him out of the disintegrating machine and allowed him to escape with just a few minor burns to his hands and face.

On another occasion a trainee, realizing that his aircraft was starting to drift off the runway, immediately shut off power. But he had already built up too much speed and was unable to prevent the machine from tearing through the wire perimeter fence and careering across the neighbouring farmer's cow pasture that lay beyond it. After only 20 metres the aircraft smashed first into a horse and cart, and then into a cow being milked by the farmer's wife. Tragically, the farmer's wife, the horse and the cow were all killed by the whirling propeller blades.

The pilot climbed uninjured from his machine, but was inconsolable when he learned that the farmer's wife was the mother of three small children. He organized a collection, which raised over 2,000 Danish Krone – a moving gesture and a considerable sum of money; but nothing when compared to the loss of a wife , and three now motherless infants. The most macabre thing about the whole unfortunate episode, however, was the behaviour of the farmer. He had been working some distance away from the scene of the accident and refused all offers of help from the rescue services, saying he couldn't come with them until he had finished milking the cow.

At the beginning of September I finally got out of my plaster and was able to take part in the training again. By now the course had moved on to gunnery practice against ground targets. The aircraft used were Arado Ar 96 trainers, each armed with a single, fixed forward-firing MG 17 machine gun. Every day we would fly the short distance across to a cordoned-off stretch of beach on Denmark's west coast and practise our marksmanship firing at the targets that had been set up there.

It was during one such exercise that one of our Arados was attacked by a British Spitfire. The enemy fighter's 20 mm high-explosive shells ripped the ground target to shreds and set the trainer's engine on fire. The pilot managed to belly land his burning machine on the beach, but the Engländer was already coming back in for a second pass. He poured a long steady burst into the by now blazing Arado. But the pilot had already leapt from the cockpit. Racing across the beach, he disappeared into one of the gunnery range bunkers just in the nick of time.

While the Spitfire had been concentrating on the downed Arado, the rest of us had scattered in all directions like a flock of hens at the sight of a fox. Our trainers were no match for a Spitfire. But the enemy pilot was not finished with us yet. The next machine he went after was that flown by recent Knight's Cross recipient Fahnenjunker-Oberfeldwebel Werner Haugk. A veteran ex-Stuka and Zerstörer pilot, Werner Haugk also happened to be the brother of the Aalborg school's commanding officer.

Although the Arado was badly damaged in the Spitfire's attack, and he himself was grazed in the neck by a cannon shell, Werner Haugk managed to land back at Aalborg. But the wound proved fatal. It had pierced his carotid artery and he bled to death while taxiing in. His lifeless body was lifted from the cockpit by his grief-stricken younger brother Hauptmann Helmut Haugk.

On 29 September Hauptmann Polzin, Oberleutnants Fleischmann and Leiterer, Leutnant Graf and I were told that we were being posted to Gelnhausen, ENE of Frankfurt-am-Main, for further rocket-fighter training. We were to report there on 2 October. But when we discovered that the transfer to Gelnhausen meant going back to yet more training on gliders, we asked Hauptmann Haugk with barely-concealed annoyance when we would actually get to fly the rocket-fighter itself.

'I'm afraid you'll have to be patient for a little while longer, gentlemen,' Haugk replied. 'What you must understand is that the Me 163 Komet is nothing more than a tiny glider equipped with a rocket engine. Once it has shot you up to an altitude of 10,000 metres in little less than three minutes, you'll have time to carry out just one firing pass at the enemy bomber you select as your target. You'll have to shoot it down during that one pass and then – because of the rocket engine's short burning time, which is eight minutes at the most – you will have to concentrate all your efforts on getting back home again ... and that means gliding! Consider for a moment the swept-back wings, their small aspect ratio and thin aerofoil section, the tail-less fuselage and compact form of this so-called 'power-egg' and then you'll begin to understand why you will need to be expert glider pilots before you can hope to master it.

'Up till now you've been flying standard Habicht gliders with their 10 and 13 metre wingspans. From here on you'll be doing your training on Stummel-Habichts, which are cropped wing versions of the same craft with spans reduced to just 6 and 8 metres. You'll have to get used to a completely different style of gliding and learn how to handle the kind of high-speed landings that will be vital to your survival when it comes to flying and landing the Me 163 with a dead engine.'

With this admonition ringing in our ears, our goodbyes to Hauptmann Haugk were brief. There were no promises to 'see you again soon'. Every one of us was fully aware that the war could not go on for much longer. But none of us knew whether he would live to see its end. Before we left the attractions of Aalborg behind, however, we all took the opportunity to stock up on every imaginable type of local delicacy: large quantities of sausage, cheese, butter and ham were stuffed into our kitbags, for back in the Reich we would soon be subsisting on basic rations again.

After an agonizingly slow train journey, made all the slower and more tedious by the numerous delays and diversions resulting from bombed-out stations and destroyed tracks, we finally arrived at Gelnhausen airfield on 2 October. To our surprise we were not accommodated in the usual communal barracks blocks, but were instead quartered in large single rooms. The washing facilities and bathrooms were also clean and in very good order. All in all, the field and the picturesque little town of Gelnhausen itself, nestling in the Kinzig Valley nearby, gave every impression of being far removed from the war.

But appearances were deceptive. The air raid sirens wailed on an almost daily basis. Gelnhausen was situated too close to Frankfurt and a number of other Luftwaffe airfields in the Rhine-Main region to remain inviolate to Allied air incursions and bombing raids.

The next three weeks were taken up by a glider programme of the kind that was familiar to me from my days at Schwarza. Only the aerobatics – rolls and steep turns in the Stummel-Habicht – were new to me. Shortly before the end of the Gelnhausen course a group of low-flying Tempests attacked a freight train on the line that ran to the south of the field. The RAF fighters employed their customary tactics; first immobilizing the locomotive by cannon fire, and then leisurely working over the closed goods wagons standing stationary on the tracks. When the rescue teams were eventually able to approach the scene some 30 minutes later they found the wagons filled with hundreds and dead or badly wounded women and children, refugees from the Reich's eastern provinces who were fleeing from the advancing Russians and seeking safety in the west.

On 27 October we departed Gelnhausen for Berlin-Rangsdorf airfield. Located on the southern outskirts of the Reich's capital, just beyond the districts of Blankenfelde-Mahlow, Rangsdorf also boasted a large lake. When the Bücker aircraft manufacturing company first moved to Rangsdorf in 1935, not only was a works airfield constructed, but also a military field for the use of the Luftwaffe and a base for seaplanes on the shores of Rangsdorfer Lake.

When we arrived there on 28 October we were met by an instructor who introduced himself as Leutnant Lutter. Wearing the Knight's Cross, he was an ex-transport pilot who had lost his left forearm while serving in Africa. At Rangsdorf we were once again housed in barracks, where we were surprised to find five Italian pilots occupying the next room. It transpired that, after the fall of Mussolini, Hitler had apparently promised to continue training Italian pilots on some of Germany's most modern aircraft. And these five – accompanied by a retinue of three orderlies, two chambermaids to make their beds, and an interpreter; one Leutnant Kirn – were part of that programme. The names of only three of them have stuck in my mind: Capitani Zuccarini, Biron and di Lollo.

During our short ten-day stay at Rangsdorf

we trained exclusively on Stummel-Habicht gliders. Launched by winch, we practised precision landings – first on the 8-metre variant, and then on the 6-metre – to get the feel of the gliding characteristics of the Me 163 which, we were told, were very similar to those of the cropped Habichts.

Our training was sometimes brought to a halt by an air raid on Berlin just to the north of us. The scenario of howling sirens, followed by the engine mutter of approaching bombers, the sound of falling bombs – at first a muted scream and then a loud roaring – the dull thud of explosions, the deep barking of the city's Flak defences, and the constant staccato stuttering of machine guns, were all too horribly familiar to me from the brief time I had spent in Berlin attending the gas-defence school. But during one particular raid the cacophony of background noise was almost droned out by a high-pitched, almost melodic whine that seemed to be coming from almost directly above our heads.

The low-hanging clouds were preventing us from identifying the source of this most unusual sound. It was only when a badly shot-up Me 109, its propeller windmilling, burst from the cloud base that we realized it was the noise of the airstream whistling through countless bullet holes.

The pilot managed to regain control of the machine at the very last moment, putting it down in a high-speed belly landing between the barracks blocks. I was only five metres away from where it finally slid to a stop. Rushing over to it I found the pilot, a Leutnant, sitting dazed but uninjured in the cockpit. I unbuckled his parachute harness and seat straps and released him. Still in a complete state of shock, he gazed at me blankly and asked: 'Where in heaven's name am I?'

'Not in heaven, old man, that's for sure. In fact, you're right in the middle of Rangsdorf airfield – and just in time for a bite to eat,' I added encouragingly in an attempt to buck him up a bit. It was only then that I took a closer look at his aircraft. The rudder had been shot away, the top of the canopy was missing, there was a gaping hole in the rear fuselage and both wings had been liberally peppered with machine gun fire. It was an absolute sieve. There were so many holes in the machine that it was no wonder it had sounded to us like some crazed aerial flautist as it came whistling down unseen through the clouds. Little wonder either, that the pilot had no appetite after such an experience. He politely, if somewhat absently turned down my repeated invitation to join us in a meal. All he wanted to do, he said, was to telephone his unit as quickly as possible. As a consequence, I never did get to know his name.

On 8 November it was announced that all trainees who had not yet flown a single-seat fighter were to be transferred to Mackfitz in Pomerania. I was one of this motley group of 20, made up of all ranks. We set out from Rangsdorf to take the S-Bahn into the centre of Berlin. But when we got to the city's main line Stettiner Station we were told that the train to Mackfitz would not be leaving until the following morning. We therefore decided to while away the time by having a stroll around Berlin. Even though the capital lay in ruins and offered little in the way of entertainment, this was still better than sitting around on a cold and draughty station platform. The only problem was our luggage. But that was a problem easily solved – a few packets of cigarettes slipped to a railway official and we were given the use of a locked room to store our things in overnight.

When we eventually arrived in Mackfitz I was assigned to share a room with Leutnant Donner. He had already been there for quite some time and, after we had introduced ourselves, we started chatting. He told me that he was the youngest of three brothers. The other two had both been killed in action. The eldest had served in Panzers; the middle brother had been General Galland's wingman and had been shot down during Defence of the Reich operations. Now he, the youngest, was the sole remaining heir to the Donner family's banking business in Hamburg.

He went on to tell me that he was fairly certain his father was pulling strings with General Galland to ensure that he was kept out of harm's way. He revealed to me in confidence how his father had come to be so close to Galland. Apparently, after his older brother had been shot down and killed, Galland had married the brother's wife – in other words, the widow of his erstwhile wingman. Not wanting anything to happen to his last surviving son, Leutnant Donner's father had managed to get him posted to Mackfitz, which is how he came to be sitting around here in this backwater doing absolutely nothing.

It may have been little consolation to my new room-mate but, in fact, we were *all* sitting around in Mackfitz doing absolutely nothing. The field's fuel supplies had been exhausted and all flying was suspended until a fresh delivery arrived. As a result we were given all sorts of ridiculous jobs just to keep us occupied. One day we were issued with saws and axes and instructed to hack a large clearing in the pine woods bordering the airfield. This was then to be covered in camouflage netting and used as a dump for the numerous wrecked and cannibalised aircraft of all types – including some 60 Fw 190s, Do 217s and Ju 88s – that lay scattered around the field.

When it became clear that no new supplies of fuel could be expected in the foreseeable future, I put in a request for leave. I was granted 11 days, from 20 to 30 November inclusive. This suited me perfectly as 28 November was the birthday of Marliese Benze, the girl I hopd to marry, and I wanted to take this opportunity to announce our official engagement.

Although hardly a great distance, the journey from Mackfitz down to Eimbeckhausen took me all of two days. After catching up on some much needed sleep, I duly marched off to the Villa Benze on 26 November. Herr Benze owned a successful chair-making factory and, as he got most of his timber from our forest, my family and the Benzes had been friends for years. I knocked on the door of my prospective father-in-law's study. 'Herr Benze, may I request the hand of your daughter in marriage?' I asked in the highly formal manner demanded by the occasion.

The benign expression on his face told me what his answer would be. It also gave me the courage me to add, far less formally: '... and everything else that goes with it?'

He nodded wordlessly and wiped away a furtive tear before giving me a bear-hug. 'At last, my boy,' he said, visibly moved, 'It's high time you sailed into calmer waters.' My parents must have forewarned the Benzes as to the purpose of my visit, for the door suddenly burst open and the rest of the family, all seven of them, came storming into the room to shower me with hugs, kisses and congratulations.

But it wasn't long before the rejoicing was cut short by a low-pitched thrumming in the skies above. The noise grew steadily louder. We all trooped outside and saw countless bundles of condensation trails being dragged across the sky by formations of heavy bombers all heading towards Hanover. Even as we watched, more and more bomber boxes were coming in from all directions and joining up with the main stream. Then German fighters fell upon the enemy armada like a swarm of angry hornets.

If I hadn't known that the spectacle unfolding above our heads was a bloody duel between life and death, I would perhaps have tried to convince my fiancée that it was an air display I had arranged especially for her benefit. As it was, our fighters had already become embroiled in a series of violent dogfights with the bombers' escorting fighter screen. Vivid skeins of tracer criss-crossed the sky in wild confusion. Here and there a bomber exploded in a gigantic fireball. And everywhere pieces of wreckage were fluttering and spiralling earthwards. The clouds of smoke as machine after machine was hit began to turn the glowing orange-red of the sky a funereal black.

Suddenly I saw an Fw 190 come spinning down almost vertically. Its guns were still hammering and it seemed to be heading straight for the house. Before I could get the family into the safety of the cellar, the machine appeared to right itself momentarily, only to crash into one of the huge piles of timber stacked in the yard of the chair factory nearby. I waited for its fuel tanks to explode, but nothing happened. When I got to the scene of the crash all I found was a water-filled crater, covered in a thick film of oil and with a few small blue flames flickering around its edge. But I could hear the ammunition going off underground. I presumed the body of the pilot was still in the cockpit buried deep in the crater. The rest of the machine lay strewn along a path between the woodpiles in the factory grounds.

I later discovered that this raid on Hanover had been carried out by 1,137 B-17 and B-24 heavy bombers, escorted by 732 P-51 Mustang and P-47 Thunderbolt fighters. Our Jagdgeschwader 301 had suffered 40 losses during the course of the action – a toll representing more than a third of its pilots. The Americans admitted the loss of 42 heavy bombers and 11 escorting fighters.

Five Luftwaffe fighters and three enemy bombers had been shot down in the Eimbeckhausen region. I had seen two machines crash in the vicinity of my parents' house and hurried off to investigate.

In one of the rides that cut through our forest I found an American airman lying next to the wreckage of his blazing machine. After dragging the burning body away from the source of the fire, I tried desperately to smother the flames, first by beating at them with branches and then by smothering them with earth. I soon realized, however, that the enemy flyer was beyond all help. I removed his papers from the pocket of his flying overalls and handed them over to a local policeman who had just arrived at the crash site on his bicycle, instructing him to inform the Red Cross of the dead man's identity without delay.

Not unnaturally, this air raid, and the aircraft that had been shot down close to Eimbeckhausen, had had a sobering effect on our little community. They had certainly cast a pall over our combined engagement and birthday festivities. In addition to this, all the guests were aware of my coming transfer to Defence of the Reich operations, and this only served to depress the party atmosphere even more. It was therefore with a sense almost of relief that I was able to escape the general air of gloom and set out by train on 30 November for the journey back to my unit.

When I reached Mackfitz airfield early on 1 December I discovered that a tanker of aviation fuel was due to arrive at any time. This had persuaded the station authorities to release the fuel reserves that they had been holding back for use only in the case of absolute emergency – so there *had* been fuel at Mackfitz all along! – and which, in turn, allowed me to start familiarizing myself on the Fw 190.

My room-mate Leutnant Donner explained the cockpit layout to me, taking me through all the instruments, switches and buttons with a great deal of care and expertise. Donner himself was scheduled to go up with an instructor and another pupil to carry out some wide circuits of the field, and the moment he had finished describing the Fw 190's handling characteristics to me the impatient instructor was urging him to get a move on. I waited while their three Focke-Wulfs taxied out and took off. My orders were not to follow them, but to restrict myself at first to straightforward circuits and bumps in order to get the feel of the Fw 190.

It was while climbing away after my fourth touchdown that I noticed two columns of black smoke climbing into the air to the north of the field. That amount of smoke could only be coming from crashed aircraft. And as the only machines in the immediate vicinity were the three other Focke-Wulfs, my first thought was that two of them must have been involved in a mid-air collision. Having no radio, I quickly landed to inform the chief instructor of what I had seen, then immediately took off again and headed for the scene of the accident.

I was hoping against hope that the two pilots might have been able to bail out, but when I reached the spot there was absolutely no sign of life in the fields below – just the smoking remains of what had been two Focke-Wulf fighters. And when the third machine came flying towards me, its markings told me that the pilots involved in the accident had been the instructor and my room-mate Donner.

The surviving trainee and I returned to the airfield, which by now was alive with activity. The station's fire-fighting vehicles and ambulances had been sent racing off to the crash site, and all other aircraft that were up on training exercises in the surrounding areas had been recalled. Still badly shaken by what he had just witnessed, the pilot of the third machine explained what had happened. Apparently the instructor, quite suddenly and without any warning, had started to climb steeply. Leutnant Donner attempted to follow him, but must have been momentarily blinded by the glare of the sun, for somehow or other the two machines came into contact. Neither pilot had managed to regain control and both aircraft went spinning into the ground.

Conversion training on the Focke-Wulf Fw 190.

A partial view into the cockpit of an Fw 190.

The accident had to be reported to higher authorities at once, of course. And from what my late room-mate had told me of his family background I guessed, quite rightly, that trouble was heading our way. Sure enough, General Galland let it be known that he would be arriving in Aalborg on 11 December. He would no doubt want the full details of his protégé's death, and someone could expect a severe carpeting at the very least. I certainly wouldn't have liked to have been in the chief instructor's shoes at that moment, for he had known of Galland's personal guarantee to Leutnant Donner's father that the sole heir to the family banking dynasty would be extremely well looked after.

Once again I had the unenviable task of packing up a room-mate's effects and sending them to his next-of-kin. Galland's visit was brief, but not without effect. By the evening of 12 December he had gone, leaving behind a very chastened chief instructor moping dejectedly about the place and a four-day ban on all further flying.

But by 17 December things were back to normal. I resumed my training on the Fw 190 and really pushed the machine to its limits; throwing it about in a sequence of flick rolls, stall turns, dives, loops and inverted flight, all to my instructor's complete satisfaction. But then something untoward happened. On my last scheduled landing approach of the day I found myself coming in too fast. I lowered my undercarriage a little earlier than normal in order to lose some speed. But the moment I activated the flaps the machine went into a sudden half roll, which I was unable to prevent despite centralizing and hauling back hard on the stick.

The aircraft's odd behaviour clearly had something to do with the operation of the flaps, so I retracted them again and carefully completed the roll. Due to my unconventional approach I was by now only five metres above the field's perimeter fence. This left me with no option but to abort the landing and go round again. I would have to try to come in without flaps. A fast landing could prove tricky, however, as the grass runway was only 800 metres long. A row of tiny pine trees had been stuck into the ground to marks its end, and just beyond these was a dangerously deep ditch.

As the ground was frozen hard and covered with a light dusting of snow, I touched down as close to the perimeter fence as possible in order to use the full lngth of the runway and immediately started tramping on the brakes. Despite this, the aircraft continued to head towards the line of 'Christmas trees' at an alarming rate of knots, and to prevent myself from ending up in the ditch I forced it round into a high-speed ground loop. Fortunately, the Focke-Wulf's wide-track undercarriage took the strain as the wheels juddered sideways across the runway. The machine turned a full 180 degrees before finally coming to rest pointing back in the direction of my touch-down.

As I sat in the cockpit recovering from the shock and thanking my lucky stars that the undercarriage legs hadn't sheared off, one of the Feldwebel instructors came running up furiously demanding to know what the hell I thought I was playing at, making such a stupid beginner's mistake. I ignored his fit of rage and merely lowered my flaps, pointing wordlessly to the tiny stump of flap projecting from beneath the trailing edge of my port wing. The instructor clasped his hands above his head and muttered something that sounded vaguely like an apology, saying that another fatal accident was all that the school needed right now.

Despite bad weather on the morning of 18 December gunnery practice on the Fw 190 went ahead as scheduled. I was sent out to a firing range located on one of the Baltic beaches. Due to the adverse conditions I was unable to find anything in the area indicated, and so began to fly west along the coast in the hope of seeing some signs of the range further on. Instead, I found myself over the island of Usedom and inadvertently entering the prohibited airspace that surrounded the highly secret Peenemünde missile test establishment. I was just about to turn round and take to my heels when I saw a large, streamlined cylindrical object with a long tongue of flame belching from its tail climb slowly into the low-hanging clouds. I had been witness to the launch of a V2 rocket, one of the 'wonder weapons' that was supposed to bring a change to Germany's fortunes in this unspeakable war.

The low cloud base that soon hid the rocket from my view also allowed me to escape detection as I hastily reversed course and got out of the danger area. If I had been discovered within the prohibited zone the consequences for me would have been dire in the extreme. As it was, I headed back eastwards, stumbled across the firing range quite by chance, and let fly with several long bursts at the ground targets set up on the beach.

However, as I had taken 44 minutes to complete the exercise, and because the number of hits registered was judged insufficient, I was ordered to do it all over again that same afternoon. Although the weather conditions were by then even worse, I managed to find the firing range after flying back and forth a few times. I went in so low that I very nearly rammed the ground targets and was certain that every one of my rounds had hit home. A third practice shoot was flown on 20 December. On this occasion the weather was perfect. I found the firing range straightaway and completed the exercise in half the time I had taken before.

I had only just got back from this third and final session on the range when I was told of my transfer to Sprottau in Silesia. I was to report there in two days' time to commence rocket-fighter training with IV./EJG 2 – the fourth Gruppe of Fighter Advanced Training Wing 2.

12 Power Eggs with No Power

When I arrived at Sprottau on the afternoon of 22 December I was pleased to see a familiar face. 'Fritze' Fleischmann and I had become firm friends during the short time we had recently spent together while glider training at Gelnhausen. Hauptmann Polzin, Leutnant Graf, several Feldwebeln and Unteroffiziere, as well as the group of Italians had also been posted to Sprottau.

I was given a room that had a small bedroom leading off it and settled in very comfortably. Fritze Fleischmann had already found a larger room that was standing empty and this we converted into a temporary mess, decorating it with a Christmas tree, candles and everything else needed to make the imminent Christmas festivities a success.

The Kommodore of Ergänzungsgeschwader 2 was Oberstleutnant Werner Andres. The Kommandeur of the wing's IV. Gruppe was Hauptmann Hans Nocher, who was succeeded shortly after our arrival by the Knight's Cross holder Hauptmann Robert Olejnik. Our chief instructor was introduced to us as Leutnant Hermann Eugen Ziegler, perhaps better known now under his pen name of Mano Ziegler. We had long admired his sporting achievements as a world champion high-diver and his flying skills as a test-pilot, and were therefore delighted that he was to be our instructor on the Me 163.

Fuelling an Me 163 '06' with C-Stoff.

In the event, our Christmas celebrations turned out to be something of a damp squib. This was due mainly to the fact that the liquid refreshments, including several bottles of wine and cognac, promised by Fritze Fleischmann's father had failed to arrive. Fritze immediately rang his father, who was a high-up in the Reich's audit office in Potsdam, only to learn that the package had been sent off in plenty of time, but must have 'evaporated' – in other words, been stolen – on its way to us. So on Christmas Eve we had to make do with 'Reich's soup', our name for the official issue of thin mulled wine that was little more than water tinted red and tasting faintly of cloves.

Nor did the weather do anything to cheer us up. Heavy snow and ice had put our long-cherished hopes of flying the Me 163 on indefinite hold. We would have to wait some little while yet, it seemed, before we would be able to take the 'Wundervogel', the 'wonder-bird', into the air. But then, when we discovered that there was neither aviation fuel for the unit's Me 110 tug aircraft, nor the highly specialized fuels required by the Me 163s – which were powered by a lethal mix of hydrogen peroxide (T-Stoff) and hydrazine hydrate (C-Stoff) – our spirits really hit rock bottom.

Beginning on 1 January 1945, 20 to 30 centimetres of fresh snow fell every day. In order to keep the runway in operation, the station commander ordered the trainees to shovel it clear. There were 130 of us of all ranks, and Sprottau's runway was a good 1,000 metres long and 50 metres wide. It was going to be no easy task. But when an NCO then proceeded solemnly to issue us with exactly five shovels and two snow scrapers we were absolutely dumbfounded. 'You'll find a few more brooms over there,' the commander said, 'but I'm afraid that's all there is.' Before disappearing back into his office he added, almost as an afterthought: 'Oh, and by the way, everyone is confined to camp until that runway is as clean as a whistle.'

We managed to clear 200 metres a day at most, with just a handful of people at a time actually working, while the rest stood around doing nothing but stamping their feet and moaning fit to bust. Not surprisingly, many came down with colds and reported sick. I suspect that a number of malingerers chose the same course of action – or rather, inaction. Hauptmann Polzin, who had been given the unenviable task of overseeing the snow clearance, caught a very nasty, feverish and genuine cold, and detailed me to take over his duties.

Shortly before the weekend an Unteroffizier of the permanent staff came to see me saying that he and his comrades had a suggestion to make; if I could get the station commander to lift the ban confining everyone to camp, the runway would be cleared within a day. When I put this proposal to the commander he smiled sympathetically: 'I've no problem agreeing to that, because you'll never do it. But it's not down to me. Let's just say that all those who help clear the runway will be given a weekend pass.'

I told the men of the station commander's promise. Hardly had I got the words out of my mouth before they were dashing off to their quarters, war-whooping like a bunch of Indians, to find something – anything – to clear the snow with. They reappeared carrying every kind of object imaginable: doors, benches, squared-off bits of timber, even chairs were pressed into service as snow scrapers. Everywhere you looked, men were scurrying around panting and sweating as they pushed piles of snow aside with the unlikeliest of implements.

The news that 48-hour passes were on offer spread like wildfire. More and more figures appeared out on the runway. Even those who had been languishing in the sick bay suddenly recovered in a manner that was little short of miraculous. And – incredible but true – in just four hours the runway had been cleared! Nor was that all: not only was the runway ready for use again, but a small quantity of aviation fuel for the Gruppe's Me 110 towing aircraft had at last arrived and, on 15 January, I was finally allowed to climb into the cockpit of one of the Me 163 'wonder-birds'.

I had already heard a great deal about the fabulous handling characteristics of the Messerschmitt rocket-fighter, but also a lot about the lethal unreliability of its rocket motor. The latter was of no concern to me at the moment, however, as we still hadn't received any deliveries of T-Stoff and C-Stoff fuel. Instead, the machines' tanks would be filled with water to provide the necessary ballast and, after being towed aloft by an Me 110, our first flights would be restricted to practising gliding and landing our unpowered 'power-eggs'.

As the Me 163 was not equipped with an undercarriage, take-offs were made with the aid of a jettisonable, two-wheel trolley attached to the aircraft's ventral landing skid. This trolley had to be released immediately after the machine had left the ground – something which most pilots forgot to do in the excitement of the moment. If the trolley was jettisoned too late – once the machine was already five or perhaps even ten metres off the ground, say – its two somewhat oversized rubber tyres would cause it to bounce anything up to 20 metres back into the air. When this happened it meant at best that a search party would have to be sent out to find and retrieve the errant trolley last seen leaping about all over the field like a demented springbok. At worst, the trolley would bounce back up and strike the aircraft that had just released it, more often than not with fatal consequences.

A cutaway drawing of an Me 163B showing the jettisonable take-off trolley and landing skid. *Lexikon der Flugzeuge, Wolfgang Bredow/artwork John Weal*

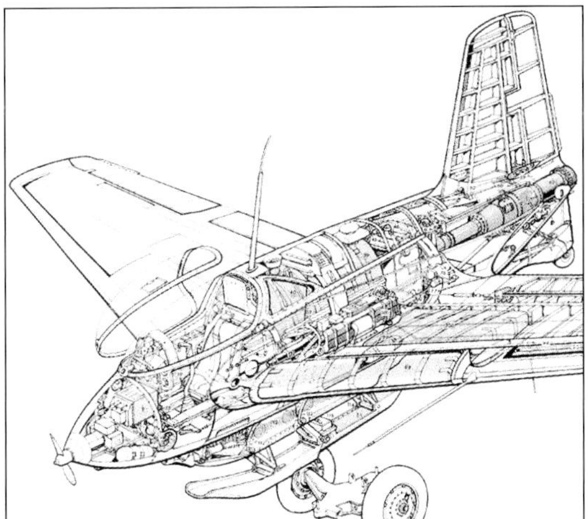

An Me 163 after landing on its ventral skid.

The Me 163 V45 prototype. *National Archives, USA*

An Me 163B wearing the 'Baron Münchhausen' badge associated with 14. Training Staffel. *Wolfgang Bredow*

The next few days were spent in practising precision landings. The Me 163 was landed like a glider on its extendable ventral skid. But the pilot had to take great care not to flatten out too far off the ground, as a heavy landing could result in severe spinal injuries. An Me 110 towed me up to a height of 2,000 metres for my first attempt. After casting off, I was to glide back down towards the field, extend the landing skid, and touch down as close to the landing cross as possible. All seemed to be going smoothly, I was nicely lined up on the landing cross, but when I lowered my flaps the Me 163 promptly sank like a stone. I managed to recover, but came to a stop an embarrassingly long way short of my intended point of landing. At least I now knew how the bird responded to the activation of the flaps, and I had no further problems in putting it down smack on the landing cross from then on.

On 24 January Fritze Fleischmann and I were told to report to the Kommodore. Oberstleutnant Andres informed us that we had passed all the necessary tests and, in theory, were ready to start flying the rocket-fighter operationally … if only the fuel for the rocket motors were available. 'But we aren't expecting the next delivery of T-Stoff and C-Stoff for at least another three months,' he explained, adding: 'There's nothing more for you to do here during that time, and so I imagine you'll want to get back on operations.'

I asked Andres if he could arrange to get me posted to a jet unit, and he promised to see what he could do. Before dismissing us he instructed me to travel by rail to Udetfeld, an airfield near Kattowitz (Katowice) in Poland, to pick up an Me 110 that the Gruppe urgently needed here for towing duties. I suggested that it would perhaps be better, and certainly quicker, if I flew to Udetfeld in one of our Me 110s and took a second pilot with me to ferry the other machine back. After all, it was at least 300 kilometres to Kattowitz and with so much of our railway network destroyed by enemy air attacks, who could say how long it would take me to get there – and besides, the Russians were already closing in on Udetfeld.

Andres heard me out, but regretted that he was unable to comply with my suggestion: 'I'm sorry, Wollenweber, but you can see for yourself just how bad things are here. I don't know how on earth I'm expected to continue with the training programme. We haven't got enough Me 110 tugs, and there's hardly any fuel left for those we *do* have. Here are your travel orders. I'm sure you'll manage to get there by train – I'm relying on you.'

The two-day rail journey from Sprottau, via Breslau, to Udetfeld was more than just hazardous; it was horrific. In those forty-eight hours I experienced more of the terrible sufferings of the civil population than in all the previous five years of war put together. Every time I had to change trains the station platforms were packed with thousands of apprehensive women, most with small children clinging to them, all hungry, freezing in the bitter cold, and desperate to escape the advancing Russians.

The hopelessly overcrowded waiting rooms were scenes of utter chaos and misery: mothers were begging for milk to feed their tiny babies, and pitiful bundles of humanity huddled or lay on the floor anxiously awaiting the train that would carry them to the west. I had never witnessed such abject misery before in my entire life. At first my feeling was one of slight disgust. But then I became angry: angry at myself and my own helplessness – angry at being able to do no more than share out my meagre travel rations of Choca-Cola, liquorice and biscuits among the children.

And everywhere the same reproachful, questioning look in the eyes of the women, why wasn't I, a fit and healthy young Luftwaffe officer, fighting at the front protecting them. It was the Berlin bunker all over again. I felt like hanging a sign around my neck: 'Give me the fuel and I'll be able to do something for you.'

When I eventually got to Udetfeld the mechanic working on the Me 110 said that Leutnant Ziegler had already been on the phone enquiring about me. He had been informed that

Oberstleutnant Werner Andres, Geschwaderkommodore of EJG 2.

the machine I was to ferry back to Sprottau wasn't ready yet as one of the oil pumps was defective. 'Then take a pump from one of the old machines standing around here that has been retired from service,' I urged the mechanic. 'An oil pump from a DB 603 engine will work perfectly well on a DB 605, they're identical. I want this machine fully serviceable and ready to go by tomorrow morning. The Russians are only 20 kilometres away from here and their tanks will soon be squashing this place flat.'

At 10.05 hours on 27 January 1945 I lifted off in the Me 110 and am pretty sure that mine was one of the last German aircraft to fly out of the Udetfeld 'cauldron'. During the flight back towards Breslau I spotted a large concentration of Panzers below me. I assumed these to be vehicles of the SS Panzerdivision that was rumoured to be about to launch a counter-attack against Tschenstochau (Czestochowa), an important rail junction to the north of Udetfeld. I went down to 50 metres and waggled my wings in greeting.

As I drew nearer, however, my jaw dropped: every tank wore a red Soviet star and the crews of the anti-aircraft vehicles in their midst were already swinging their quadruple Flak guns in my direction! To avoid their fire I pressed my machine even closer to the ground and sought the cover of the trees to make my escape.

After a flight lasting 80 minutes I landed at Sprottau, only to be immediately buttonholed by Leutnant Ziegler: 'Glad to see you made it safely. We're transferring to Esperstedt at noon and we need every Me 110 pilot we can muster to help get our rocket-fighters there.' After we had towed all our Me 163s the 300 kilometres or so back to Esperstedt in Thuringia, we were quartered in every kind of billet imaginable in the surrounding area. Oberstleutnant Andres and the senior officers took up residence in a small castle on the edge of town while I, for example, was allotted private accommodation in a farmhouse at Ringleben, some 45 kilometres away.

Esperstedt airfield in the middle of winter was totally unsuited for glider-tug operations and, as there was no fuel available anyway, all training activity came to a complete stop. After two weeks of sitting around twiddling my thumbs, I'd had enough. I went to badger Oberstleutnant Andres again: 'Herr Oberstleutnant, back in Sprottau you very kindly said that you'd put in a word for me regarding a posting. With the greatest respect, may I once more request that I be released from my duties here and be permitted to transfer to a jet fighter unit.'

'Gently does it, Wollenweber. You're in far too much of a hurry to join the Reich's Eagles and get your feathers singed. But, as it happens, you've come at exactly the right moment. The orders transferring you to the Defence of the Reich command for further duties have just landed on my desk. You're to report to the office of the General of Fighters in Berlin-Kladow without delay. They'll tell you where you are to go next,' Andres said, handing me my transfer orders in a sealed envelope.

The brief look we exchanged as I took my departure said everything, and yet said nothing: what fate awaited us, would we survive the war unscathed, or be shot down and killed? Perhaps we would 'only' be wounded and, if so, how serious and life-changing would our injuries be?

13 To Jagdgeschwader 1

I spent the best part of 12 February on a train which, due to the usual diversions and delays, didn't get into Berlin's Friedrichstrasse Station until after midnight. I had hardly arrived when the sirens started their mournful wail; yet another air raid warning! I was hungry and dog-tired, but what was that when compared to the privations, sleepless nights and all the suffering that those living in the capital had had to endure over the past months.

After the all-clear had sounded I caught the S-Bahn out to Rangsdorf, hoping to find a bed for what was left of the night at the airfield there. I lugged my kit across to the barracks block where I had stayed the previous October. Luckily, the door was unlocked but there wasn't a soul about. The water, lighting and heating had all been turned off and everybody seemed to have left. I found a room that still had a locker and a bed covered with a woollen blanket in it, and dropped off to sleep with my stomach rumbling.

The next morning there were still no signs of life anywhere around and so I set off, unwashed and still hungry, to take another S-Bahn across to Fighter General Staff HQ at Kladow. There I was given a room in the visitors' guest house. After a thorough wash and shave, and with a good breakfast inside me, I began to feel human again. I was next directed to the office of the head of postings. A sign on the door told me that this was a Hauptmann Müller.

I knocked on the door, waited for the 'Enter!', then went in, handed over my documents, came to attention and reported: 'Oberleutnant Wollenweber, transferred from IV. Gruppe, Ergänzungsjagdgeschwader 2 for further duties.' The Hauptmann looked up at me and glanced at my papers. A broad grin spread across his face. 'Heavens above, Wollenweber! I never thought we'd meet up again – and both in one piece at that!' Hauptmann Müller was clearly pleased to see me.

Then the penny dropped. This was the same Müller, then a Leutnant, who had been my course officer at the Fürstenfeldbruck war academy back in 1941.We had got on very well together. He was a keen huntsman and knew that I came from a forestry background. He had asked if he might accompany us on a hunt some time, to which I had readily agreed. Unfortunately it never came off, as he was taken ill shortly afterwards and I had been posted elsewhere by the time he returned to duty.

'You must tell me what you've been doing with yourself over the past few years. What unit of our Reich's Eagles have you been stooging around with? I'm dying to hear all about it – take your time,' Müller said as he fished a bottle of brandy out of a cupboard. It turned into a long session, during which we brought each other up to date on our recent experiences. At the end of it I described how much I was now looking forward to the chance of finally getting into a jet fighter unit.

'But it doesn't say anything about that here,' Müller said as he leafed through my papers again. He showed me the section recommending my transfer to an Fw 190 ground-attack unit. 'That can't be right … the admin office must have made a mistake … Oberstleutnant Andres promised me that I would be …' I began to stammer.

'Don't get yourself worked up, Wollenweber, I can quite easily sort this out for you,' Müller said. He went on to explain in a conspirational tone: 'Jagdgeschwader 1 is about to be converted on to the new Heinkel He 162 turbojet fighter. I've gone through your service record with some care and it's my opinion that, with all your training and experience, you're exactly the right kind of man they'll need. Come back here tomorrow morning and see Oberleutnant Seitz, he's just three doors down the corridor. By then I'll have everything fixed.'

We parted with mutual good wishes for the future. I could hardly believe my luck: after so many years, to have stumbled across somebody who was not only an old friend, but also the one person who seemed to have the necessary clout to be able to arrange the posting of my choice for me!

The next morning I tapped on Oberleutnant Seitz's door. Not hearing an 'Enter!', I barged straight in – we were, after all, both of the same rank. Seitz was sitting at his desk, but was talking to three officers, each of whom was sporting the Knight's Cross around his neck. I tried to duck quickly back out again, but was brought to a halt by one of the Knight's Cross wearers: 'Don't you ever bother to wait until you are invited to enter a room?' he snapped at me.

'No, Herr Oberstleutnant – er, I mean yes, Herr Oberstleutnant,' I stuttered in confusion, seeing visions of my transfer to turbojets fading rapidly. 'Not only is he impolite, now he wants to demote me into the bargain,' the other said, raising his eyebrows. I looked more closely at my questioner and almost froze to the spot in awe – it was none other than Oberst Gerhard Barkhorn, the legendary fighter 'ace' who had shot down more than 300 enemy aircraft!

'No, Herr Oberst, please accept my apologies, Herr Oberst,' I managed to say in a strangulated voice as I clicked my heels together. 'That's perfectly all right, we're finished here anyway,' Barkhorn replied. He turned to his two companions: 'Shall we go, gentlemen?' The three of them left the room grinning and chuckling.

I got the impression that Oberleutnant Seitz had also been somewhat amused by my making such a bloody fool of myself. He certainly had more than a hint of a smile on his face as he handed me my travel warrants, saying: 'You're to ferry a Focke-Wulf 190 from Schönefeld up to Garz/Usedom on the Baltic coast. That's where you'll find I. Gruppe of Jagdgeschwader 1 "Oesau", the unit to which you have been posted with immediate effect.'

This resulted in another arduous and depressing journey by train through the rubble and ashes of Berlin. The trip from Kladow across to Schönefeld on the south-easternmost outskirts of the city on that 16 Jnuary took me past endless rows of burnt-out houses and apartment blocks. The gaping holes that had once been doors and windows in their now hollow facades stared back at me like the eyes of the dead.

At one of the stations en route I happened to bump into Oberleutnant Krös of the Gatow gas-defence school. He informed me that the school was about to be transferred to Blankenburg in the Harz Mountains now that the Russians were getting close to the capital.. He clearly regarded this as tantamount to running away. The other instructors were a bunch of cowardly swine, he said. They would hang on to their cushy little jobs like glue. Not one of them was prepared to pick up a weapon and do his bit towards ensuring the 'final victory'. I expressed no opinion, simply wishing him well as I picked up my luggage and continued on my way through the devastated city towards Schönefeld airfield.

There I was told that I would not be assigned a machine until the following day as there were several other pilots from JG 1 already waiting to ferry Fw 190s up to Garz. After sharing a room overnight with a Leutnant Reinhard, I reported to the flying control office at nine-o-clock the next morning ready and eager to take over an Fw 190A-8. Instead, I found myself being harangued by a woman of indeterminate status and advancing years. In a strident voice that would have been the envy of any drill sergeant, she proceeded to inform me that I should have been there by seven, and that now all available machines had already been assigned pilots. She went on in a similar vein, grumbling and grousing nineteen to the dozen until I finally shut her up by saying: 'Alright, alright, I'll come back again tomorrow – at least I've gained another day's grace on my way towards a hero's death.'

And so, on 18 February, I was there at seven on the dot. I was given a machine that had only 13 minutes of static test running time on the clock and was yet to be fuelled. By the time all the formalities of acceptance and clearance, fuelling, the collection of a parachute and stowage of my kit had been completed, it was already 11.20 hours. The Berlin that I then found myself flying over looked even more dreadful from the air than it had done from ground-level. It was a scene of total destruction. I wondered to myself whether people could actually be living down there in the middle of all that devastation and, if so, how they could possibly exist without heating, water, power and all the other basic necessities of life.

I had got as far as Prenzlau, some 90 kilometres to the north of Berlin, when the engine of my Fw 190 developed ignition problems. It produced a series of loud bangs and began to belch smoke through every crack and crevice in the cowling. Soon it was misfiring so badly that I momentarily lost power every time I as much as touched the throttle. I knew from my earlier days that there was an airfield at Prenzlau, and I decided to land there in the hope that the mechanics could sort out my troubles. But as I curved in on final approach, I saw that there were cows grazing in the middle of the field. So Prenzlau had been abandoned too. Now I would have to see if I could coax this wheezing and backfiringing bird the rest of the way to Garz.

As I continued to head northwards I fiddled about with the throttle until I found a setting that kept the misfiring within acceptable limits. I had already decided to put down at Garz as if I were landing a glider: a nice smooth, clean three-pointer – but on the concrete runway. This should hopefully prevent any wobbling about or bouncing back into the air upon touchdown, and should also avoid my having to blip the throttle and risk the engine's cutting out altogether.

The plan worked. And after getting down safely I taxied towards the dispersal area where a group of pilots and mechanics were standing around in front of several Fw 190s of various series. As the engine had started backfiring again and was emitting a succession of even louder bangs, the whole crowd turned to look in my direction. After I had switched off and slid back the canopy a familiar figure approached: 'I'd heard you'd become a big noise in the Luftwaffe,' Leutnant Berger laughed.

I was delighted to find Hans Berger here. He and I went back a long way. We had done our training together at the Zerstörer school in Memmingen when he was still an Oberfähnrich, or senior officer-cadet. He had arrived at Garz a few days earlier and already knew the ropes, and so was able to put me in the picture as to what I had to watch out for and whose word was law around here.

Firstly, however, I wanted to report to my new Geschwaderkommodore, Oberst Herbert Ihlefeld. But when I heard that he was away at the moment, I accompanied Berger across to the mess hall to get a bite to eat. There he introduced me to the other pilots of the Gruppe and to the Kommandeur, Oberleutnant Karl Emil Demuth. I was to be assigned to Leutnant Berger's 3. Staffel. Leutnant Gerhard Hanf

Winner of the Oak Leaves with Swords to the Knight's Cross, Oberst Herbert Ihlefeld, Kommodore of Jagdgeschwader 1, was credited with 132 aerial victories.

commanded 2. Staffel, and 1. Staffel was led by Leutnant Heinz Künneke. The latter was the brother of the well-known musical star Evelyn Künneke, whose songs we used to play over the loudspeakers at Kirkenes before every bombing mission to help the armourers' and ground crews' work go with that extra bit of a swing.

The fact that the Gruppe's three Staffeln were commanded by Leutnants, rather than by officers of Oberleutnant or Hauptmann rank, was an inescapable sign of the times. Losses among experienced pilots and formation leaders had been growing at an alarming rate over recent months. In Operation 'Bodenplatte' alone – the New Year's Day attack by Luftwaffe fighters on Allied airfields in the Low Countries and France, in which Jagdgeschwader 1 had participated – over 200 pilots, including 14 Staffelkapitäne, had been lost.

We had hardly finished eating when a Feldwebel came into the mess to announce: 'The pilot who has just landed is to report to the station commander.' That can only mean me, I thought, as I looked enquiringly at Berger. He merely shrugged his shoulders and grinned. The pilots at the other tables also seemed to find the situation funny, but were unsuccessfully trying to pretend that their scarcely concealed mirth stemmed from the amusing conversations they were having with their neighbours. Puzzled, I asked Berger: 'What's the station commander's rank?' 'Oberstleutnant,' he replied. 'Get going then, he won't bite your head off,' he added, suppressing a gurgle.

I followed the Feldwebel across to the station commander's office and knocked on the door. 'Enter!' a voice rasped from within. I stepped into the room. 'Aha! So *you're* Oberleutnant Wollenweber. Do you always land in that manner?' the commander demanded in the same rasping tone. He didn't wait for a reply, but went on: 'Donnerwetter, you don't often see – and hear – landings like that. Where did you fly operationally?' 'In Kirkenes on the Arctic Front, Herr Oberstleutnant,' I answered, still at a loss to know what he wanted to see me for.

It was only when he produced a bottle of cheap brandy from a filing cabinet and invited me to take a seat, saying he wanted to drink a toast to my successful landing, that I began to catch on: he was one of those desk-bound tipplers who looked for any excuse to satisfy their need for a drink. The other pilots had all been through the selfsame charade with him; hence their knowing grins. After he had poured me a glass of the raw spirit, he speedily and efficiently emptied the rest of the bottle himself. Then I was dismissed.

Back in the Mess the other officers asked me what it was he had wanted to see me about. Nothing at all really, he just wanted a reason to knock back a bottle of booze, I explained to general laughter. Then I was informed that, during my brief absence, orders had arrived transferring the Gruppe down to Parchim in Mecklenburg-Vorpommern. Oh no, I thought, not another damned train journey – please, anything but that. After my gypsy wanderings of the past few weeks, I had really hoped that I would now be able to stay in one place for more than just a few days. But it was not to be. Part of the Gruppe left for Parchim by road in a convoy of Kübelwagen and other assorted vehicles. As for me – what else? – I was issued with a travel warrant and told to proceed there by rail.

One of the unit's trucks took me the 35 kilometres from Garz to the railway station at Anklam. From there it was by train, via Pasewalk to Berlin-Karow. This meant I was back almost to where I had started. And on the way I once again had to endure the constant changing of trains at small wayside stations, the endless waits on crowded, freezing platforms and, worst of all, the demoralizing sight of hundreds of wounded soldiers and the vacant, apathetic stares of hungry and exhausted refugees fleeing from the east.

At Karow I bumped into Leutnant Finner who had been at Mackfitz with me. He had just completed another course and had now been posted to our 1. Staffel. We travelled together from Karow out to Parchim. But we had hardly put a foot through the gates before fresh orders were received sending us, and all the other pilots who had arrived in Parchim before us, off on our travels again – and this time we would *all* go by rail. It was 23 February and our destination was the Heinkel works at Rostock-Marienehe where we were to be given a familiarization course on the He 162.

The train took us to Warnemünde, where we learnt that we were to be billeted not at Rostock, but in Warnemünde's very elegant and high-class 'German Reich's Chancellor' Hotel. There we were met by a Leutnant Büttner, who had been transferred across from II./JG 1 to join our Gruppe. The seaside resort of Warnemünde seemed to have been spared the horrors of war. There was none of the frantic hustle and bustle that I had experienced in many other towns. All was peace and quiet. Even the air raid sirens were silent. That evening I went to the cinema with Büttner. I was struck by the fact that no newsreel was shown during the programme. But I could guess the reason why: footage of glittering military parades, a staple of all newsreels in the past, would not have gone down very well with the audience if the troops were shown marching through ruined and rubble-strewn streets. Nor were there any more heroic victories for the announcer to boast about in ringing tones – perhaps even Göbbels & Co. no longer believed in their own exhortations to see things through to the end?

14 The Birthplace of the 'Salamander'

On 24 February we travelled the short 14 kilometres by train from Warnemünde to Rostock-Marienehe, site of the historic Ernst Heinkel Aircraft Manufacturing Works. It was from here that the world's first jet-powered aircraft, the Heinkel He 178, had taken off on its maiden light on 27 August 1939.

When we detrained directly in front of the factory we saw that many of its buildings and much of the grounds had suffered severe damage from Allied bombing. While we were waiting for the necessary formalities to be gone through before we could be issued with our works security passes, we were given our first 'specialized briefing' on Heinkel's own 'Wundervogel'.

Truth be told, we knew precious little about the He 162 and were all naturally eager to get our first glimpse of this new secret weapon. One thing that confused us was the plethora of names that had been bestowed upon the machine. Because of its small size and limited weight, its manufacturers referred to it as the 'Spatz', or 'Sparrow'. Another of its titles, the 'Salamander', was derived from the code name of the original lightweight jet-fighter programme that had resulted in the He 162. Not surprisingly, perhaps, the regime preferred the much more bombastic 'Volksjäger', or 'People's Fighter'. When I first set eyes on the He 162, I thought the name 'Pfeil', or 'Arrow', would suit it admirably – a view apparently shared by others, for many He 162s would later have large red arrows painted on each side of their noses – but the name 'Pfeil' had already been allocated to Dornier's push-pull Do 335.

We were also a little sceptical as to whether Heinkel's turbojet fighter, which had been designed and built in record time, would live up to the high expectations placed upon it. After all, little more than seven weeks had elapsed between the awarding of a production contract on 15 September 1944 and the machine's maiden flight on 6 November 1944.

Of one thing we *were* sure, however. A jet-powered fighter was not something that could be flown by any and every Hitler Youth who happened to possess a gliding certificate. Yet this was precisely the mad scheme that the Party propagandists were trying to sell to the civil population when they dubbed Heinkel's machine the 'Volksjäger'.

It was Generaloberst Keller, the head of the NSFK (the Nationalsozialistisches-Fliegerkorps, or National Socialist Flying Corps) who had first put forward the proposal to Göring. If those youngsters of the Hitler Jugend who had been trained to fly gliders were given a short familiarization course, he suggested, thousands of them could be sent up in He 162s to combat the American bomber streams. Göring liked the idea. He ordered the leader of the Hitler Youth organization, Reichsjugendführer Artur Axmann, to set up an appropriate training unit at Trebbin, south of Berlin.

A number of engine-less He 162s were, in fact, delivered to Trebbin. These were to be used to provide the boys of the Hitler Youth with the 'feel' of the machine in the air while being towed behind another aircraft. But with the war situation worsening daily, the project was soon overtaken by events and the course terminated. This undoubtedly saved many members of the Hitler Jugend from almost certain death at the hands of the Allied air forces. And the only thing that remained of the whole hare-brained scheme was the name 'Volksjäger'.

While being conducted around the factory, we were made even more aware of the enormous amount of damage inflicted by the many Allied bombing raids that had been made on it since 1942. Only three of the works' large sheds were still in operation, and it was in Shed 2 that final assembly of the He 162s was taking place. When we entered the hangar-like shed we saw a row of machines all carefully covered by tarpaulins. The scene somehow reminded me of my childhood Christmases when, as a boy, I had gazed at my presents piled under the tree wondering what was hidden underneath all that wrapping.

When the tarpaulins were removed, our group's reactions were mixed. Faces at first reflected surprise, and then either enthusiasm or scepticism. My initial thought: if that clumsy, almost misshapen great lump of a turbine hadn't been stuck on top of its neat little fuselage, this could have been the most beautiful and elegant aircraft I had ever clapped eyes on. I was also hugely impressed by the manner in which the most basic of materials – due to the shortage of metals, the wings and part of the tail unit were, after all, simply made of glued wood – had been combined with such a revolutionary concept.

Located immediately behind the nose cone, the cockpit's large, cleanly-moulded Plexiglas canopy promised excellent forward and lateral visibility, the instruments had been reduced to a bare minimum and were clearly laid out, and the pilot had even been provided with an ejection seat. The wooden wings had a thin aerofoil section and terminated in downswept, detachable aluminium tips that looked for all the world like a pair of droopy ears. While the leading edges of the wings were straight, the trailing edges displayed negative sweep. The span of the tiny, shoulder-winged machine was just 7.20 metres and its take-off weight a mere 2.5 tonnes. This meant that it was not only 2.70 metres smaller, but also some 700 kilograms lighter than the already trimly compact Me 109G.

Right: The ejection seat of the He 162. *Museum Flugsicherheit- und Rettung, Baden-Airpark*

Below: The He 162 was a shoulder-wing machine with negative sweep on the wing trailing edges. (Model by H. Engelhard)

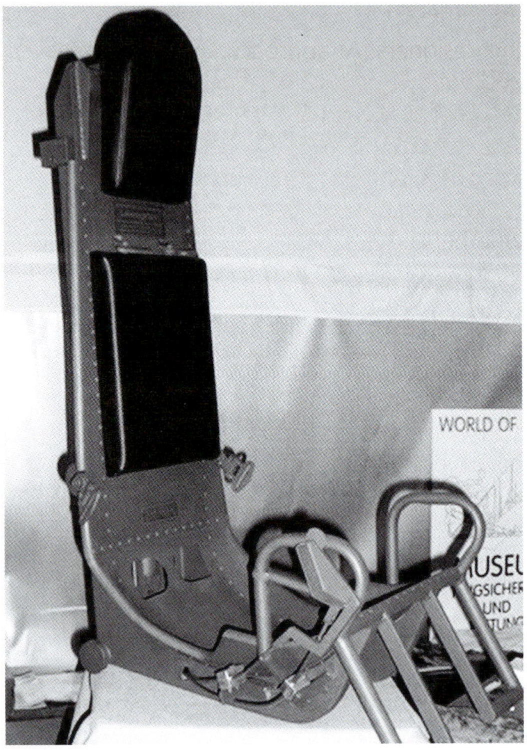

Revolutionary features were the so-called 'Lippisch ears', the downswept wingtips, and the dorsal mounting of the engine. (Model by H. Engelhard)

The Plexiglas teardrop canopy offered exceptional visibility.

A noteworthy feature was the pronounced dihedral of the tailplane. This arrangement was apparently necessary to deflect the exhaust gases of the dorsal-mounted turbine. But for me it raised the questions as to what kind of control forces would develop at high speeds, and whether or not the exhaust turbulence would affect the operation of the twin rudders. What I did find ingenious, however, was the undercarriage: the machine's mainwheels were those of an Me 109, while its nosewheel was the tailwheel of a Ju 88 – shouldn't be any supply difficulties there then.

The firepower of the two fuselage-mounted, forward-firing 30-mm MK 108 cannon should also prove more than adequate to bring down the enemy's 'Flying Fortresses', although I would have liked to have seen more than the 50 rounds per gun provided for by the designers. At approach speeds in excess of 700 km/h, a pilot would have to open fire at a range of at least 300 metres if he wanted to be sure of scoring hits on the bomber he was attacking, and 50 rounds didn't last long.

What concerned me even more was whether the 670 kilogram weight of the BMW 003 jet engine perched on top of the fuselage was properly distributed. And, if it was, would this solid mass – however streamlined its casing – have an adverse effect on the machine's aerodynamics? And how would it affect the He 162's handling characteristics, say in a dogfight or in a deadstick landing?

But by far the biggest problem of all, I was told, was the aggressive reaction of the adhesives used to bond the aircraft's wooden components. The current gluing techniques were far from perfect, as the separation of wing leading edges and ailerons during high-speed flight trials were all too regularly proving – often with fatal results. All suppliers of glues and wooden parts had been ordered to improve their products without delay. But, given the constant disruptions in the deliveries of raw materials, the daily bombing and destruction of road and rail networks, and the dearth of specialist joiners and carpenters, this was a time-consuming and well nigh impossible exercise.

After this first visit to the Heinkel works we returned to Warnemünde, where Leutnant Büttner, Leutnant Genske of the Geschwaderstab and I took a stroll along th promenade. The war was finally beginning to intrude on this once fashionable seaside resort. In the shallows just off the beach the burnt-out wreck of a small freighter was rolling gently in the swell; its carcass slowly being reduced to a skeleton by the waves breaking against it. The sorry spectacle that it presented reminded me very much of our own present military situation and the inevitable collapse of Germany, whose leaders still clung to their belief in 'final victory' and who were prepared on each and every day that was still left to them senselessly to sacrifice yet more of the nation's most valuable asset ... its people.

An ingenious solution in times of material shortage: the tailwheel of a Ju 88 served as the nosewheel of the He 162. The two MG 151/20 cannon fired through troughs on either side of the machine's nose.

On 26 February Flugkapitän Heinrich of the Heinkel works gave us a talk on the development of the He 162, the hopes that were being pinned on it, and the results achieved in the test flights to date. When Heinrich went on to describe the He 162's having approached the speed of sound in timed flight, we could scarcely contain our excitement. This led even the most sceptical among us to hope perhaps that, if enough machines could be built – it was estimated that we would need a permanent force of 300 fully operational He 162s, together with a corresponding number of well trained pilots – a change in the war situation might yet be possible, even at this eleventh hour.

But when I paused for a moment and started to go through these cloud-cuckoo land figures in my head, I quickly came to the conclusion that, if they hoped to make any impression whatsoever on the Allies, every single one of those 300 He 162 pilots would have to shoot down at least one enemy aircraft a day out of the many thousands that were now parading almost at will across the skies of Germany. And as only 30 machines at the very most had been taken on charge to date, and new assembly and logistical problems were cropping up almost daily, it was obvious to me that such calculations were totally meaningless.

On top of that, the Heinkel's limited flight endurance of just 30 to 45 minutes meant that an entirely new set of combat tactics would need to be worked out. We also brought up the subject of what we felt were the inadequate number of rounds for the two MK 108 cannon. Flugkapitän Heinrich answered this by saying that the new He 162A-2 variant was to be armed with two of the almost equally effective 20-mm MG 151/20s, which would be provided with 120 rounds per gun.

We had already heard that no two-seat trainer versions of the He 162 had yet been built. Lacking any previous experience on jet fighters, how were we supposed to fly them, we asked. 'There's not going to be a two-seater,' Heinrich explained, 'the building of single-seat interceptors has absolute priority under the emergency fighter programme.'

'But you *will* be given a set of pilot's handling notes,' he continued. 'These you will have to read and learn thoroughly. You will also receive instruction on the ground. One of our works pilots will explain all the controls to you. He will show you how to start the engine, how to handle the throttle, and point out which instruments you need to keep a special eye on. He'll talk you through what you have to do at take-off, after lift-off, while in the air, and when landing. When the He 162 is demonstrated to you, fix firmly in your minds the exact point of lift-off, watch how the pilot handles the approach when he comes back in, and note precisely where he touches down.'

I looked at the other pilots. From the expressions on their faces I could tell what they were thinking. The gamut of emotions ranged from utter dismay, through disbelief, to obvious impatience to fly this machine at the earliest possible opportunity.

The days that followed were taken up with lectures and theory. Works engineers and designers filled our heads with enormous amounts of data, figures, test results and flight reports. But all the theory in the world was no substitute for one actual training flight. Between lectures we were sometimes shown around other parts of the factory. On one occasion we were ushered into a hangar in which stood a very curious beast indeed.

The Heinkel He 111Z consisted of two twin-engined He 111s joined together by means of an additional constant-chord wing centre-section carrying a fifth engine. The resulting machine, with its enormous wingspan of more than 35 metres, had a crew of seven. The pilot flew the aircraft from the left-hand fuselage. The second pilot, who also acted as navigator, was in the right-hand fuselage, which was little more than one huge fuel tank with a capacity of 8,250 litres. The He 111Z – for 'Zwilling', or 'Twin' – had originally been built as a towing aircraft for the Messerschmitt Me 321 Gigant, or Giant, heavy transport glider. But the

The He 162's flying instrument panel was neatly and clearly arranged. *Archiv AK Junkerswerke und Fliegerhorst Bernburg*

machine we were gazing at in awe and wonder was the Z-2 variant, a projected long-range bomber that could fly a distance of 8,000 to 10,000 kilometres and thus conceivably carry an offensive load of four 1,850 kg bombs as far as America. A couple of know-alls in our little group even hinted that the He 111Z-2 was being readied to drop an atomic bomb.

In another corner of the same vast hangar stood a long-legged, twin-engined He 219A-2. I was captivated by this sleek beauty at first sight and, to this day, have never been able to understand why the He 219, a 650 km/h night-fighter which would also have made an excellent all-weather fighter, was not given the highest priority.

Finally, we were taken out onto the runway and shown an He 162 all fuelled-up and ready for take-off. Standing next to it was Dipl-Ing. Wilhelm Gundermann who, together with Hans Joachim Pabst and Max Hahn, had played such an important role in the development of Germany's earliest jet engines. Gundermann explained to us that the BMW 003 turbine produced in excess of 800 kilopond thrust, which was enough to lift the He 162 off the ground after a take-off run of about 650 metres. Take-off speed was in the region of 200 km/h. Landing speed was a minimum 170 km/h and no lower. Any kind of aerobatics in the He 162 was strictly forbidden. Nor was it permissible to exceed the 600 km/h maximum speed stipulated by the manufacturers, or to drop below the stated 300 km/h minimum speed in level flight.

All this we accepted without question. But when Gundermann then went on to say that, in the immediate foreseeable future, BMW would not be in a position to deliver the 1,000 jet engines per month as required, but only 100 at the very most, our spirits took a nosedive.

Also built at Rostock-Marienehe was the five-engined He 111Z, two fuselages joined together by a new wing centre-section.

Although we didn't talk about it much any more, every one of us was by now perfectly aware that the end of the war could not be far off.

The situation was indeed catastrophic. In the east the Russians stood on a line along the River Oder from Breslau up to Stettin. In the west the Americans had reached the Rhine and the British were already in Westphalia. The once peaceful seaside resort of Warnemünde had undergone a complete change in the last few days. Ships of all shapes and sizes were constantly arriving with thousands of refugees and wounded soldiers from the eastern front. They should have been taken on by ferry to Denmark, but because the sea routes to the west were heavily mined, they were left stranded in Warnemünde.

There were hardly any supplies remaining in the overcrowded town to feed the hordes of refugees that were still pouring into it every day. Hungry and without medical attention, these unfortunates therefoe had no option but to attempt to continue their journey westwards by train rather than by boat. This put enormous additional pressure on an already overburdened railway network and led to frequent disruptions in the deliveries of fuel and ammunition to the fighting front.

The BMW 003A-0 engine mounted on a mock-up He 162 fuselage during trials at Rechlin. *Manfred Griehl*

The BMW 003E-2 engine weighed about 670 kg and delivered up to 930 kilopond thrust.

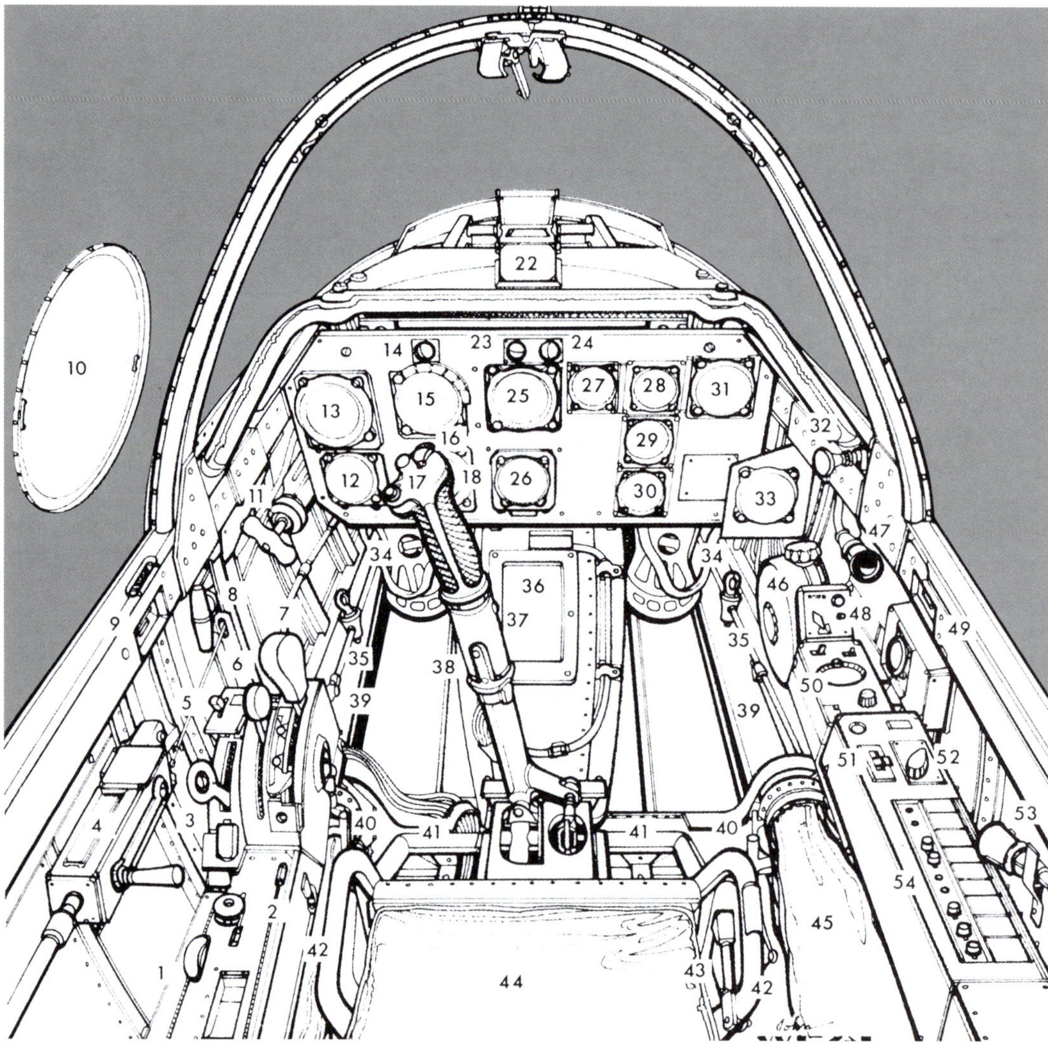

Heinkel He 162A-2 cockpit

1 Rudder trim control
2 Take-off rocket jettison
3 Undercarriage selector
4 Elevator trim control
5 Take-off rocket activation switch
6 Fuel cock
7 Throttle lever
8 Undercarriage operating lever
9 Port undercarriage indicator
10 Ventilation/clear vision disc
11 Flap manual control pump
12 Flap indicator
13 Turn-and-bank indicator
14 Pitot indicator
15 Airspeed indicator
16 Firing button (A-Knopf)
17 Gun-charging button (B-Knopf)
18 Altimeter
19 One-piece windshield
20 Canopy release
21 Canopy lock
22 Revi gunsight
23 Port cannon indicator
24 Starboard cannon indicator
25 Rate of climb/descent
26 Compass
27 Oil pressure gauge
28 Jet pipe temperature
29 Fuel pressure gauge
30 Fuel contents
31 Revolution counter
32 Oxygen valve
33 Oxygen contents
34 Rudder pedals
35 Rudder pedal adjustment screws
36 Nosewheel well window (visual check)
37 FuG 24 transmit button (front of column)
38 Control column
39 Cannon blast tubes
40 Cannon forward mounts
41 Foot stirrups
42 Seat handles
43 Seat ejection trigger
44 Ejection seat
45 Canvas recoil-spring cuffs
46 Oxygen supply
47 Flare pistol holder/chute
48 FuG 25a control box
49 Starboard undercarriage indicator
50 FuG 24 (R/T) and AFN 2 (radio-navigation) control box
51 Starter switch
52 Engine setting
53 R/T socket
54 Electrics switch panel, reading from front: battery, fuel pump, weapons and gunsight, pitot heating, ignition, turn-and-bank/ rocket take-off, FuG 24, FuG 25a, starter

I began to get the impression that some of our group were no longer wholeheartedly committed to the task facing us. I also felt that a sense of hopelessness was spreading among our superior officers. But what were we to do? We could only continue the fight if we were given the right weapons. Without them, we simply had to resign ourselves to our fate in the full knowledge that this could well mean losing our lives in the closing days of he war.

On 5 March our introductory course at the Heinkel works in Rostock came to an end. Leutnant Büttner handed out travel warrants for our return to Parchim. He himself would be staying a few days longer at the Heinkel factory, while we sat around killing time at Parchim waiting for our new machines to arrive. Under the circumstances, it is perhaps not surprising that our main topic of conversation was the He 162. What would this unknown quantity be like to fly, would we be able to handle the totally new experience of jet propulsion, could we tolerate the high speeds?

Here again I got the distinct feeling that a number of my comrades, some formation leaders included, were far from enamoured with the He 162 and showed no great interest in getting to know it any better. By this time our Geschwaderkommodore, the Swords-wearing Oberst Herbert Ihlefeld, was back at Parchim and I was finally able to report my presence to him. It was at dinner in the mess a few evenings later that Ihlefeld informed us we were to receive a visit from Oberst Walter Dahl. Since his success as leader of the Rammjäger – pilots who had vowed to bring down enemy bombers by ramming them if all else failed – Dahl was known to one and all simply as 'Rammdahl'. His official title was Inspekteur der Tagjäger, or Inspector of Day Fighters, a post to which he had been appointed in late January 1945.

Proudly sporting his recently acquired Oak Leaves, Dahl duly arrived in Parchim on 17 March. He gave us a rousing, not to say inflammatory speech, in which he portrayed us as the 'chosen ones', personally selected by the Führer himself who, because of his firm belief in our abilities, was entrusting to us one of the most advanced weapons in his entire arsenal.

'If you deploy the He 162's technological advantages to the full, you will break the stranglehold of Allied air superiority and so play a vital part in achieving final victory,' he intoned with almost religious fervour.

To underline his point about the importance of modern technology in helping us win the war, he had laid on a demonstration of the Luftwaffe's new R4M air-to-air rockets. An Me 262 came screaming in to fire its battery of underwing rockets at an old Savoia-Marchetti SM.79 parked out on the field's perimeter. The violence of the explosions as the rockets struck home was very impressive. All that was left of the Italian tri-motor was a few ribs and spars and a smoking pile of metal.

Before he departed Oberst Dahl asked each of us about his previous training, his operational missions and successes. But there turned out to be very few experienced fighter pilots among our number. The majority were recent arrivals, either posted in from disbanded bomber units or trainees sent straight from flying schools to make good the Geschwader's recent heavy losses. Most of the ex-bomber types had never even sat in a fighter, let alone flown one. And the youngsters, although firebrands and thirsting for action, only had some 10 hours flying time under their belts, which meant they could just about take off and land without coming a cropper, but were capable of little more.

And then, of course, there were the wounded among us; scarcely recovered from their injuries but already being thrown back into the battle. Quite a collection, I thought to myself, I wouldn't give odds on any one of them surviving his first combat mission, yet here they are being used as cannon-fodder without a thought being given to the losses they would inevitably suffer.

Precious little happened over the next few days – if one discounts the constant power failures that robbed us of heat and light. Boredom set in. We still hadn't received one single He 162 and nobody was able to tell us when we would actually start to convert on to the new machine. We were itching to use the many Fw 190s standing idle around the field to go up and join in the air battles that often raged above our heads, but we were forbidden from doing so – the reason given being that we couldn't afford to suffer losses while awaiting the arrival of our promised jet fighters.

During this period our time was mainly occupied by playing cards or chess. Some of us read books or thumbed through magazines, while others ignored the official ban and listened to foreign radio broadcasts. It was from these that we first learned of the Morgenthau Plan, which envisaged the reduction of a defeated Germany to the status of a non-industrial, purely agricultural nation. We were appalled at this news. By broadcasting their intentions, which held out no future for us, the Allies were playing straight into the hands of

To the best of my knowledge Oberleutnant Demuth never flew the He 162.

Hitler and his warmongers, giving backing to the latter's calls to fight to the last bullet, even if it meant total self-destruction.

Now and again the monotony would be broken by the sudden appearance of Mustangs over the airfield. But the attackers were always driven off by Parchim's Flak defences before they could inflict too much damage. Once we heard the banshee howl of four Me 262s overhead and watched as they brought down five B-17s in very short order. On 19 March two Me 262s being delivered to Parchim crashed while coming in to land, killing both ferry pilots.

The following day Leutnant Büttner arrived back from Rostock. He told me in confidence that a number of woodworking companies had recently been 'conscripted' into producing components for the He 162. Among the companies he mentioned was the Benze chair-making factory, the firm owned by my future father-in-law. 'So we'll soon be flying in beech-wood from my family's forest,' I remarked, explaining the connection to him.

On 22 March all officers were ordered to attend a meeting with the Gruppenkommandeur in the officers' mess. Leutnant Werth of the Geschwaderstab had just returned from a visit to the personnel department in Berlin and had brought notification of several promotions back with him. When we entered the mess at 17.00 hours in full uniform there was quite a party atmosphere about the place. As glasses were being handed round I noticed hopeful looks on one or two faces.

Two of the likeliest candidates for promotion were the Geschwaderkommodore and the Kommandeur of our I. Gruppe, Oberleutnant Demuth. Somewhat to our surprise, however, neither one of them was on the list. The first name to be announced was that of Oberleutnant Bleser, who was made up to Hauptmann. This was followed by Leutnant Künneke, who was first upped to Oberleutnant, and then immediately afterwards likewise promoted to the rank of Hauptmann. Then came Oberfähnrich Stiemer, who was commissioned Leutnant.

After each announcement glasses were refilled and a toast drunk to the newly promoted officer, although Oberleutnant Demuth seemed to be not so much enjoying the schnapps as drowning his sorrows. When the formalities were over we all trooped into the mess lounge, where the festivities grew decidedly more boisterous. Oberleutnant Demuth soon found his taste for schnapps again; either that, or he was still trying to forget his disappointment in drink.

Whatever the reason, he was certainly knocking it back. And when, after several more glasses, he suddenly declared that he wanted to drink 'Brüderschaft' with me, it put me in rather an awkward spot. In Germany, the ritual of intertwining elbows and drinking 'brotherhood' was a declaration of close friendship. The two participants would thenceforth use the familiar 'Du' form of address to each other rather than the more formal 'Sie'. To be invited to drink 'Brüderschaft' was therefore something of an honour. Conversely, to turn down that invitation was at best a snub, and at worst an insult – hence my present predicament.

'To my utmost regret, Herr Oberleutnant, I'm afraid I must decline. We may hold the same rank, but as Gruppenkommandeur you are my senior officer. My use of 'Du', I feel, might undermine your authority, and that I wish to avoid at all costs.'

Despite my attempt to explain the reason for my refusal as politely as possible, Demuth immediately flew into a rage: 'What impertinence! How dare you deny your Gruppenkommandeur the use of 'Du', it's unheard of!' But he calmed down again very soon afterwards and wandered off mumbling something that I didn't quite catch. When the time came to bid each other goodnight he had, it seemed, given the matter some more thought. He appeared to accept my explanation – who knows, perhaps he even preferred it to having yet another 'yes-man' added to his retinue.

15 Kommando 'Bernburg'

On 23 March Oberleutnant Demuth informed me that I was to go with nine other pilots to the Junkers subsidiary factory at Bernburg an der Saale the next day to collect ten brand new He 162s off the production line there and ferry them back to Parchim. I was placed in command of the group and we should start packing straightaway he said, before adding that each pilot would be allowed to take only one item of hand baggage with him.

I passed these instructions on to Leutnant Büttner, Leutnant Finner and seven other pilots, explaining that, due to lack of space, they could only take one briefcase, or something similar with them, as nothing bigger would fit behind the ejection seat of the He 162.

Hauptmann Bleser of HQ company organized a small open-bodied truck and two trailers for us and advised us to travel during the night in order to avoid being strafed on the road by enemy fighters. Bernburg is situated between Magdeburg and Leipzig some 230 kilometres to the south of Parchim. On our way there we passed Wittenberge at around midnight. The town had just suffered a heavy bombing raid and its famous Singer sewing machine factory was burning so fiercely that you could have read a newspaper by its light.

When we arrived at the Junkers works at Bernburg at about three in the morning everybody seemed to be fast asleep. After we had been hammering on the gates for some time a civilian employee eventually appeared. He apologized for taking so long and explained that he was blind, having lost his sight in the First World War. Even though he moved with the slow deliberation of a sleepwalker, we found this hard to believe at first. But when asked if he might run his fingers over my face and, having done so, declared: 'You are a kind person, Herr Oberleutnant,' we were really taken aback.

The caretaker had been informed of our coming and showed us to Block 7 where we were all accommodated together in one large room. It contained a number of two-tier bunk beds and was rather spartanly furnished, but after our long night's journey we were dog tired and not particularly choosy. Very soon we too were fast asleep.

Early next morning we took ourselves on a tour of the works to try to get some idea of how production was going. But the doors to the assembly shops were all closely guarded and, as we had no special passes, we were not allowed in. Later, over breakfast, we got into conversation with an engineer who broke the news that no machines were ready for us yet and that we would have some while to wait. He appeared to be quite well informed about the state of production and the delays caused by the erratic deliveries of the jet engines. One interesting thing he told us was that in the time the factory took to produce one Junkers Ju 88 it could turn out 100 He 162s – if the materials, particularly the jet engines, were available. When I asked him how long that was, he replied: 'Ten days.'

Interesting perhaps, but of little relevant help to us at the moment. It looked as if we were in for yet another wait; would it never end?

At midday a Hawker Tempest suddenly roared by just 20 metres above our heads aiming for the works' flying control building. The Flak defences opened up with everything they had and for one moment we thought they were scoring hits on the wings of the attacking fighter. But it was the muzzle flashes of the Tempest's four wing cannon, whose shells were already slamming into the flying control office. The Flak gunners had obviously been poorly trained. Their fire had, in fact, been wide of the target throughout the brief attack and when it was all over we heard that one man had been killed.

On 26 March Dipl-Ing. Pankratz from the the Luftwaffe's main test centre at Rechlin came to issue me with blanket orders for the coming ferry flight. This seemed a trifle odd to me, and when I read through the documents that Pankratz had handed over to me I was even more at a loss to understand what was going on. Now, instead of taking ten machines back to Parchim, we were being instructed to ferry *fifteen* machines all the way down to Lechfeld, not far from Munich, with an intermediate stop at Unterschlauersbach near Nuremberg on the way!

Dumbfounded, I asked Pankratz how on earth we were supposed to fly 15 machines to Bavaria with just ten pilots. He could do no more than shrug helplessly, but he did say that we would be getting two of the works' own test pilots, Oberfeldwebel Strauss and Feldwebel Seeling. He also gave me a code number that would enable me to make priority phone calls in the case of dire emergencies.

I immediately gave this a try and asked to be put through to the OKL – the Oberkommando der Luftwaffe, or Luftwaffe High Command – in Berlin, hoping that they could shed some light on this now totally different situation. Amazingly, I was connected within seconds and a voice on the other end of the line announced itself to be an Oberst Eschenauer.

When I expressed my misgivings about our new orders, explaining that not one of us had yet flown the He 162, that we didn't know the airfield at Unterschlauersbach and that, even if we did manage by some miracle to land safely at Lechfeld, there was still the problem of how we were to get back to our unit at Parchim, I was totally unprepared for the violent reaction my words provoked. Eschenauer started ranting and raving down the phone at the top of his voice. The tongue lashing I was getting seemed never ending, but he did eventually run out of steam and concluded by yelling that if I didn't follow the flight orders to the letter, immediate action would be taken and I would find myself facing a drumhead court-martial.

After recovering somewhat from this almighty rocket, I sat down with my little group to discuss what we should do. The unanimous consensus was that we needn't lose any sleep over things at present. After all, the people here at Bernburg hadn't handed over one single He 162 to us as yet. I then asked Feldwebel Seeling, one of the pilots whose job it was to test fly the aircraft coming off the production lines – a procedure more commonly referred to as 'flying-in' the machines – whether he could perhaps tell us anything new about the He 162. But Seeling didn't know any more than we had already picked up during our short course at Heinkel's Rostock-Marienehe works.

On 27 March we were taken across to an He 162 standing out on the perimeter of the field, where we were introduced to Flugkapitän Hermann Steckhan, one of the civilian pilots engaged in 'flying-in' the newly-built Heinkels. Steckhan was an experienced test pilot. Since 15 February he had successfully flown the He 162 on no fewer than seven occasions. Today he was taking up the machine with the Werknummer (serial number) 310 001, and had agreed to let us listen in via the works' loudspeaker system to his in-flight R/T exchanges with ground control.

When Steckhan pressed the button of the Riedel two-stroke starter motor, the turbine caught immediately with a high-pitched whine. This gradually rose in pitch to a shrill whistle and then a long tongue of flame shot from the exhaust outlet. Steckhan taxied to the runway threshold. The hellish din of the jet engine reached a crescendo as he accelerated and lifted off.

But at height of just 150 metres the turbine abruptly cut out. We heard Steckhan calmly report that he was doing 240 km/h and was having problems with the automatic thrust nozzle control settings. After completing a half circuit he came in at 50 metres for a deadstick landing. This was much too high, and he had too much speed. We watched as the tiny machine smashed down hard onto the runway. The turbine was ripped off upon impact and went sailing off to the right. Then the two wooden wings snapped off, the cockpit was squashed flat and the fuselage broke into several pieces.

Prior to his accident on 27 March 1945, Flugkapitän Hermann Steckhan (left) had successfully completed 15 flights on the He 162, including two by night. *This and the following six photos courtesy of Archiv AK Junkerswerke und Fliegerhorst Bernburg*

Above: He 162 Werknummer 310 001 is towed to the take-off position.

Hermann Steckhan makes his preparations for take-off.

Points of interest in this picture include the dihedral on the horizontal tail surfaces, the inwardly-canted twin fin and rudder, and the negative sit of the mainwheels.

Above: Steckhan is in the cockpit and issuing his final instructions.

Left: The BMW jet engine starts up – a very rare photo.

It was little short of a miracle that Steckhan was able to extricate himself from the 95 percent destroyed machine. He managed to stagger a few paces, but then collapsed in a heap. We immediately rushed to the site of the crash and found him lying unconscious and horrifically injured beside the wreckage of the Heinkel. He had been flung violently forward by the crash and his face had hit the control column. His teeth had been pushed through his upper lip, one incisor had been broken off and the other front teeth all pushed inwards. The right side of his upper jaw had been dislocated, his spine badly compressed, and his right leg was a bloody mess.

By the time Steckhan had been taken away by the medics for emergency treatment, my pilots' initial shock at witnessing such a scene had turned to stunned consternation. Unteroffizier Dobrat was the first to find his voice: 'If the test pilots can't even fly this crate, you're not getting me into it. It's plain suicide, and no one can ask that of me,' he muttered rebelliously.

Hermann Steckhan's last take-off in an He 162.

Not wanting a mutiny on my hands, I tried to calm things down a bit by saying that technical faults could never be ruled out on a new aircraft, and especially not one as revolutionary as the Heinkel. But it was a very sombre and thoughtful group that slowly made its way back to quarters. What they had just seen had clearly reinforced the doubts of those already 'anti' the He 162, and what enthusiasm there *had* been among its supporters had totally disappeared.

Weather conditions were so bad on 28 March that flying was out of the question. Perhaps this short break would help my pilots get over the events of the previous day. I went across to flying control to find Gruppenkommandeur Demuth. He was still unaware that we had been ordered to fly to Lechfeld rather than back to Parchim and was clearly irritated when I reported the fact to him.

On Maundy Thursday, 29 March, the weather was greatly improved and the field was soon bustling with activity. Two He 162s were towed out of the production sheds. One was to be 'flown-in' by works pilot Osterwald, the other was being prepared for Oberfeldwebel Strauss, now part of our little band, who was scheduled to go up on a training flight.

We stood watching as the pair took off, spent ten minutes in the air and then landed again; all smoothly and without any fuss. Strauss had been one of the staunchest supporters of the He 162 and this flight seemed to restore his earlier confidence in the machine, which must have taken quite a knock after Steckhan's awful accident. I hoped he might perhaps also be able to lift the spirits of the doubters among us.

It was 30 March by now and there was still no sign of the 15 machines we were supposed to ferry down to Lechfeld. We were told that they were not yet ready to fly, although I was, in fact, later to discover that there were at this time 20 operational He 162s tucked away in the sheds which, for some reason or other, were to be kept out of our sight.

In an attempt to raise our morale, however, it was implied that three machines *would* be ready for us to fly to Lechfeld in the very near future. Unfortunately, no exact date could be given as Easter was just around the corner and the factory didn't work over the holidays. That really was the last straw! I began to boil with rage; every day thousands were dying under the hail of Allied bombs and yet, because it was Easter, we were expected to sit around doing nothing while we waited for the weapon that might perhaps help bring an end to the terror bombing.

Still fuming, I marched off to flying control where I worked myself up into a real fury: 'I *insist* that the three machines mentioned be made ready by the day after tomorrow at the very latest. Furthermore, I *insist* on being allowed to carry out a test flight in an He 162 tomorrow – something that has consistently been denied me thus far. And if these demands are not met, meine Herren, I shall have no hesitation in telephoning the OKL in Berlin forthwith and informing Oberst Eschenauer that the Junkers staff at Bernburg consider a cosy Easter holiday with their nearest and dearest far more important than making their contribution to the final victory. And if I know the Herr Oberst, he will not take kindly to such news. I think I can state with confidence that the entire management of these works will quickly find themselves wearing field-grey and fighting the Russians.'

My outburst had the desired effect. Suddenly the tempo was upped. The general air of lassitude disappeared at a stroke and everything started functioning smoothly and efficiently.

There was no holiday for the factory on Easter Saturday, 31 March 1945. He 162, Werknummer 310 006, stood ready and fully fuelled for my first jet-powered flight. A works test pilot took me through all the controls and important operating procedures one last time. Because I wasn't even sure in my own mind how, or in fact whether, I would be able to cope with the coming flight, I had given the pilots of my group permission to go into town. I didn't want them to be infected by my nervousness, to witness me behaving like a raw beginner, or perhaps even see me crash. Most of them had jumped at the chance of a few hours in Bernburg, and those who had elected to stay behind I had put on duty manning the telephones.

I've no idea how many times I'd gone through the sequence of my first jet fighter flight in my mind. But I did know how hard I had worked to achieve this end – how much training I had undergone and how much aimless waiting around I'd had to put up with. I had performed every control and operating movement over and over again in my head. Whenever I heard reports on the inadequate state of jet engine technology, I had brushed all doubts and thoughts aside. Now there was no going back. I climbed into the machine and connected the R/T.

When, at 18.10 hours precisely, I pressed the starter switch, I heard through the closed canopy once again that peculiar high-pitched whine as the turbine blades began to revolve. I slowly increased power. The whine gave way to a piercing whistle as the revs increased. I was tramping hard on the brakes and could feel the tiny machine quivering as I held it in check. Then I pushed the throttle forward, released the brakes, and the He 162 went howling down the runway like a scalded cat! Perhaps I had erred on the side of caution by running the engine up so slowly and carefully, for I needed the whole of the runway to get her off the ground and only just cleared the road running along the field's western boundary.

At 300 km/h I retracted the undercarriage and flaps, set the jet nozzle control to 'F' (for 'Flug', or 'Flight'), poured on full throttle and pulled the stick back into my stomach – now the He 162 was in her true element. In the few seconds that I had been concentrating on the taps and switches, the machine had already reached an altitude of 2,000 metres. Even though I was still climbing, the needle of the airspeed indicator was showing 700 km/h. Over the R/T I heard a confused background babble of voices that told me there was quite a dogfight in progress not too far away. I called ground control and asked for the exact location, but received no reply. Only then did it dawn on me that I was on a training flight and my guns weren't even loaded!

I reversed course, went down low and thundered across the rooftops of Bernburg at 800 km/h. I would have given a lot to hear the comments of those pilots who had opted to go into town. They would doubtless be staring up at the machine flashing past above their heads, not having a clue who was piloting it.

I was filled with elation. I would never have believed that the He 162 could be flown so easily, and at speeds that no enemy fighter could possibly match. With this little beauty we need no longer worry about what sort of opposition we were up against: be they Mustangs, Thunderbolts, Lightnings, Mosquitoes, Spitfires, Typhoons or Tempests, all they would see of us would be our backsides as we shot past them. And if we *did* run into trouble, we could always use our superior speed to climb or dive away.

But while trying out a few turns I discovered one worrying weak point in the He 162's behaviour. It was something that I would have to warn my pilots about without fail: application of too much rudder resulted in large amounts of slip and skid. Even more dangerous, the outside wing simultaneously displayed a strong tendency to lift, which could result in the machine's flipping over onto its back and the pilot's losing control. I could only guess at the reasons for this: perhaps the downswept wingtips affected the machine's aerodynamics, increasing the pressure of the airflow passing *under* the wings, or maybe sharp turns deflected the engine's exhaust gases against the canted rudder surfaces.

Whatever the cause, I avoided any possible problems by using only the ailerons when turning, even if this did mean that I was reduced to performing so-called 'Schiebekurven', literally 'push-turns': steady and sedate flat turns with little or no bank.

Another drawback related to the BMW 003 power unit and its extremely high fuel consumption. If the He 162 was flown at low level 'with all the stops out' – as I was now doing – the fuselage fuel tank would be emptied after just 15 minutes' flying time. But we would be operating at altitudes of between 8,000 and 10,000 metres with a 'cruising speed' of some 600 to 700 km/h and, for longer range missions or ferry flights, would carry additional fuel in our wing tanks. By flying 'sensibly' and using less gas, we would thus be able to stay aloft for 35 to 45 minutes.

But my priority at the moment was to get back down again. As I headed back towards the airfield I made a conscious effort to study the terrain for prominent landmarks. In the last 15 minutes I had covered a distance of 150 kilometres. At this kind of speed I couldn't see there being much time for map reading! Although the He 162's undercarriage was neat enough, it didn't strike me as being the most robust of designs, and so I put her down very gently. As I was taxying towards one of the earth blast pens that provided protection against strafing attacks, the pilots who had been on telephone duty came running out to meet me. They crowded around the cockpit, shouting each other down in their excitement and all demanding to know how the flight had been. Not wanting to go through the whole story twice, I asked them to be patient until the rest of the group had got back from town, and then I would tell them all about it.

When we were all gathered I made a point of warning them about the He 162's highly individual behaviour when it was given rudder. I also described the problem, entirely of my own making, that I had experienced during take-off: 'You've got to run the turbine up slowly – but not too slowly. Hold the machine on the brakes for as long as you can while you're building up to full revs. Don't release the brakes until you've got enough thrust for take-off and you can feel the machine straining to move. Don't forget, either, that lift-off speed is between 180 and 200 km/h – and remember to switch the jet nozzle control from 'S' for Start to 'F' for Flug.'

They had been hanging on my every word, and now all of them – the doubters and the grousers included – were clamouring for the chance to fly the machine as soon as possible. 'Tomorrow is Easter Sunday,' I announced, 'and I've a little present for Leutnant Büttner, Oberfeldwebel Strauss and Unteroffizier Dobrat. You will fly the first three He 162s down to Lechfeld in the morning.' I arranged with them to phone me the moment they landed at Unterschlauersbach, their intermediate stop, to let me know how they had fared thus far. Then I went across to the flying control office to discuss the route the three should take, to find out about the weather and to collect the documents they would need for the flight.

Easter Sunday, 1 April, brought with it beautiful spring weather. The sun was shining and there was not a cloud in the sky. Even so, things didn't go quite as smoothly as I had hoped. The bowser was late in arriving and didn't have enough fuel to allow the three pilots to carry out an initial practice circuit of the field and then land again to top up for the ferry flight itself as I had planned. So that was one safety check that had to go by the board. Despite this, it was still getting on for midday by the time the three Heinkels finally lifted off for the first leg of their flight to Unterschlauersbach.

I tried to contact them by phone later in the afternoon, but without success; the lines had been destroyed. Then, suddenly, the works' sirens began their mournful wailing and a disembodied voice boomed over the loudspeakers: 'Air raid alert! All personnel to the shelters immediately!'

I dashed back across to flight control and asked if any He 162s were ready for take-off. They told me there was one: a demonstration machine from the Vienna-Schwechat 'Languste' production facility. I hastily grabbed two ground crewmen, organized a starter trolley, found a parachute for myself, and drove out to the pen where the Heinkel was standing.

As I was climbing aboard I asked the mechanics how much ammunition the machine was carrying. There was a moment's awkward silence. Then they explained to me that this was an He 162A-1, the variant armed with 30-mm MK 108 cannon. And as the aircraft produced here at Bernburg were all A-2s, which were equipped with 20-mm MG 151/20s, there was no ammunition available for 'my' A-1 apart from a few practice rounds.

In the meantime, a formation of B-26 'Marauder' bombers was busily plastering the railway sidings some two kilometres away, sending several tanker wagons of precious and

The He 162 assembly line in the underground facility at Vienna-Schwechat, code-named 'Languste' ('Lobster').

'White 20', Werknummer 120 095, parked in a bombproof hangar.

urgently-needed aviation fuel fireballing into the air. Having little to fear from the ground defences, their escorting fighters were flying around just 500 metres above our field waiting to pounce on the slightest sign of movement. Even if I *did* succeed in getting off the ground without being shot down – which was most unlikely – it would have been sheer madness to go up against them in an unarmed machine. Frustrated, I had no option but to clamber back out of the cockpit and join the others watching helplessly as the enemy fighters disported themselves above our heads.

The state of affairs here at Junkers' Bernburg factory was unbelievable: there were no properly trained Flak gunners, hardly any ammunition, no organized works' defences to speak of, let alone a factory-based industrial defence Staffel of fighters such as were employed to protect many other aircraft manufacturing plants. On top of this, there was the almost total lack of power plants and the dire shortage of aviation fuel that was preventing the production of the jet fighters and their delivery to front-line fighter units.

Only much later did I learn from reliable sources that, at this time, over 100 BMW jet engines had been completed and were awaiting collection from Nordhausen only some 100 kilometres away – but that no notification had been sent to Bernburg informing them of this fact. Since then I have tended to believe that the situation was not the result of chronic mismanagement or negligence, but was much more likely to have been down to sabotage.

I was back in the flying control office very early on on the morning of 2 April, still trying to find out what had become of my three ferry pilots. After numerous attempts I finally managed to get through to Lechfeld. I was informed that the three had been unable to land at Unterschlauersbach as the field had already been captured by the Americans. Against all the odds, Oberfeldwebel Strauss had made it all the way down to Lechfeld, but his machine, Werknummer 310 002, crashed on landing and was destroyed by fire. He himself had suffered serious injuries, including a fractured skull and severe burns. Lechfeld didn't know what had happened to my two other pilots.

I was thoroughly depressed. Somehow I felt personally responsible for the two missing men. But by this late stage of the war everything was chaos and confusion. Nobody had the time or the inclination to worry about the fate of others. The only concern seemed to be the saving of one's own skin.

Which is why I felt like hugging Unteroffizier Dobrat when he suddenly turned up in front of me on the morning of 3 April with his parachute under his arm. Filthy and exhausted, he described what had happened to him: 'After take-off we got into loose formation and set course for Unterschlauersbach. On the way I somehow lost sight of Leutnant Büttner and Oberfeldwebel Strauss. Despite our arranging to stick together, they must have gone off on their own. Anyway, when I tried to land at Unterschlauersbach I saw that there were American tanks on the field. They started shooting at me, and so I headed eastwards looking for an alternative place to put down, but couldn't find anywhere. I finally ran out of fuel and had to belly land in open country somewhere to the east of Nuremberg. I tried to phone you from the nearest village, but couldn't get a connection. So I made my own way back here to Bernburg, partly by train and partly by hitching lifts.'

Sadly, I never did discover what became of Leutnant Büttner.

At midday on that 3 April Major Geyer from the Rechlin test centre arrived in Bernburg. Although he himself wasn't a pilot, I hoped to gain his support in trying to get the people at the OKL to change their minds and let the remaining Heinkels be ferried to our Gruppe at Parchim rather than down to Lechfeld. I explained the difficulties we had been having over the last few days and said that we could no longer use Unterschlauersbach as a refuelling stop. All he could suggest, howver, was that I get in touch with Berlin again to tell them that the situation had changed and that the ferry mission was no longer possible.

I duly contacted the OKL and – as I feared – was put straight through to my old 'friend' Oberst Eschenauer. To my surprise, he didn't immediately start bawling me out this time, but he did insist that the order to ferry the He 162s to Lechfeld be carried out come what may. When I asked where we were supposed to land to refuel en route now that Unterschlauersbach was in enemy hands, he had a ready answer: 'You'll have to fly to Eger in the Sudetenland. It's a bit further to the east, admittedly, but still roughly halfway to Lechfeld. I'll make sure that there will be fuel there waiting for you. Now perhaps you'll finally follow the orders you've been given. Ende.

Bloody armchair warrior, I muttered to myself, you sit there on your fat behind in the OKL and it doesn't matter a damn to you that my Geschwader up in Parchim desperately needs these He 162s. All you and your kind care about is: orders are orders. And anyone not obeying an order ends up facing a court-martial.

On 6 April the next four machines were ready to be ferried down to Lechfeld. The pilots I picked for the job were Leutnant Finner, Feldwebel Häusl, Feldwebel Seeling and Unteroffizier Dobrat. I had advised Dobrat to take it easy for a while after his recent nasty experience, but he insisted on being included in this second group. He was one of those who was totally captivated by the He 162 and, as he had had at least *some* experience flying it, I acceded to his request. The four completed their preparations, worked out a flight plan and took off between 11.00 and 12.00 hours for Eger.

I hurried back to the flight control office, hoping to be able to keep tabs on their progress. I also wanted to have a word with the met officer. I knew that our 'weather frog' surreptitiously listened in to Allied radio broadcasts. This was strictly forbidden, of course, but he justified his actions by saying it helped him in compiling his own forecasts. I asked him to tune in to BBC London, only to hear to my horror: 'this morning Allied bombers attacked industrial targets and the airfield at Eger causing extensive damage.'

It was enough to drive anyone mad. Today of all days, just as my four pilots were on their way there – and without the slightest inkling of what was awaiting them. I badgered ground control to call up the four machines and order them to return to Bernburg immediately. But despite repeated attempts to contact them, they failed to answer. Nor could Eger be reached by telephone; it was as if everything was jinxed. It was bad enough that Oberfeldwebel Strauss was lying badly injured in hospital and that Leutnant Büttner had disappeared without trace, I didn't even want to think about what kind of danger my other four pilots might be flying into at this very moment.

Under the circumstances, it was perhaps just as well that I had something else to take my mind off things. I was scheduled to take He 162, Werknummer 310 078, up on a test flight that afternoon. Remembering my first take-off six days earlier, I decided to try for myself the tip about the brakes that I had passed on to my pilots.

So this time, as the engine slowly built up revs, I kept my feet firmly on the brakes until I could barely hold her. When I finally let her go, the He 162 went shooting down the runway with her engine screaming like a soul in torment. I was able to retract undercarriage and flaps long before reaching the airfield boundary. Then I pointed the machine's nose upwards in a steep climb and gave her full power. When I next checked the altimeter I was already at a height of 4,000 metres.

Once again I was absolutely enthralled by the ease with which the He 162 clawed her way into the sky, and once again I was overwhelmed by the intoxicating feeling of speed – the sensation was simply indescribable. But today, before returning to earth and my sombre reflections on the possible fate of my four comrades, I wanted to take this machine to the limit of its capabilities and determine its true maximum speed.

Although we had been forbidden to fly any faster than 600 km/h, I pushed the throttle fully forward, put her nose down at an angle of ten degrees, and went into a high-speed dive. I was watching the airspeed indicator intently. It crept up to 800 km/h – and then the needle suddenly dropped back to zero. At the same time it felt as if the machine had received a hammer blow, and the hissing of the engine fell silent.

Shocked out of my wits, I immediately pulled back the throttle and carefully lifted her nose. Just as suddenly as it had unwound, the airspeed indicator began registering properly again. And I could also hear the engine's steady whistle. So it couldn't have flamed out after all. Several engineers had assured me that once the BMW 003 jet power plant had come to a stop, it was impossible to re-start it again in the air. I could only assume that the aircraft had edged a little too close to the critical Mach number. The sound barrier was something that had only been talked about. No pilot had yet experienced its effects.

Not knowing if the Heinkel had suffered any damage from the apparent blow, I flew straight back to Bernburg. After an uneventful landing I walked around the machine but, despite a thorough inspection, I could find nothing outwardly amiss with it. I didn't mention my little escapade to the works' engineers, but I did describe what had happened to my remaining comrades. I say 'remaining' advisedly, for flying control still had no news of the four missing pilots and by now I feared the worst.

On 7 April we were told that two more He 162s were ready and waiting for us, but I had no intention of letting these machines be ferried down to Lechfeld. The OKL's Oberst Eschenauer could court-martial me if he liked, but I was determined that my last two pilots weren't going to pay the price of following this half-wit's idiotic orders.

The two in question were Oberfähnrich Köttgen and Fähnrich Mann, neither of whom had yet flown the He 162. To give them a chance to get to know the aircraft, I ordered them to do a few circuits and practise flying together as a loose pair. But just as Oberfähnrich Köttgen was taking off, the air raid sirens sounded. Some way to the south of the field a fierce dogfight had already broken out between a number of German and English fighters. I aborted Fähnrich Mann's take-off and tried to reach Köttgen over the R/T to order him to return to base immediately. But he hadn't switched his radio on.

As he later explained to me, he was, in fact, busy searching the sky for Fähnrich Mann. He spotted an aircraft in the distance and headed towards it. When he got closer, he saw the machine was wearing British roundels and realized it was a Tempest. Köttgen immediately climbed away at full power. The Tempest had already been joined by several of its fellows, but the enemy pilots – clearly awed by the Heinkel's turn of speed – promptly scattered like startled rabbits and made off at low level. It would no doubt have been a very different story had they known that Köttgen was carrying out an unarmed practice flight. As it was, he was able to land unmolested.

Köttgen and Mann may have been safe, but I still didn't know what had become of my four other pilots. I still couldn't get through to Eger, and Lechfeld had no news of them.

It must have been around midnight when I was woken by the sound of sirens: another air raid warning! Outside it was as bright as day. Parachute flares marked all four corners of the factory grounds. I hurriedly got into my uniform, ran down the stairs and dashed across the courtyard to the nearest air raid shelter. Before ducking into it, I glanced up into the sky again.

Directly overhead a glowing red flare was slowly descending at the end of a parachute. This must be a warning signal, I thought, dropped by a pathfinder aircraft as a signal to the approaching bombers not to attack the works. And, sure enough, it was not long before bombs were raining down on the nearby town of Bernburg instead. It was clear to me that the only reason the factory was being spared was because the Allies wanted to capture the jet fighters intact.

Several members of the works' management team were sitting in a corner of the shelter quietly discussing among themselves who their next employers were likely to be. When hostilities ceased would they be 'snapped up' by the Americans or the Russians? Anxious to know what the current situation on the ground was, and which enemy forces were the closest, they asked me whether I would be willing to undertake a couple of reconnaissance flights in the He 162 to find out. 'You provide me with a machine that's been thoroughly flown-in and well serviced, and I'll be glad to,' I replied.

At 18.55 hours on 9 April I took off in He 162, Werknummer 210 011, for a recce of the region to the southwest of Bernburg. The area I was to cover was roughly triangular in shape and bordered by the towns of Nordhausen, Mühlhausen and Bad Langensalza. I had been asked to look out for signs of American activity, and it wasn't long before I found them.

In fact, Langensalza airfield was packed with B-26 Marauder bombers and all kinds of fighters. As I whistled across the field at a height of 300 metres the enemy was spraying Flak up at me from all directions. But the lines of tracer were all criss-crossing the air behind me. It was if I was dragging a fiery necklace in my wake. I was doing a good 700 km/h, and if the gunners wanted to hit me they'd have to rethink their angles of correction and allow for much more 'lead'. Just to be on the safe side though, once out of their sight I went down even lower. This would offer me greater protection if I encountered any more enemy troops. At this speed, I'd be past them and gone before they even heard me coming! I bet the 'Amis' had never experienced anything like it, and I had to smile at the thought of the expressions of disbelief they must have had on their faces.

On the other side of the coin, *we* had no experience of identifying, let alone attacking ground targets at such speeds. At the rate I was travelling, I was covering 750 metres every three seconds and in that short a time it was simply not possible to distinguish a target with absolute certainty and engage it effectively.

The rest of the flight passed without incident. I landed back at Bernburg at 19.30 hours and reported what I had seen to the works management. The next day – at 18.30 hours on 10 April, to be precise – I took off again in the same machine. I headed in the same south-westerly direction as before, but this time did not venture quite so far, concentrating instead on the areas around the towns of Aschersleben, Sangerhausen and Frankenhausen. Throughout the 30-minute flight I was continually coming under fire from our own Flak. But this was hardly surprising; how were the Flak gunners supposed to recognize an aircraft that was unfamiliar even to most Luftwaffe pilots?

Late that same evening I was called to the phone. On the other end of the line was Fritz Sauckel, the Gauleiter, or regional political head, of Thuringia who, in his other role as Hitler's 'General Plenipotentiary for Labour', had earned himself a bloody reputation while presiding over the Reich's slave-labour programme. His speech had the same slightly slurred inflection usually associated with heavy drinkers: 'I've just heard that you're the person who's good at flying jet fighters. I hereby appoint you my private pilot. Pick me up at Erfurt in your jet machine first thing in the morning – the Americans are knocking on the gates. I'll tell you where we're going after that when you get here.'

'I'm sorry, but I'm engaged on another mission by special order of the Führer,' I tried to explain. 'Let me worry about that,' he replied, 'I'll speak to the Führer personally. He grants my every wish. By the way, how many people can this new machine of yours carry?' When I said: 'Just me – it's a single-seat fighter,' there was a moment's silence. And then a 'click' told me that he had hung up. Well, well, I thought to myself, so the criminal wants to do a bunk and is looking for the quickest way to go about it!

On 11 April the Bernburg works were a scene of frenzied activity. The place was like a disturbed ants' nest: machines were being pushed out of the sheds and fuelled up, people were running about with boxes and cartons stuffed with blueprints and documents, smoke was curling into the air all over the field as factory records were burned in empty oil drums, some workers were in the food stores stocking up on reserves for the days and weeks ahead, and suddenly I found myself bumping into works test pilots I had never set eyes on before.

The factory was being evacuated. The Americans were closing in on Bernburg!

Three days earlier, on 8 April, our Gruppe's base at Parchim had suffered a heavy American bombing raid. Despite emergency repairs the runway there was still unusable. And so this evening we were to ferry six He 162s to Ludwigslust, an alternative field some 30 kilometres to the southwest of Parchim.

I took off at 17.55 hours in He 162, Werknummer 310 023. As I circled above the field I witnessed an impressive, not to say unique sight. The machines of Oberfähnrich Köttgen and Stenschke, Fähnrich, Mann and Unteroffizier Hartung and Riemer were all lined up one behind the other waiting to take off. As each aircraft accelerated down the runway I watched the shimmering exhaust gases turn into long bright lances of flame. The thunderous noise of their departure was a fitting adieu to Bernburg, for none of these machines would ever return to their place of manufacture.

I continued circling at a height of 300 metres until the last of them had lifted off, waiting to lead the little group north-northwest in close formation as had been agreed at briefing. But they weren't yet confident enough to tuck in really close and each pilot was careful to keep a safe 50 to 100 metres between himself and the machine nearest to him. It would clearly take a few more practice flights before they mastered their new mounts and started to have faith in their own abilities.

As we skirted west of Magdeburg at 2,000 metres I noticed Fähnrich Mann's machine slowly beginning to lose height. A thin stream of white smoke was coming from his engine. This could mean that there had been water in his fuel tank which had now entered the combustion chamber, bringing the turbine to a stop and leaving Mann with no chance of restarting it. I immediately followed him down, urging him to try the ignition switch anyway. The engine wasn't smoking any more, but Fähnrich Mann didn't answer and the machine's rate of descent was increasing. At 1,000 metres we were fired on by Flak and I reluctantly broke away.

By this time the rest of the formation had disappeared and I set out to chase after them. At 18.35 hours, after a flight of 40 minutes, I was the last of our now depleted group to put down on Ludwigslust airfield. Oddly, despite all our recent trials and tribulations, the thing that most sticks in my mind from my arrival in Ludwigslust was the sight of the Gruppe's pilots strolling about in the mess in their smart new leather flying suits. I remember feeling distinctly shabby in my ordinary cloth overalls.

It wasn't until much later that I discovered what had happened to Fähnrich Mann. Apparently, he had managed to make it as far as the airfield at Salzwedel, but had brushed the tops of some trees as he came in to land. The He 162 hit the ground like a stone, instantly caught fire and was completely burnt out. Mercifully, it was thought that Mann had been killed on impact.

On 12 April Gruppenkommandeur Demuth appointed me leader of 2. Staffel. In actual fact, the few machines we had received from the Heinkel works so far were only enough to equip a single Staffel anyway. But it was not only aircraft that we were lacking. Here at Ludwigslust I again had the feeling that many of our senior officers still nurtured a deep dislike of the He 162.

At midday Oberleutnant Demuth's driver came to take me out to the airfield. Demuth was standing beside an He 162 trying to explain the controls to a young Fähnrich sitting in the cockpit. When I asked the driver what was going on – I was pretty sure that Demuth had never flown the He 162 himself – he simply pulled a face and said: 'That's why I had to come and fetch you. The young sprig is from a very good family. His father is one of the top medical officers in the Luftwaffe. The boy was taught to fly by Hanna Reitsch. Now he wants to go onto jets, and Oberleutnant Demuth is supposed to show him how.'

Aha, so that's the way the land lies. Demuth doesn't want to make a fool of himself, so I've been roped in to take over. As I went through the various controls with him, I soon realized that the youngster was trying to conceal his nervousness by affecting a blasé attitude towards the whole tedious business. Anyone else I would have yanked out of the cockpit without a second's thought. But here I gave him the benefit of the doubt, suspecting that hormones might be playing a part in adding to his superior air of bravado. So I carefully explained all the operating procedures: the importance of running the engine up slowly, the trick with the brakes, when to retract and when to lower the undercarriage and flaps – in short, everything he needed to know to be able to take off and land.

But I got the impression that he still wasn't listening properly, and so I went over everything again and then asked him if he had really understood all the points I had made. He assured me he had, at the same time making it abundantly clear that he was bored with the whole business and impatient to get going at long last. So the engine was fired up and he began to roll. But he wasn't picking up speed quickly enough. Demuth and I could both see what was coming. We jumped into the Kübelwagen and raced off down the runway after the He 162.

The machine was already more than halfway along it, but still accelerating far too slowly to permit lift-off. At the far end of the runway there was a low embankment, behind which were a number of slit trenches and a concrete taxiway leading to the dispersal area. He's going to crash, I thought – and almost at that very instant, he did. The He 162 slammed into the earth embankment, somersaulted, and went skidding along the taxiway on its engine nacelle. The right wing broke off and the whole load of J 2 fuel poured over the Fähnrich hanging upside-down in the cockpit.

Fortunately, there was no fire. The Fähnrich was able to extricate himself from the cockpit. Sodden and stinking to high heaven of aviation fuel, he stood in front of us wordlessly holding up his broken index finger! Because of the appalling stench we didn't want him in the car with us, so Demuth ordered him, soaked in fuel as he was, to make his way back along the runway on foot.

In the meantime, several other pilots had arrived on the scene. The sorry sight of the He 162, resting upside-down on its engine and left wingtip, led to more heated arguments about the machine's unpredictability. To settle the matter once and for all, I obtained Demuth's permission to take an He 162 up on a demonstration flight.

Ground crew prepare 'White 21', Werknummer 310 021, for take-off.

Ludwigslust, 13 April 1945: Feldwebel Friedrich Enderle is about to take off in 'White 5', Werknummer 120 013. He crashed on the airfield boundary and was killed.

At 15.25 hours I lifted off in He 162, Werknummer 120 078, to show the doubters just what the machine was capable of. I first gained height and flew off for some distance until I was out of sight of those watching. Then I turned back, dived at full throttle and screamed at maximum speed low across the field. Hold onto your hats, gentlemen, I grinned to myself. They had seen me approaching and watched me fly past without a sound, but they weren't hit by the full thunderous roar of the turbine until I was already shooting steeply back up into the heavens again. As I climbed I performed four upward rolls – two to the left and two to the right.

At 3,000 metres I tipped over into another dive and hurtled back across the field at low level again, pulling such sharp high-speed turns that condensation trails streamed from the machine's downswept wingtips. After a final 180 degree turn I executed a slow half roll to come back over the heads of the spectators in the inverted position. At the end of the run another half roll brought me back onto an even keel.

After 20 minutes of throwing the machine about all over the sky I came in to land. While I was taxying towards dispersal I could see the ground crews excitedly throwing their caps into the air in a sign of appreciation at my performance. As display flights, and particularly aerobatics, with the He 162 were officially prohibited, this one went into my logbook as a 'flying-in'.

My demonstration must have impressed the individual in charge of the clothing stores as well, for it was not long after this that he issued me with an almost brand new flying suit made of soft, light-brown leather. Admittedly, it was an item of 'war booty' taken from a downed American flyer, but it fitted me like a glove. For that reason I chose not to dwell on the possible consequences if I happened to be shot down myself while wearing it and was mistaken for an 'Ami' by a bunch of irate farmers.

Upper left: Gruppe badge of I./JG 1. *Upper right:* Staffel badge of 1./JG 1 (*drawing by Simon Schatz*). *Lower left:* Staffel badge of 2./JG 1. *Lower right:* Staffel badge of 3./JG 1

16 Last Stop Leck

On 14 April we were given orders to transfer from Ludwigslust up to Leck in North Friesland, a part of Schleswig-Holstein. Situated just a few kilometres to the south of the Danish border, Leck was also only 20 kilometres from the North Sea coast.

Gruppenkommandeur Demuth detailed me to lead the pilots to our new base, while he took command of the ground party. There was a simple explanation as to why he himself didn't fly at the head of the Gruppe: if he had ever been up in the He 162 at all – which I still seriously doubted – it was only to do a single circuit at the very most. And yet he claimed to have scored a victory while flying the machine. Even my armourer was puzzled by this. 'Herr Oberleutnant,' he had asked me one day, 'could a pilot have shot down an enemy aircraft if the muzzle covers of his guns were still in place?' 'What sort of stupid question is that,' I had snorted, 'Who put that ridiculous idea into your head?' 'Oberleutnant Demuth,' he had replied.

The transfer to Leck was to be made with an intermediate stop at Husum. As we had no maps of the area, and because most of the pilots had flown no more than a few circuits, we all trooped off to study the large map hanging on the wall of the flying control office. I told the group to impress on their minds the route to be taken, at the same time keeping my fingers crossed that visibility would be good – I wasn't at all sure how they would manage if we had to fly a compass course.

Lifting off at 14.00 hours on 15 April, I was the last to leave Ludwigslust. Flying He 162 'Red 22', Werknummer 120 074, I touched down at Husum just 20 minutes later. During my approach I had spotted the wreckage of an He 162 under the trees close to the airfield boundary, with the apparently lifeless body of the pilot lying next to the shattered cockpit canopy. And as I taxied towards the dispersal area another He 162 came floating in behind me. But its pilot had completely misjudged his hold off. The machine was at an impossible angle, flying much too slowly, was much too high and on the point of stalling. From a height of 10 metres it simply fell out of the air and crashed almost horizontally onto the ground.

The lowered undercarriage dug itself deep into the soft earth. The engine was wrenched off the top of the fuselage and went flying across the field all by itself like some giant smoking cigar. I brought 'Red 22' to a stop, jumped out of the cockpit and started running back towards the scene of the crash. I recognized the pilot as Unteroffizier Josef Rieder, one of the group who had flown from Bernburg to Ludwigslust with me three days earlier. He was still in the cockpit, unconscious and with blood streaming down his face. Luckily the canopy had been torn off as well, so I was able to unstrap him and, with the help of some others who had also come rushing across, lift him out of his seat.

Shortly afterwards an ambulance drove up and the medics laid Rieder on a couple of blankets before taking him off to station sick quarters. There it was discovered that he had broken his jaw. By now he had regained consciousness, and while he was being given a shot of morphine to deaden the pain he clung to me tightly: 'I don't want to stay here, Herr Oberleutnant. Please don't leave me here. I'll be flying again by tomorrow,' he beseeched in a thick voice. But when the doctors also diagnosed a suspected fracture of the spine, Rieder was taken off to hospital in Neumünster for examination.

Later, in the flying controller's office, I learnt that the body I had seen while coming in to land had been that of Unteroffizier Hartung. Like Josef Rieder, Wolfgang Hartung was another of the pilots who had ferried an He 162 from Bernburg to Ludwigslust.

The day's events had shaken me up more than I realized and I had trouble getting to sleep at the end of it. After a restless night I quickly briefed the remaining pilots on the final leg of our flight to Leck. Once again, I saw everybody else safely off before lifting 'Red 22' from the runway at 10.00 hours. Bidding farewell to Husum with a barrel roll over the centre of the field, I set off on the 12-minute 'hop' up to Leck.

Five kilometres short of my destination I spotted an He 162 standing in a tiny meadow and assumed this to be the landing ground. I was just about to lower my wheels when I realized that there was a herd of cows grazing in the field. This can't be right, I thought, it must be the Lütjenholm gliding school – but what's an He 162 doing down there?

I regained height and resumed course. And there, right in front of my nose, was the 'proper' Leck airfield. It was enormous, with several huge hangars, a large number of aircraft blast pens and a maze of taxiways; the whole being surrounded by extensive areas of woodland.

After I had landed a weird, three-wheeled contraption came puttering along the runway towards me. It hooked up my He 162 and towed it to an empty revetment. One of the ground crew told me that this vehicle – looking something like a cross between a tractor and a motorcycle – was, in fact, an aircraft tug. It was originally built by the firm of Scheuch specifically to recover Me 163 rocket-fighters that had had to put down in open country, but was being employed here at Leck to conserve aviation fuel. So critical had the situation become that, whenever possible, aircraft were towed in order to save even those small amounts of fuel they would otherwise have used by taxying under their own power. There were also a couple of Kettenkräder, half-track motorcycle combinations, serving the same purpose. These were in special demand in times of emergency, such as when the field came under air attack, for they could tow aircraft about at speeds of up to 30 km/h!

The machine I had flown to Leck, He 162 'Red 22', was soon renumbered and repainted as 'Yellow 11', although of course it retained its Werknummer 120 074. But it was in He 162 'Yellow 3', Werknummer 120 098, that I was ordered up on an emergency scramble on 18 April. As it turned out to be a false alarm, however, I took the opportunity to carry out a private test flight, which was to go into my logbook as another 'flying-in'.

In case I ever needed to use the ejection seat in earnest, I decided to test the machine's handling at or near stalling speed. I therefore took her up to a safe 4,000 metres, gradually reduced throttle bit by bit, and extended the flaps. I wanted to find out at what speed the aircraft started to feel mushy, and how she

The 'Scheuch' tug was employed to tow both the Me 163 and the He 162.

An unretouched original photo of 'Yellow 3', Werknummer 120 072, with my briefcase resting on the nose cone in front of the windscreen. The lion badge of 3. Staffel was not introduced until the last days of the war and was carried by only a few machines.

behaved immediately prior to the stall. It was while pulling a slightly tighter turn than usual at about 250 km/h that the nose came up and she showed all the signs of an incipient spin. I knew that the He 162 could not be recovered from a spin, and so gently put her nose down, retracted the flaps and carefully added a little more power.

Once I had her straight and level again and there was no possible danger of the engine's 'choking' itself, I wound her up to maximum speed. When the needle reached 850 km/h I experienced that same peculiar thump that I had felt during the high-speed flight back at Bernburg. And again the needle fell back to zero – but this time the elevators stopped working as well! I hastily pulled the throttle right back. The airspeed indicator suddenly came back to life and the machine started responding normally to my control movements.

Wanting to make sure that the aircraft hadn't been damaged in any way, I flew back to Leck and prepared to land. On the approach I noticed that my rate of descent was a little faster than usual and that my landing speed was also slightly higher. When I climbed out of the cockpit I saw that the metal fairing between

'My Yellow 3', Werknummer 120 072. *Profile copyright Simon Schatz, based on original drawing by Miroslav Billy and Michal Bradac*

the fuselage and engine nacelle was no longer there. I didn't think the damage had been caused by my nudging too close to the sound barrier. It was much more likely that the 5 mm retaining screws had been unable to withstand the high pressure and had been simply torn out, taking the metal panel with them.

Because 'Yellow 3' had to go in for repair, 19 April saw me back in 'Yellow 11'.This was the same 'Red 22' that I had flown up to Leck a few days earlier but which, after its renumbering, now formed part of my 2. Staffel. Although aerobatics on the He 162 were still officially prohibited, and even though the shortage of fuel was by this time more acute than ever, I felt that we had to get to know the machine's absolute limits if we wanted to come out of any future dogfights in one piece. Today I therefore intended to try looping the He 162. Once again, I first climbed to 4,000 metres to allow myself a good margin of safety.

After picking up speed in a dive, I pulled the machine up into a steep climb. But, however much elevator I used, the He 162 refused to go over onto its back at the top of the loop. Instead, the jet engine suddenly cut out! I quickly executed a half roll to regain normal flight attitude. Luckily, I still had ample altitude to reach base by gliding if necessary and so started working out the best line of approach. As I slowly lost height I constantly kept trying to restart the engine by flicking the ignition switch. And, wonder of wonders, at 1,700 metres – and after a few hesitant wheezes – it burst back into life. This test flight had taught me two things. One: you couldn't loop an He 162. And two: despite the BMW engineers' dire warnings, you *could* relight a dead engine in the air.

At midday we got a report that a group of low-flying enemy aircraft was approaching from the direction of Niebüll, a small town to the west of the field. The Alarmrotte – the readiness section of two machines, flown on this occasion by Leutnant Gerhard Stiemer and Feldwebel Günther Kirchner – was immediately scrambled. Kirchner's machine had barely lifted its wheels from the runway before it came under attack from a Tempest. Rather than trying to escape, he committed the cardinal error of getting involved in a dogfight at a height of only 50 metres.

The He 162 was totally unsuited for sharp turns at ground level. Its great advantages lay in the ease with which it could climb to great heights and then attack its enemy from above using the benefit of its superior speed. Several witnesses thought they saw Kirchner shoot down the Tempest. But this was not so. What actually happened was that he attempted to make a steep 180 degree turn by use of rudder. This was something the He 162 simply would not stand for. It instantly flipped over onto its back, the airflow separated, and it fluttered earthwards like an autumn leaf. Kirchner then made his second, and final mistake of the day. He immediately jettisoned his canopy and fired the cartridge of his ejection seat. But, because the machine was inverted, he was shot not up into the air, but straight down into the ground.

The Tempest pilot had opened fire on the tumbling Heinkel, presumably so that his gun-camera would provide a record of his would-be victory over this strange bird. But he never got the photographic evidence of his 'kill' back to base. The Tempest was brought down by Leck's Flak defences almost immediately afterwards.

The field was still in total uproar when a Kübelwagen screeched to a halt beside me. Sitting next to the driver was Oberleutnant Demuth: 'Get in,' he yelled at me above the tumult, 'and bring your machine-pistol with you. We're off to Niebüll to pick up a downed American.'

Upon our arrival in Niebüll we were directed out to the area where it was believed a P-47 had made an emergency landing. When we got to the spot, however, we found not a Thunderbolt, but a seemingly intact English Tempest which showed no evidence of combat damage of any kind. And as there were no signs of the pilot anywhere about either, we decided to drive back into Niebüll.

Outside the town's police station an angry crowd had gathered. The English pilot had been brought here and the mob wanted to lynch him. 'Kill the dirty swine, string him up here and now,' they were chanting. My machine-pistol cleared a path for us through the jostling mass. At the entrance to the station the local policeman was clinging to the handrail visibly trembling with fright. Behind him stood the pilot, his face chalk-white, his hands clutching the waistband of his uniform trousers – the policeman had removed his belt to stop him escaping.

I asked the terrified policeman why the crowd was in such an ugly mood. 'The Tommy shot up a train full of refugees,' he managed to explain, 'a whole load of them were killed.' I gave the Engländer his belt back, telling him in his mother tongue that we had come to collect him for questioning. I assured him that he need have no fear, nothing would happen to him while he was in our charge. My machine-pistol got us back out through the furious crowd without incident. We jumped into the Kübelwagen and sped away back to Leck.

As my English was pretty fluent I was given the job of looking after him and so invited him to my quarters for a chat. I knew that he wouldn't divulge his unit, base or any other of his service details, and so I tried to convince him that this wasn't part of the interrogation process, just a normal conversation between two flyers. But he was very mistrustful at first, and when I asked him for his home address he wouldn't even tell me that. He seemed to appreciate the fact that I had rescued him from a possibly very nasty fate at the hands of the lynch mob in Niebüll, but it wasn't until I promised to have his next-of-kin notified that he was safe and well that he began to loosen up.

We were soon chatting away quite animatedly, asking one another who or what had brought us to our present unhappy state of being mortal enemies who were quite prepared to shoot at each other on sight. We talked about the imminent end of the war, and what was likely to happen afterwards. We discussed the strengths and weaknesses of the aircraft that we flew, and what sort of hobbies we pursued in our spare time. He remained with us overnight and was collected by the field police the following mooning. They were taking him off to a prisoner-of-war camp and I never heard what became of him after that.

On 20 April I was detailed as leader of the three-aircraft readiness flight; the other two pilots being Leutnant Hans Berger and his wingman. At 11.30 hours a report came in of low level enemy air activity in the Husum area and we were given the order to scramble. We ran to our machines, but while the turbines of the other two He 162s were soon whining up to full power, the engine of my 'Yellow 3', Werknummer 120 098, simply refused to start. Rather than delay the take-off any longer, I passed command to Leutnant Berger, telling him and his wingman to get going at once. The pair lifted off at 11.35 hours, leaving me still trying to coax my engine into life.

It was another 20 minutes before the mechanics eventually succeeded in persuading the Riedel starter motor to do its job, by which time Berger and his wingman were already coming back in to land. I called Berger over the R/T and was told that they had had no contact with the enemy.

At 12.05 hours I was finally able to take off. While climbing away I switched on my guns. 'Yellow 3's' new Revi 16G gunsight failed to light up, but I assumed the fault was just a broken bulb. Having reached an altitude of 600 metres I could see below me a number of burning vehicles littering the main road leading into Husum. Some kind of enemy activity had obviously been going on down there. Seconds later, shortly before Husum airfield, I caught sight of a single Tempest. It was flying at low level and its pilot was clearly intent on attacking some ground target or other that he had spotted.

I'll soon spoil your fun and games, I thought to myself, closing in to just 100 metres behind and slightly above him. I flicked up the cover guard and pressed the firing button of my two MG 151 cannon. He hadn't noticed me yet ... nor was he about to – my guns had failed to fire! By this time I was so close that I almost rammed him. I hauled back on the stick and put the He 162 into a steep climb as I whistled past him. That woke him up! The Engländer stood his Tempest on its nose, went down even lower and shot off at high speed.

At an altitude of 1,100 metres I saw a second Tempest and curved in towards it. But this pilot wasn't going to be caught napping – perhaps he had already been warned of the presence of my 'Wunderwaffe' by his colleague. For as I approached he executed a sharp stall turn and disappeared into the depths. With my guns U/S there was little point in chasing after him. I turned back towards Leck, scarcely able to contain my anger at the two missed chances. I almost felt like crying out loud. If the stupid so-and-so of an armourer responsible for my weapons' failure had been there at that moment, I would have throttled him without a second's thought!

I had been robbed of one, perhaps even two easy and near-certain victories by the negligence of some cretin or other. I might have been hailed a hero – instead, I felt a total failure. And I knew there was bound to be someone, either at debriefing or later in the mess, who would be only too eager to cast doubts on the story of my 'bad luck'. Rather than returning to base in triumph, waggling my wings to signify two kills, I was now worried that the two Tempests might be tailing me back, ready to pounce on my defenceless machine as I brought her in to land.

That's why I kept a careful eye on the sky all around me as I neared Leck. And just to be on the safe side, I even flew straight past the field at first to make sure no-one was following me, before pulling a shallow low-level turn and coming in much too fast. With the brakes smoking and the stick pushed fully forward, I managed to bring the bird to a stop just short of the boundary. There couldn't have been much rubber left on the tyres.

I climbed out of the machine in a filthy temper and called my mechanic over. I could still remember all too well the occasions on the Arctic Front when the guns of my Me 110 had jammed just as I was in a perfect position to attack. I had put those failures down to the slackness of some armourer or possibly icing. But this latest incident was a complete puzzle. While trying to trace the fault, we discovered that one of the electric wires leading to the gun charging switch had been neatly cut through, which pointed very strongly to deliberate sabotage.

It was a great pity that on the A-2 variant of the He 162 we were not allowed to charge our two cannon until after take-off. This was as a direct result of earlier teething problems with the machine's weapons system. Several times in the past, when the guns had been charged on the ground the cannon had suddenly, and without warning, started firing of their own volition, often sending their entire salvo of shells either into another aircraft parked nearby or into one of the hangars on the far side of the field.

On 22 April we received a report of an unidentified aircraft approaching Leck at very high speed. I happened to be on readiness and was immediately sent up to intercept the 'bogey' – presumed to be a 'Mosquito' – that was coming in fast from the south. As 'Yellow 3' was still undergoing inspection in the workshops, I took off in 'Yellow 1', Werknummer 120 223, and climbed under full power to 5,000 metres.

When I reached the given altitude I could see the contrails, but the machine itself was already well past our field. I set off in pursuit, but was amazed at the time it took before I started to overhaul it. I knew that the 'Mosquito' had a maximum speed of some 600 km/h, but the machine ahead of me was doing well over 700 km/h! As I drew closer I realized from the jet nacelles slung underwing and the periscope projecting above the glazed nose that the 'bogey' I had been chasing was, in fact, an Arado Ar 234 Blitz. It was probably a long-range reconnaissance machine of 1.(F)/33 on its way up to Stavanger in Norway.

The pursuit had taken me the length of Denmark and I could already see the waters of the Skagerrak ahead. Although the He 162 used less fuel at 5,000 metres and could remain in the air for up to 40 minutes or more at this altitude, it was high time that I turned round. Before reversing course, however, I couldn't resist flying past the Ar 234 and waving cheerfully at its astonished pilot. Then it was the long haul back to base with the engine set to a much more economical 'cruising speed'.

On 23 April Feldwebel Rolf Ackermann took off in He 162, Werknummer 120 021, for a practice flight. For some unknown reason he flew dangerously and unnecessarily closely past the flying control building. Then he began to climb. It could have been that he was intending to perform an upward roll, but he made the fatal mistake of using rudder as well as aileron. The Heinkel was having none of that. It wobbled out of control, flicked onto its side and smashed one wing low into the ground, exploding in flames on impact.

Some of Ackermann's comrades were convinced that he was putting on a private show to impress his girlfriend who worked in the flying control office. And if the behaviour of the young female signals auxiliary who immediately came rushing out of the building screaming hysterically was anything to go by, they could well have been right.

I promised myself that, when the opportunity arose, I would tackle the Heinkel designers to ask when they were finally going to sort out this lethal weakness in the He 162's rudders. In the meantime, there was work to be done. 'Yellow 3' had had a complete engine change and late that afternoon I took her up for an air test.

17 The Final 'Volksjägers'

During the evening of 23 April I was summoned to Gruppenkommandeur Demuth's office. As the Russians were rapidly closing in on Rostock, he instructed me to take a group of ten pilots to Heinkel's Marienehe works as quickly as possible, pick up the last of the He 162s produced by the factory, and ferry them back here to Leck. He stressed the utmost importance of this mission and handed me a Führer order to underline the fact.

First I selected my group of ten. This consisted of Leutnants Gerhard Stiemer and Adalbert Schlarb, plus eight other pilots of varying ranks. Then I started hunting around for suitable transport for the journey to Rostock. But these days 'suitable' was used to describe anything not yet actually rusting away on the scrapheap, and all I could find was a clapped-out, wood-burning old Hanomag prime mover, a sort of four-wheeled tractor, and trailer.

Because of the danger from low-flying enemy fighters, which controlled every square metre of Germany during the hours of daylight, we did not set out until midnight. The other pilots had loaded the trailer with some bundles of straw which they burrowed into to keep out the night cold. Schlarb, Stiemer and I rode in the cab of the ancient Hanomag, which had a second bench seat behind the driver.

As we lurched and rattled along the road the driver explained that he didn't dare switch the engine off should we make a halt. There were problems with the starter, and once the engine had stopped he would have the devil's own job getting it going again. To minimize the risk of being detected by any patrolling night fighters we drove without lights. Luckily, the road showed up fairly well under the full moon, but the driver had his work cut out whenever it disappeared behind a cloud.

The very real threat of daylight air attack meant that all traffic now travelled by night. Consequently the road was solid with troop transporters, supply trucks and civilian vehicles of every kind all jam-packed with refugees. To make matters worse, the wreckage of numerous abandoned and burned-out cars lined the edges of the already narrow country roads. It was not surprising that we now and again scraped the sides of oncoming vehicles.

Suddenly I heard the pilots on the trailer behind us yelling: 'Stop! Stop at once!' I got the driver to halt and jumped down from the Hanuman. The pilots were by now all standing in the road pointing up into the sky. 'Enemy bombers!' they shouted before diving as one into the roadside ditch. I dragged our driver into the back yard of a nearby house. The enemy machines came roaring along the road at low level. We heard a bomb explode 100 metres beyond us – just where we would have been if we hadn't stopped to take cover. As it was, a bus took the full blast. But no harm was done; it was already a charred wreck from a previous attack. After ten minutes all was quiet again and we could resume our journey.

The continual jolting of the old Hanomag meant that none of us could get any proper rest, and the driving was showing signs of total exhaustion. Shortly before Lübeck it was therefore decided that we would take a short break and grab forty winks. We parked the Hanomag behind a high stone wall. But the throbbing of the engine must have attracted the attention of the field police, for within five minutes one of them was hammering on the driver's door with the butt of his machine-pistol: 'Who's in charge here?' he shouted. When the driver pointed at me, the MP barked: 'Come along with me and be quick about it!'

I followed him to a concrete bunker that had been camouflaged to look like an ordinary house. We went down a few steps and into a room where an SS Sturmbannführer – the equivalent of a Luftwaffe Major – was sitting behind a desk. 'Hand over your papers!' he snapped, swivelling the desk lamp so that its glare was directed straight into my face. I pulled my travel orders out of my greatcoat pocket and laid them on the desk together with the special Führer order that I had been given by Gruppenkommandeur Demuth. The SS man cast a perfunctory glance at my documents before launching into what was obviously a well-rehearsed tirade.

'You're all a bunch of deserters, cowards and traitors to the Fatherland!' he suddenly bawled at the top of his voice. 'Planning to clear off, I'll be bound. But we'll soon make short work of you. Scharführer, remove this man's pistol belt!'

The SS sergeant laid his machine-pistol on a table and came towards me. As he was now unarmed, and because I was reluctant to part with the travel rations that were stuffed in the holster on my belt, I took my own pistol from my pocket and bellowed back: 'Not one step further! And you, Sturmbannführer, will now kindly read aloud the Führer order that is lying on the desk in front of you!' The SS officer inched his hand towards a desk drawer that no doubt contained a weapon. 'Don't even think about it,' I warned, 'this ridiculous business has gone on long enough and I'm rapidly running out of patience.'

I turned the lamp back so that it now shone in the SS officer's eyes as he picked up the Führer order. As the name suggests, these orders were so called because they were personally signed by, or on behalf of the Führer. They gave the bearer absolute priority in carrying out the mission he was engaged upon, and ordered all public officials, other authorities, military personnel and party members to offer him every possible assistance. It couldn't be any clearer than that. I collected my papers together but, before leaving the room, I read the last sentence of the Führer order to the two SS men again: 'Any failure to comply or refusal to help will be punished by summary court-martial or the equivalent thereof.' 'Understood,' muttered the Sturmbannführer.

Even so, it had been a very nasty little incident. As I climbed the steps out of the bunker I could feel the goose-pimples running down my back. These dangerous lunatics – nicknamed 'Heldenklaue, 'hero-pinchers', by the general public on account of their relentless, not to say rabid pursuit of deserters – had the right to arrest anyone they found not carrying the proper papers and string them up on the nearest tree or lamp-post without trial.

Once I was safely back in the Hanomag the driver put his foot to the floor. Everyone out on the street had heard the yelling and shouting in the bunker and we all wanted to get away from there. As we continued along the coast road towards Warnemünde we passed thousands of refugees trekking the other way. Women were pulling tiny handcarts piled high with all their worldly goods packed into suitcases, parcels and untidy bundles. Their children were either walking beside them or were perched on top of the swaying mounds of luggage. It was a scene of such abject misery – the despair on the faces of the women and old people, the crying babies, the hungry children – that I felt both sick and angry at the same time. Would this abominable, accursed and filthy war never end?

I was ashamed at being a healthy young man riding in a vehicle, however decrepit it may have been, while these terrified masses, who had nothing to do with the war, were forced to flee on foot in such a pitiable state. 'On your way back take as many of the weakest as you can with you,' I said to the driver. 'Goes without saying,' he grunted. The sight of the pilots in the trailer sharing out their travel rations among the refugees we passed also made me feel a little better.

We reached Heinkel's Marienehe works in the early morning, which was just as well as the Hanomag, belching smoke and steam from every orifice, wouldn't have made it much further. We were told that the officers were again to be accommodated in the 'German Reich's Chancellor' Hotel in Warnemünde, while the NCOs would be billeted on the airbase just outside of town. But first we remained in Marienehe as I wanted to find out exactly how many machines were ready for ferrying back to Leck.

I was informed that there were just two waiting for us, and that the factory would be producing only one machine a day from now on. After sending Leutnant Stiemer and another pilot off to Leck in the two available He 162s, I had a nose around the works to see if there were any other aircraft we might 'borrow' if the need arose. Russian tanks were getting ever closer and it made sense to have some alternative means of escape available if we had to leave here in a hurry. While rooting around I came across a Fieseler Storch and an

Me 108 Taifun, two types that I had often enjoyed flying in the past.

For the last two weeks or more – since 8 April to be exact – II. Gruppe of JG 1, under the command of the Knight's Cross-wearing Hauptmann Paul-Heinrich Dähne, had also been converting onto the He 162 at Heinkel's Rostock-Marienehe works. They had not been having an easy time of it either. And on 24 April, the day of our little group's arrival, I witnessed the latest in the long string of accidents that were directly attributable to the He 162's weak point: the rudder assembly.

Hauptmann Dähne was on a practice flight over Warnemünde when, at a height of just 500 metres, he attempted a steep left-hand turn. The machine stood on one wing for a moment, then flipped the rest of the way over completely onto its back. Out of control, it tumbled out of the sky and crashed into a boggy area of marsh at the mouth of the River Warnow.

As it fell white smoke was pouring from its engine. Then hundreds of tiny glittering fragments came raining down as well. Hauptmann Dähne had probably tried to eject, but had forgotten to release the canopy before triggering the ejection seat cartridge, breaking his neck as he smashed through the moulded Plexiglas. That would at least explain the sparkling shower of crystal-like shards. All attempts to recover his body failed and the remains of his machine sank into the swampy ground.

Unfortunately, Dähne had been one of those pilots who had distrusted and rejected the He 162 from the very outset. He had therefore never tried to come to terms with its strengths and its weaknesses. I suspect he didn't even know of the dangers posed by the misuse of rudder. The Heinkel designers were clearly under enormous pressure to rectify this fault as quickly as possible, but this would mean redesigning the whole tail unit.

In an effort to find at least a temporary solution, they consulted both their own works test pilots and the pilots of JG 1, myself included, who had successfully flown the machine. After Dähne's accident I was buttonholed by the head of the Heinkel design bureau Siegfried Günter: 'You must have given some thought as to how we can get a grip on this situation. We urgently need to come up with a method of doing it quickly. The way the war's going, we simply don't have the time to rebuild the entire tail assembly from scratch. It must be possible to get the machine out of a tailspin somehow. Have you got any suggestions?'

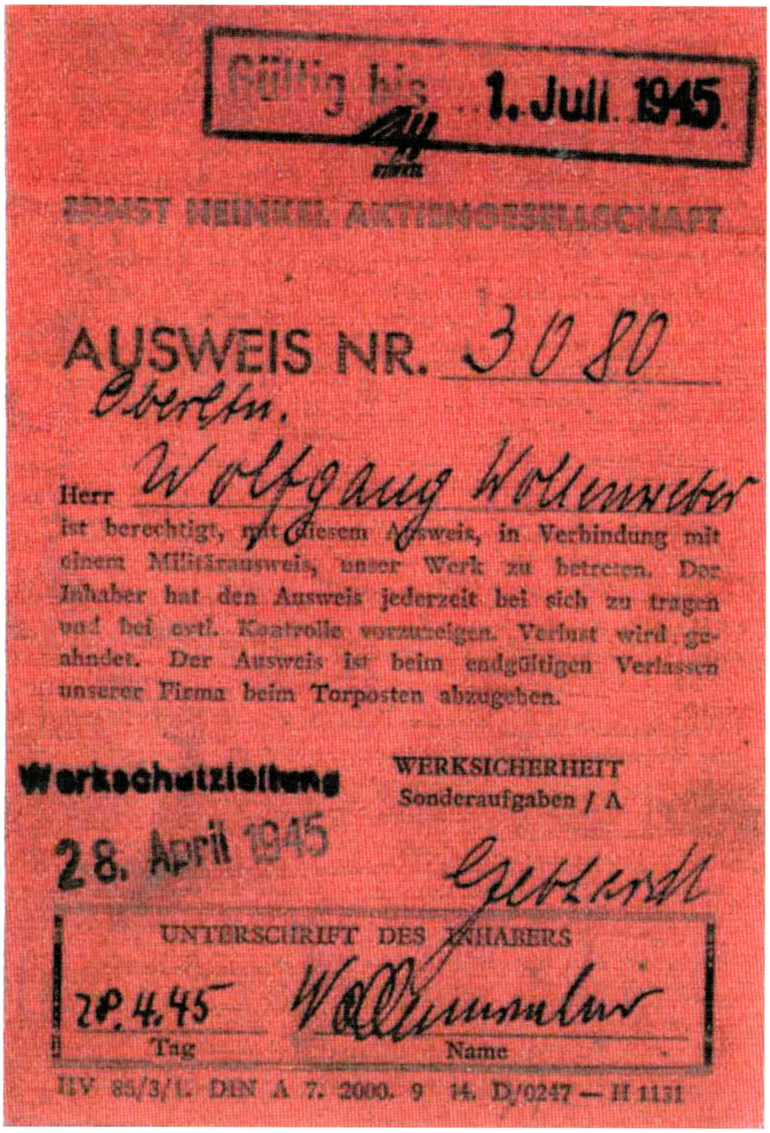
Gültig bis 1. Juli 1945.
ERNST HEINKEL AKTIENGESELLSCHAFT
AUSWEIS NR. 3080
Oberltn.
Herr Wolfgang Wollenweber
ist berechtigt, mit diesem Ausweis, in Verbindung mit einem Militärausweis, unser Werk zu betreten. Der Inhaber hat den Ausweis jederzeit bei sich zu tragen und bei evtl. Kontrolle vorzuzeigen. Verlust wird geahndet. Der Ausweis ist beim endgültigen Verlassen unserer Firma beim Torposten abzugeben.
Werkschutzleitung
WERKSICHERHEIT
Sonderaufgaben / A
28. April 1945
UNTERSCHRIFT DES INHABERS
28.4.45
Tag
Name
HV 85/3/1. DIN A 7. 2000. 9 44. D/0247 — H 1131

One of the last 'Special duties' passes issued by the Heinkel works. Although the Russians were almost at the factory gates by this time, it was stamped 'Valid until 1 July 1945'.

'Wouldn't lowering the undercarriage perhaps restore the centre of gravity?' I replied. Günter thought about this for a few seconds and then said: 'Would you like to give that a try for us?' I agreed, but added: 'You've got to realize that this could cost you a machine if it doesn't work.'

The news from Leck wasn't good either. On 25 April Leutnant Gerhard Stiemer, who had ferried one of the two completed He 162s back from Marienehe, had taken off together with Leutnant Hans Berger to intercept a formation of P-47 Thunderbolts. Due to lack of fuel the pair were unable to engage the enemy and so returned to base. Leutnant Stiemer's machine somersaulted on landing and he was lifted from the cockpit unconscious and with both legs broken. An ambulance took him to hospital in Leck where he found Unteroffizier Josef Rieder, who had also crashed on landing at the end of his transfer flight from Ludwigslust to Leck on

14 April and was now back from his examination by the specialists in Neumünster and recovering in the town's hospital.

During the short train ride from our quarters in Warnemünde to the Heinkel factory in Rostock on 26 April we saw the wreckage of an He 162 scattered alongside the tracks. As my own group was all present and correct, and no pilots of II./JG 1 had been reported missing, we could only assume that the machine was being flown by a works test pilot at the time of its accident. So design leader Günter hadn't been able to wait for me to try out my theory about the undercarriage affecting the He 162's centre of gravity. One of his own pilots had been sent up presumably to investigate another possibility – with the results that we had just seen from our carriage window.

At least it was now possible for me to get one machine a day away from Marienehe and ferried up to Leck, although I had to ask myself just how much good this daily drop in a bucket was actually doing.

At about 11.00 hours on 30 April Leutnant Adalbert Schlarb took off from Marienehe to fly He 162, Werknummer 120 099, to Leck. Conditions were hazy, but it was shortage of fuel – probably due to a faulty fuel contents gauge – that forced him to belly land at Lütjenburg, east of Kiel. Schlarb got away with minor injuries, but it was another machine written-off.

By this time there only were four of us, Fähnrich Köhler, Unteroffiziere Riehl and Riemer, and myself waiting for a machine to ferry back to Leck. But now a works engineer informed me that we would be getting just one, perhaps two at most, of the last He 162s to come off the assembly line at Marienehe before production was shut down for good. These machines had an increased fuel capacity, which meant that they would be able to stay in the air for 45 minutes without any difficulty. I assigned Fähnrich Köhler to ferry one of these improved He 162s, warning him that I would make mincemeat of him if anything happened to this precious piece of hardware.

While Köhler and the two Unteroffiziere went off to round up some J 2 aviation fuel, I made my way to the Fieseler Storch that I had earmarked earlier for our possible return flight to Leck. To show that I had 'confiscated' the machine, I laid my leather greatcoat, my belt and briefcase on the pilot's seat and then set off myself to find some fuel for it.

My strong suspicions that we wouldn't all four be leaving in He 162s were confirmed by the sudden arrival of a Ju 52 transport that afternoon. It came sweeping in low over the field, landed and taxied to the middle of the grass runway. The door was opened and a large number of cases, bags, parcels and packages of every description was quickly unloaded. God knows who it all belonged to, but a wall of luggage some two metres high was soon piled up alongside the runway.

While all this had been going on a crowd of women, children and men in civilian clothes had dashed out across the field towards the three-engined Ju 52 and were now jostling to get aboard it. I presumed these were members of the works' senior staff and their families anxious to get away from Marienehe and the approaching Russians. But I doubt if they made it. No matter in which direction they flew, Germany's rapidly shrinking airspace was full of enemy fighters eager to pounce on anything that moved, and a lumbering transport machine would have presented a very juicy target indeed.

Although the exodus of the management no doubt signalled the end of He 162 production at Rostock-Marienehe, the Luftwaffe had other weapons up its sleeve. But these were desperate times, and some of the weapons in question revealed to just what

Despite the hefty turbine perched on its back, ...

desperate straits the Luftwaffe High Command had now been reduced.

Standing near the perimeter fence at Marienehe, for example, was a Bücker Bü 181 trainer. Nothing particularly unusual in that, perhaps. But strapped to the little machine's wings were a pair of Panzerfaust rocket launchers, the German infantry's equivalent to the American bazooka. In the mess I met the pilot of this unlikely contraption. He told me he belonged to 3. Panzerjagdstaffel – the 3rd Anti-tank Squadron – and explained that the rockets were fired by means of two thin wire cables attached to a lever in the cockpit.

His intention was to take off after dark and use the two Panzerfäuste to knock out a couple of Russian T-34 tanks. Didn't he realize that even at night the Russians advanced in groups of anything up to 50 or 60 tanks strongly supported by their own anti-aircraft units, I asked. 'Yes,' he replied, 'but I'm relying on the element of surprise!'

I could only shake my head at such suicidal insanity.

My search for fuel, meanwhile, had proven fruitless. Amidst all the hubbub and feverish activity that was going on nobody would, or could tell me where I might find a fuel bowser. When I went back to the Storch to get my things, my leather greatcoat and travel rations had disappeared. The thief had removed the epaulettes from my coat and left them in the machine together with my belt.

But there was at least one piece of good news. *Two* He 162s would be ready for ferrying out tomorrow after all. I detailed Unteroffiziere Riemer and Riehl to take off at first light on 1 May and fly the machines back to Leck.

...the He 162 made a streamlined and elegant picture in the air.

Kommodore Herbert Ihlefeld flies an air defence mission in his 'White 23' in the Flensburg area. This painting, titled 'Jet Interceptor', is by the well-known aviation artist Nicholas Trudgian.

18 May's 'Dance of Death'

At 5 o'clock on the morning of 1 May I was awoken by the rumble of artillery. When I looked out of the window the sky was a flickering blood-red from shell explosions and fires. The Russians were only about ten kilometres from the factory gates and it was high time to make a move. At 07.15 hours Unteroffizier Anton Riemer took off for Leck in He 162, Werknummer 120 100. But when Unteroffizier Helmut Riehl followed him off 15 minutes later in Werknummer 120 104 – the last ever He 162 to be built in Heinkel's Rostock works – it seemed as if the machine had a mind of its own. Once in the air it began to weave and jump about all over the place.

Riehl managed to wrestle it round and returned to the field in a series of barely controlled rollercoaster hops; sinking towards the ground, adding power, gaining height and then losing it again. As he approached the runway the He 162 decided it had had enough and ploughed into some thick shrubbery just outside the boundary. Luckily, Riehl was unhurt. But we heard later that Unteroffizier Riemer had also crashed on his way to Leck and had sustained severe injuries both to his arms and legs.

The artillery fire was getting closer all the while and it was imperative that I find some fuel for the Storch. With a machine-pistol slung over my shoulder and Riehl at my side, I trotted back to the fuel depot where I found a Flak-Major and several airmen setting demolition charges. When I asked the Major where I could get hold of some aviation fuel he pointed at a bowser that was just about to drive off towards the main gate.

'You'd better make it snappy,' the Major shouted, 'this whole lot, including the runway, is going to go up at any minute. We can't afford to let it fall into the hands of the Russians!' We hared off after the tanker, yelling at the tops of our voices for it to stop. But the driver kept accelerating away seemingly oblivious to us. It was only when I pointed the machine-pistol at his tyres and threatened to shoot that he braked and turned back.

'I didn't notice you there, Herr Oberleutnant. My son's in the forces too, you know,' he mumbled incoherently. The man was completely drunk. 'You can have some fuel, but only in exchange for schnapps,' he wheedled, before finding the muzzle of my machine-pistol stuck halfway up one of his nostrils. 'You'll drive across to that hangar over there at once and refuel the Storch that's inside it,' I shouted.

Despite his befuddled state he seemed to have received my message loud and clear. Following my instructions to the letter, he drove into the hangar and up so close to the Storch that there was hardly a millimetre to spare between the tanker and the machine's wing. Then he handed me a hose and staggered back to the cab of his vehicle to turn on the pump motor. When the aircraft's tanks were full to the brim I called out: 'Switch off!' but nothing happened. The pump kept chugging and the fuel kept pouring out of the hose, streaming first across the wing of the Storch, and then over the floor of the hangar where it started to form a highly explosive pool in one corner.

I let go the hose and ran round to the front of the bowser to find the driver, but there wasn't a sign of him; it was as if he'd disappeared off the face of the earth. As I didn't know how to turn the pump's motor off, I simply yanked out the ignition lead. I got one hell of an electric shock, but at least it stopped the flow of fuel. We could count ourselves lucky that we hadn't gone up in flames.

Just as Riehl and I were stowing our things away in the Storch, a little DKW saloon came clattering into the hangar on four flat tyres. At the wheel sat the He 162 development engineer Wilhelm Gundermann with one the works test pilots next to him. They asked if we would take them along in the Storch with us, as they weren't likely to get very far in the battered DKW. 'Of course,' I replied, 'climb aboard, otherwise you'll soon find yourselves in Siberia. You'll have to squeeze up a bit because of all the luggage.'

I knew that the pair's additional weight would mean that take-off might prove a tad difficult and would require the whole length of the runway. But what I hadn't noticed before starting to taxi out of the hangar was that one of the Storch's tyres was also completely flat and that the other had hardly any air in it either. There was nothing to be done about that now, however, so I lowered the flaps to their full extent and set off down the runway at the speed of an old man on a bicycle. The Storch kept wanting to swerve to either left or right. If only that flat tyre would come off there wouldn't be so much drag, I thought to myself, holding the stick back into my stomach the whole time. We were about halfway along the runway when both tyres shredded and flew off.

The Storch immediately started to pick up speed, rumbling along at 60 km/h on its wheel rims. But with the weight we were carrying that was still far too slow for lift-off. Then, suddenly, we were swept upwards as if by some giant hand. A powerful pressure wave, produced by the Major setting off his demolitions, had wrenched us off the ground and flung us up into the air! Behind us huge chunks of concrete, hangar doors, parts of aircraft, lumps of iron and all sorts of other bits and pieces were already tumbling back down to earth as an enormous cloud of smoke and dust enveloped the entire factory site.

My original plan to follow the coastline westwards, so that we could put down in a hurry if enemy fighters appeared, wouldn't work now that we had no tyres. If I attempted to land the Storch on a sandy beach in this state, the wheel hubs would immediately dig in and throw the machine onto its back. So instead I headed inland a little, only to find the coastal road packed with endless columns of refugees. This was the sort of target that would be bound to attract the attention of enemy aircraft before very long. But I comforted myself with the thought that we'd soon reach Lübeck Bay, where there were sure to be some German warships to provide us with cover.

A Fieseler Fi 156 Storch.

I couldn't have been more wrong – hardly had we turned into the bay before every vessel in the vicinity opened fire on us! Even the larger warships joined in, their huge shells sending columns of water 50 metres into the air. It would have been pointless to waggle my wings to show them I was a 'friendly'. I knew only too well from my days up on the Arctic Ocean that once the German Navy started firing at you, it wouldn't stop until you were either in the drink or out of sight.

It was at this point, just to fill the refugees' cup of misery to overflowing, that English fighters began to attack the traffic on the nearby coast road. But it was a lucky break for us. The ships immediately switched their fire to this new target, while the enemy fighters – presumably in the belief that German warships wouldn't be shooting at one of their own – took us for an English spotter aircraft and didn't bother us either. While no-one was looking I quietly slipped the Storch into a long bank of cumulus and we stayed in this until the whole gruesome nightmare of fire and flying lead was well behind us.

The rest of the 80-minute flight to Leck passed without further incident. But there still remained the ticklish business of getting the Storch back down onto the ground again. To alert the station fire section to my predicament I flew low and slow past their building, tilting first the left wing and then the right wing so that they couldn't fail to see that my machine had no tyres. And, in fact, several firemen were already running out on to the field, waving and pointing to indicate that they had understood my problem. Now if I somersaulted while attempting to land, there would at least be somebody on hand to get us out of the machine in double-quick time.

I floated in very gently, flaps fully extended, holding her just above the ground and letting the tailwheel touch down first. With the stick pulled back, I kept her nose in the air and the mainwheels off the ground for as long as possible. As soon as the rims made contact, screeching over the concrete and sending sparks flying, the abrupt deceleration caused the tail of the machine to start lifting, threatening to flip us over onto our back. Luckily, the additional weight of my back-seat passengers prevented us from going over completely. The nose slid along the ground for a few more metres and then we came to a halt, the tail sticking up into the air to form what was known in the Luftwaffe as a 'Fliegerdenkmal', or 'flyer's monument'.

It hadn't been one of my better landings, but at least we were all down in one piece. At first, my comrades in the mess refused to believe my story of landing on the wheel rims – but I had three witnesses to back me up.

In Leck I heard for the first time the rumours that Adolf Hitler had shot himself in his Berlin bunker on 30 April. This news had escaped us amidst all the confusion of the final days at Heinkel's Rostock-Marienehe works. The cowardly swine, I thought – he sets the entire world ablaze, causes the deaths of millions, condemns whole generations to unimaginable suffering, and then evades all responsibility by committing suicide.

When I think back today on the Hitler era, the words of Achilles before Troy spring unbidden to my mind: 'If we obey the orders of a fool, we are lost!' At all events, the German nation will not forget Hitler's 'Totentanz in den Mai' – his 'Dance of death into May' – all that easily or all that quickly. And I'm sure that his crimes against humanity will remain with us for a long time to come.

Kommodore Oberst Ihlefeld informed us that Hitler had appointed Grossadmiral Karl Dönitz as his successor and that the latter was now both Reich President and head of the Wehrmacht, and thus our supreme commander.

On 2 May I. and II. Gruppen of JG 1 underwent reorganisation. I./JG 1 became the Geschwader's 'Einsatzgruppe', or 'operational group', while II./JG 1 was designated as a so-called 'Sammelgruppe', literally 'assembly' or 'catchment'; in other words, the unit's reserve group.

Apart from creating a number of new posts, and necessitating a change of personnel in others, I didn't quite see the point of this restructuring. On 3 May the Gruppenkommandeur of I./JG 1, Oberleutnant Karl-Emil Demuth, was replaced by Major Werner Zober. At the same time Hauptmann Wolfgang Ludewig succeeded Leutnant Gerhard Hanf as the Käpitan of our 2. Staffel.

It was while at readiness on this same 3 May that I saw the long fingers of contrails beginning to creep across the sky, heralding the approach of a huge formation of four-engined bombers from the southwest. A single readiness section would be worse than useless against such numbers. But if I wanted to take up a stronger force of jet fighters from the considerable number of He 162s now being 'hoarded' here at Leck, I would first need to obtain permission from the newly created Central Operational Control. This was commanded by the Oak Leaves-wearing Oberstleutnant Karl-Gottfried Nordmann in his role as 'Inspekteur der Tagjäger Ost', or 'Inspector of Day-fighters East'. But when I contacted his office I was curtly forbidden to fly any such mission with the words: 'Take-off prohibited, non-compliance a court-martial offence!'

So the end of the war's that close is it, I said to myself. The high-ups don't want to spoil their chances of negotiating a lenient capitulation by spilling any more blood. Well, at least that means we won't be senselessly sacrificed during these final days – perhaps there's a hope we might come out of it alive. At the same time, I could tell just how nervous the gentlemen in the corridors of power really were by their increasing reliance on courts-martial. But even this threat, so often used and abused over the last few years, would soon be deprived of its power to terrify and intimidate.

Nonetheless, at 11.38 hours on 4 May Leutnant Rudolf Schmitt actually did take off in He 162 'White 1', Werknummer 120 212, on another operational mission. When he landed back at Leck at 11.56 hours he reported the shooting down of a Hawker Tempest, but his claim was not allowed. And while on the subject of 'kills' scored on the He 162, let me state quite categorically … There weren't any. Full stop!

All assertions to the contrary are pure fantasy. Any talk of victories achieved on the He 162 comes either from questionable combat reports containing claims submitted by pilots eager to make a name for themselves, or can be attributed solely to propaganda.

I also happened to make my last flight in an He 162 on 4 May. At 15.00 hours I was ordered up in 'Yellow 3', Werknummer 120 072, to escort Grossadmiral Dönitz's personal transport over Kiel. I landed again just 30 minutes later – no great excitement, certainly no victories. But it did turn out to be the last flight by a German pilot in an He 162 from Leck, perhaps even from anywhere in what was left of the Reich. On the other hand, bearing in mind the importance of its occupant, to provide the new Reich President's plane with an escort of just one jet fighter was more of a joke than anything else.

That night we received notification from the Generalstab Mitte, General Staff Central Region, that all fighting in the Schleswig-Holstein area was to cease on 8 May. Kommodore Ihlefeld called us together to address us one last time. He explained that the war was over for us, saying: 'I can't keep you here, every one of you is free to go wherever he likes. But I would advise you all to stick together until the Allies – and I'm assuming this will be the English arrive to take possession of the airfield. There is less danger for you here than if you set off somewhere and fall into the hands of the Russians.' As far as I was aware, not one of us left the camp.

However, when it was discovered that Hauptmann Ludewig was nowhere to be found, I was ordered to take over as quasi-Kapitän of our 'orphaned' 2. Staffel in order to retain some semblance of discipline within its ranks during these final few days. Then a whole load of promotions were handed out, presumably to give the recipients the chance of claiming a higher pension in years to come. Thus, for example, all Fähnriche were upped to Leutnants, which meant that suddenly there were four more officer pilots to add to the three already serving in the Staffel.

There was a certain amount of confusion about what was to be done with the many now unemployed aircraft standing around on the field. At first it was announced that all the He 162s were to be destroyed. Then, after the demolition charges were in place, we were ordered to remove them again. It was obvious to all of us that the victorious powers, be they American, English, Canadian, French or Russian, would be itching to get their hands on this revolutionary technology. And as it was now certain that our area was soon to be occupied by the English, we didn't want to run the risk of being harshly treated as prisoners-of-war by presenting them with a pile of wrecked jet fighters. We therefore left these objects of Allied desire practically intact; contenting ourselves with merely removing the Riedel starter motors and blocking the rudders. This effectively immobilized them, but meant they could quite quickly and easily be made airworthy again.

Far right is 'my Yellow 3', Werknummer 120 072.

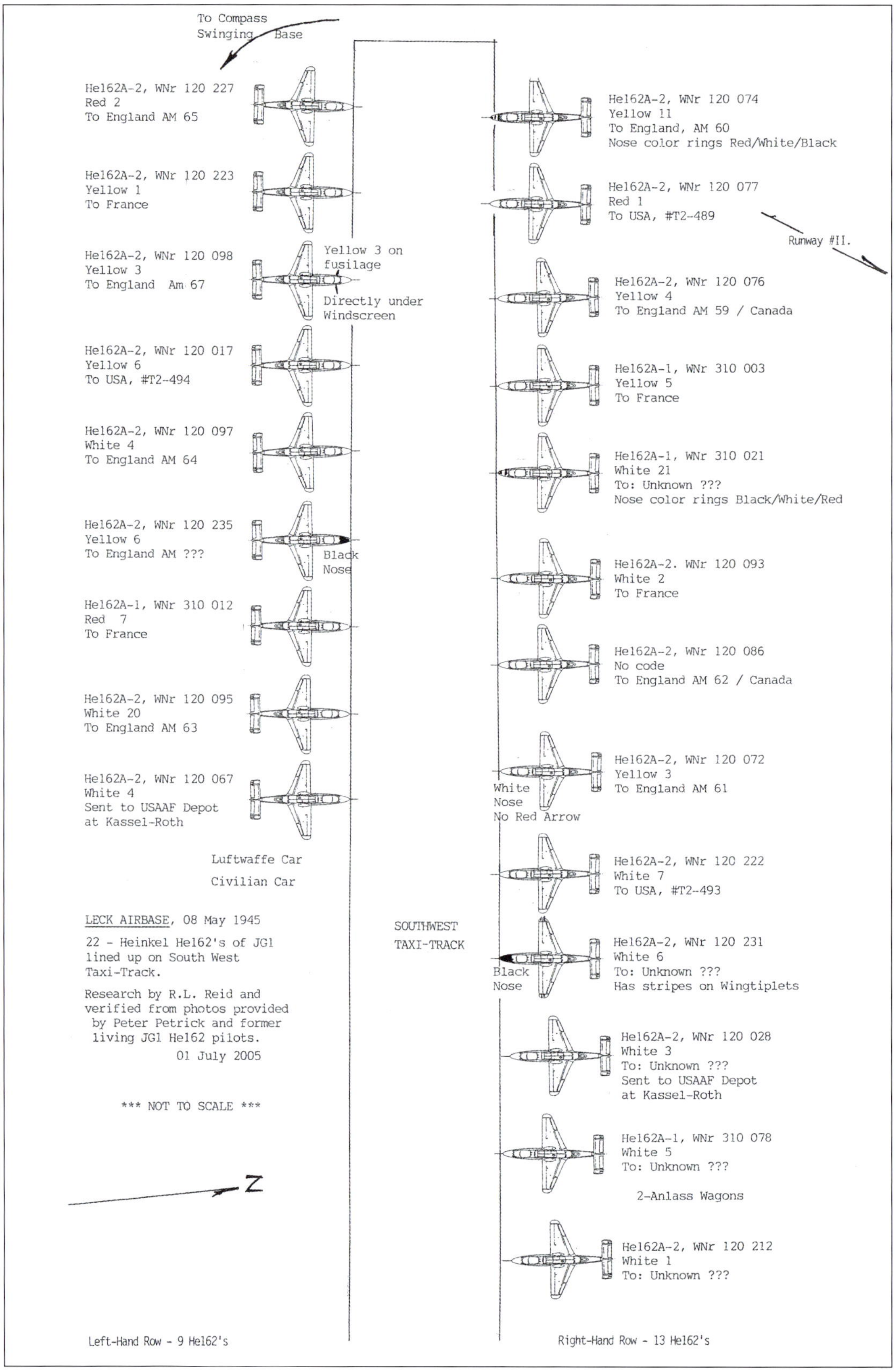

Diagram showing the positions of the 22 He 162s lined up to left and right of the taxi-track at Leck on 8 May 1945 awaiting handover to the Allies. *Richard L. Reid*

Oberleutnant Heinz Künneke, Staffelkapitän of 3./JG 1, in front of 'White 5', Werknummer 310 078.

Wheels and flaps down, an He 162 comes in to land at Leck.

An extract from my flying logbook for March-April 1945.

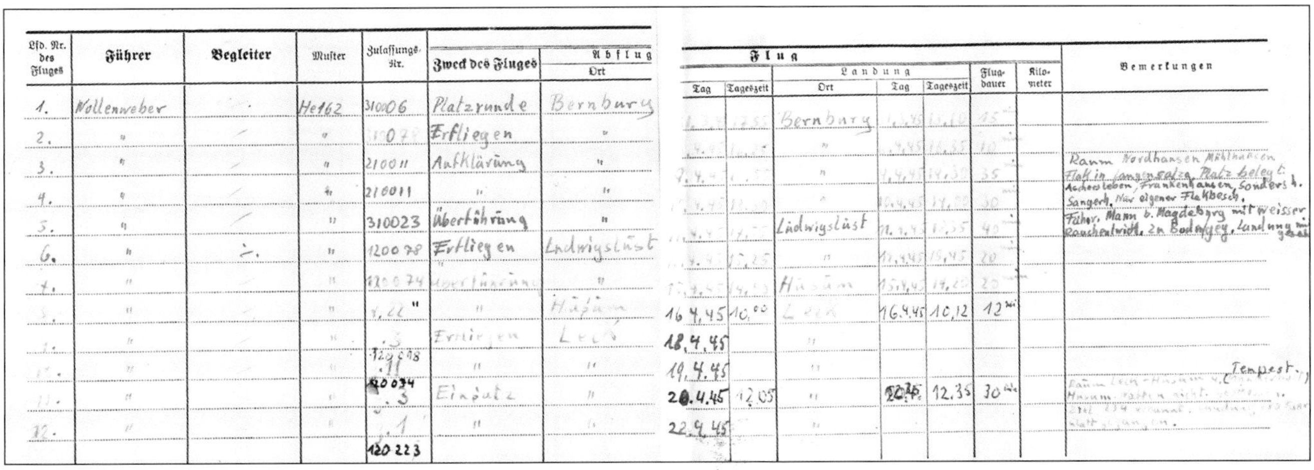

Lfd. Nr. des Fluges	Führer	Begleiter	Muster	Zulassungs-Nr.	Zweck des Fluges	Abflug Ort	Abflug Tag	Abflug Tageszeit	Landung Ort	Landung Tag	Landung Tageszeit	Flugdauer	Kilometer	Bemerkungen
1.	Wollenweber		He162	310006	Platzrunde	Bernburg	[illegible]	[illegible]	Bernburg	[illegible]	[illegible]	15 min		
2.	"	/	"	310078	Erfliegen	"	[illegible]	[illegible]	"	[illegible]	16.35	10 min		
3.	"	/	"	210011	Aufklärung	"	[illegible]	[illegible]	"	9.4.45	14.30	35		Raum Nordhausen Mühlhausen Flak in Langensalza, Platz belegt. Aschersleben, Frankenhausen, Sondersh. Sangerh. Nur eigener Flakbesch. Führ. Mann b. Magdeburg mit weisser Rauchentwickl. zu Boden gez. Landung [illegible]
4.	"	/	"	210011	"	"	[illegible]	[illegible]	"	10.4.45	[illegible]	30		
5.	"	/	"	310023	Überführung	"	[illegible]	[illegible]	Ludwigslust	11.4.45	[illegible]	40		
6.	"	÷	"	120078	Erfliegen	Ludwigslust	[illegible]	15.25	"	11.4.45	15.45	20		
7.	"		"	120074	Überführung	"	[illegible]	[illegible]	Husum	15.4.45	[illegible]	20		
8.	"		"	" 22 "	"	Husum	16.4.45	10.00	Leck	16.4.45	10.12	12 min		
9.	"		"	" 3	Erfliegen	Leck	18.4.45		"					
10.	"		"	120098 " 11	"	"	19.4.45		"					Tempest.
11.	"		"	120034 " 3	Einsatz	"	20.4.45	12.05	"	20.4.45	12.35	30 min		Raum Leck–Husum [illegible]
12.	"		"	" 1 120223	"	"	22.4.45		"					

The 'vanished' Hauptmann Ludewig got in touch with me a little later, telling me in confidence that he was living in a hut not far from the airfield and that, once things had settled down a bit, he intended trying to make it to Brazil. For us the next couple of days were spent awaiting the arrival of the English. The noise of battle had ceased. There were no air raid alarms, no sirens, no orders echoing tinnily across the field from the loudspeakers. And the He 162s parked neatly to left and right of one of the taxiways looked for all the world as if they had been lined up for public viewing at some civilian air display.

This was a tranquil interval indeed at Leck. We played cards or simply lazed about in the sunshine. The weather was good and we had enough to eat. If it hadn't been for our very real worries about the fate of our loved ones and the uncertainty of the future, we could almost have convinced ourselves that we were enjoying a pleasant break at a health farm.

Once the airfield had been cleared, tidied up and made ready for handing over, the Staffels were billeted out in nearby villages. Our 2. Staffel was quartered in what had previously been the schoolhouse in the village of Stadum, some six kilometres to the southeast of Leck. The men occupied the sports gym, the NCOs were distributed among various classrooms, and my officers and I settled into the geography lecture hall, whose bookshelves and wall maps had now been replaced by two-tier bunk beds.

The former headmaster of the Stadum school was an amateur archaeologist and keen collector of ancient artefacts, who kept the stone axes, spear tips and pottery shards he had found locked away in a small room leading off the main hall. He entrusted me with the key, imploring me to look after his prized collection and make sure that nothing was stolen.

On 6 May the duty NCO came rushing into the building in a state of great agitation to report that two English tanks had just driven into the schoolyard. I ordered everyone to fall in in the gym hall. We had just gathered when a British major came striding into the hall accompanied by an interpreter. He was carrying a riding crop in his hand and looking around him with a very self-satisfied air.

But when I barked a loud 'Achtung!' and the assembled officers and men all crashed their heels together in unison, he was so startled that he jumped back a pace in alarm and glanced anxiously at the exit. 'Werewolves?' he asked me uneasily. Many of the Allies were convinced that the so-called 'Werewolves' were a partisan-like organization set up by the Reichsführer der SS Heinrich Himmler in the closing months of the war specifically to carry out assassinations and attacks on Allied troops in occupied Germany. 'No, Herr Major,' I answered him in my very best school English, 'Here there are no Werewolves. Our salute to you was made many times louder by the echo in this hall.'

I then had to conduct him on a tour of the building, showing him into every room. By the

When American troops occupied the German airfield at Kassel they found this He 162 A-2 *Werknummer* 120 076, White 4, of 1./JG 1 which had been flown in from Leck and also attracted much interest by the occupying US troops.

time we reached the locked door of the side-room housing the headmaster's collection, he seemed to have recovered his composure: 'Werewolves inside?' he enquired jokingly. When I held the door open for him I noticed two suspicious-looking crates that hadn't been in the room earlier. The major was so fascinated by the antique objects on display that he started to pick and choose the best ones for himself.

This put me in a real fix: I didn't want to lose the good will of the British major, but what about the promise I had made to the headmaster to look after his cherished treasures. I took my courage in both hands and explained to the Engländer that these were important items relating to the cultural history of Germany and that we knew English officers were gentlemen and not thieves. He put everything back like a well behaved child, but then pointed his riding-crop at the two grey crates on the floor and asked what they contained.

'More antiquities, presents for Field Marshal Montgomery,' I lied, trying to ignore the butterflies in my stomach. He nodded. 'Okay, let's go,' he said to the interpreter, completing his inspection and leaving the school grounds with his entire retinue in tow.

The moment they had gone I dashed off to find the Staffel's chiefy to ask him what was in those two ominous crates. He didn't have the faintest idea either, nor did he know who had smuggled them into the room containing the exhibits since we had last been in there. When we opened the crates to have a look we almost had a heart attack: nestling in each of them, carefully wrapped in oiled paper, were 12 brand new Panzerfäuste! With that little lot we could have blown a whole regiment of enemy tanks to kingdom come.

God knows what would have happened if the major had insisted on looking into the crates. We might well have been stood up against a wall. As it was, we couldn't wait to get rid of the damned things quick enough and dumped them on a nearby rubbish tip at the earliest possible opportunity.

On 16 May Kommodore Ihlefeld summoned me back to Leck airfield. A group of English officers together with a whole crowd of technical engineers and a test pilot had suddenly turned up there. I was to explain the workings of the He 162 to them and then give a demonstration flight. 'White 3' had been made ready and I went through the operating handbook with the English pilot. He was not only highly interested in what I had to tell him, but also gave me the impression that he understood all the necessary controls and would be perfectly capable of handling them.

I am standing back to camera (far right) as 'White 3' is prepared for a flight by an English test pilot.

The end of the 'Eagles of the Reich'. The remains of an He 162 are seen below the left wing of an Fw 190.

But when it came time for me to change into my flying gear, the English officers shook their heads. It seems we Germans weren't to be trusted. They were worried that I would fly off somewhere in their precious, fully-fuelled He 162 never to be seen again. I could understand their concern, but nonetheless felt cheated out of this one last flight.

In my place the English test pilot would be taking 'White 3' up. It was a tragic decision, for which he would soon pay the price. He took off, performed a very creditable circuit and landed again, expressing himself absolutely delighted with the He 162's handling. The machine was then refuelled and he was ordered to fly it down to Lüneburg to demonstrate it to some Allied top brass. We later heard rumours that he had crashed while landing at Neumünster en route. It was said that he had used rudder while flying at reduced speed – yet another victim of the He 162's one notorious and never-resolved weak point.

The last two months of my Luftwaffe career are quickly told. From 16 May to 25 May my Staffel and I were stuck in a group of huts at Schmörholm, then billeted on the Stolte's farm at Hennstedt until 29 May. From there we were sent to the demobilization camp at Bredstedt where we were employed until 8 July in helping with the harvest. On 9 July we passed through the Russian camp at Celle, before finally parading on the Hanover sports arena and being handed our discharge papers on 10 July 1945.

They taught us how to fly. They showed us how to fight. But they didn't tell us that this would mean killing people who might one day have become our friends (HK)

Appendix 1 Pilot's Notes for the Heinkel He 162

Bedienvorschrift
für den
Flugzeugführer
He 162

He 162, A - 1, A - 2.

Bedienungsvorschrift für den Flugzeugführer.

Inhalt :

Pilot's Notes

Contents:

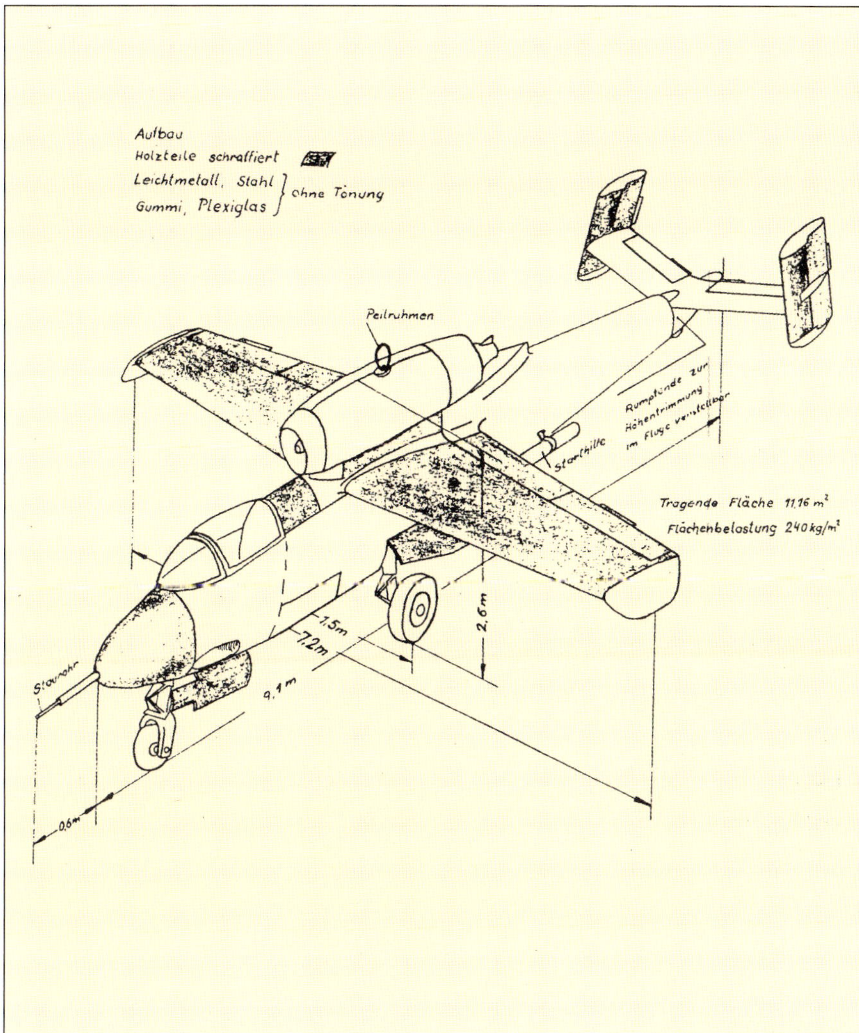
Aufbau
Holzteile schraffiert
Leichtmetall, Stahl
Gummi, Plexiglas
ohne Tönung
Peilrahmen
Rumpfende zur Höhentrimmung im Fluge verstellbar
Starthilfe
Tragende Fläche 11,16 m²
Flächenbelastung 240 kg/m²
2,6m
1,5m
7,2m
9,1m
Staurohr
0,6m

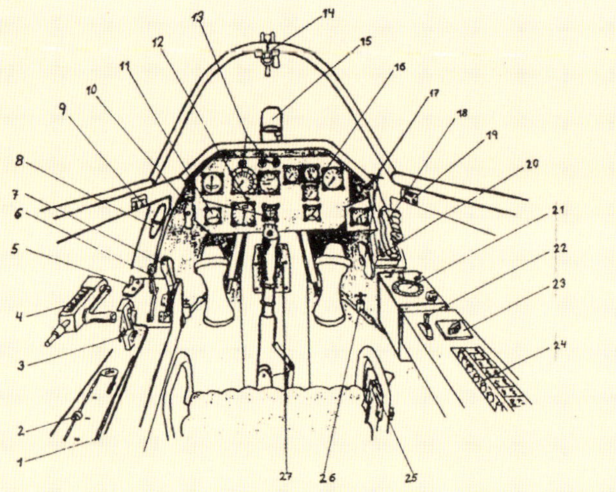

1. Abwurf der Starthilfen
2. Seitentrimmung
3. Fahrwerkschnappschalter
4. Höhentrimmung
5. Starthilfen-Auslösung
6. Brandhahnhebel
7. Leistunghebel
8. Fahrwerkentrastung
9. Fahrwerksanzeige links
10. Landeklappen-Handpumpe
11. Navigationsgeräte
12. Flugüberwachungsgeräte
13. Schauzeichen für Staurohr u. Waffen
14. Dachverschluss
15. Visier
16. Triebwerksüberwachung
17. Atemanlage
18. Leuchtpistole
19. Fahrwerksanzeige rechts
20. Bediengerät Fuss 25 a
21. Empfänger FuG 24
22. Anlasskippschalter
23. Verstelldüsenschalter
24. Selbstschalter
25. Katapultsitz-Auslösung
26. Pedalverstellung
27. Fenster am Bugrad

Selbstschalter :

Sammler
Kraftstoffpumpe
Waffen, Revi
Staurohr-Heizung
Anlass-und Messanlage
Wendezeiger, Starthilfe
Verstelldüse
FuG 24
FuG 25 a
Anlasser.

1. Take-off rocket jettison
2. Rudder trim control
3. Undercarriage selector
4. Elevator trim control
5. Take-off rocket firing switch
6. Fuel cock lever
7. Throttle lever
8. Undercarriage operating lever
9. Port undercarriage indicator
10. Flap manual control pump
11. Compass course indicators
12. Flying instruments panel (turn-and-bank indicator, ASI, rate of climb/descent, altimeter)
13. Pitot and cannon indicators
14. Canopy lock/release
15. Gunsight
16. Fuel and engine gauges
17. Oxygen valve and contents gauge
18. Flare pistol
19. Starboard undercarriage indicator
20. FuG 25a control box
21. FuG 24 receiver
22. Starter switch
23. Jet nozzle setting switch
24. Electrics switch panel
25. Ejection seat trigger
26. Rudder pedal adjustment screw (starboard)
27. Nosewheel well window (visual check)

Electrics switch panel (from front to back):

Battery
Fuel pump
Weapons and gunsight
Pitot heating
Ignition/calibration
Turn-and-bank; rocket take-off
Jet nozzle
FuG 24
FuG 25a
Starter.

I. Allgemeines.

Masse :

Spannweite	7.2 m	Spurweite	1.5 m
Länge	9.08 m	Tragfläche	11.16 m^2
Höhe	2.6 m	Flächenbelastung	240 kg/m^2

Baumerkmale:

Rumpf: Ganzmetallbauweise (Schalenbau), Führerraum teilweise gepanzert, verglaste Überdachung.
Tragwerk: Freitragender Tragflügel mit Haupt-und Endholm, Kraftstoffbehälterräume brennstoffest konserviert.
Leitwerk: Höhenflosse mechanisch verstellbar (Trimmkurbel), Doppelseitenleitwerk, sämtliche Ruder mit Bügelkanten, dynamisch voll massenausgeglichen.
Fahrwerk: Haupt-und Bugfahrwerk, letzteres nicht bremsbar.
Druckölanlage: betätigt Fahrwerke, Radbremsen, Landeklappen.

Triebwerk:

Ein TL-Triebwerk, Baumuster BMW 109 003 E-2
zwei Starthilfen R/502, können unter dem Rumpf eingehängt werden.

Elt.-Anlage:

Ein 2000 Watt-Generator am Triebwerk, ein Sammler 24 NCL 10 hinter Spant 5 auf Behältertraggerüst.

Bordfunkanlage:

FuG 24, UKW-Funkgerät für BzB und BzE-Sprechverkehr und Zielflugverkehr, FuG 25a Kennungsgerät.

Schusswaffenanlage:

A-1: 2 MK 108 Kal. 30 mm, Durchladung elektro-pneumatisch, Zündung elektrisch
A-2: 2 MG 151 Kal. 20 mm, Durchladung elektrisch.

Rettungs-und Sicherheitsgerät:

Katapultierbarer Flugzeugführersitz mit Sitzmulde für Sitzfallschirm 550 mit Füllungsbremse, Perlongurte und Höhenatmer, Bauchgurt, Schultergurt, 1 Leuchtpistole.

I. General:

Measurements:

Span	7.20 m	Track width	1.50 m
Length	9.08 m	Wing area	11.16 m^2
Height	2.60 m	Wing loading	240 kg/m^2

Construction details:

Fuselage:	All-metal (monocoque), cockpit partially armoured, glazed canopy.
Wings:	Cantilever wing with main and rear spars, integral fuel tanks anti-leak impregnated.
Tail unit:	Horizontal stabilizers mechanically adjustable (trimming crank), twin rudder unit, all control surfaces with trimming tabs, dynamically fully mass balanced.
Undercarriage:	Mainwheels and nosewheel, latter non-braking.
Hydraulics system:	Activates undercarriage, mainwheel brakes, flaps.

Power plant:

One BMW 109 003E-2 axial-flow turbojet,

Two R/502 take-off assistance rockets can be attached to rear fuselage.

Electrics:

One 2,000 Watt engine-mounted generator, one 24 NCL 10 battery on mounting behind Frame 5.

Radio equipment:

FuG 24, VHF for air-to-air and air-to-ground R/T and homing, FuG 25a IFF device.

Armament:

A-1: Two 30-mm MK 108 cannon, electro-pneumatic charging, electric firing

A-2: Two 20-mm MG 151 cannon, electric charging.

Rescue and safety equipment:

Pilot's ejection seat with seat pan for Type 550 seat parachute with canopy brake, Perlon straps and oxygen mask, belly strap, shoulder straps, 1 flare pistol.

Beladevorschrift :

Die Schwerpunktlage darf zwischen den Grenzen 19.7 - 26 % - bezogen auf mittlere Flügeltiefe - liegen. Folgende Beladezustände sind zugelassen.

	A-1 Schusswaffen 2 MK 108, Schuss 2 x 50					A-2 Schusswaffen 2 MG 151, Schuss 2 x 120			
	gr.Rumpfbeh.		kl.Rumpfbeh.			gr.Rumpfbeh.		kl.Rumpfbeh.	
	ohne Flügel	mit Flügel	mit Flügel	mit Flügel u. Reserve		ohne Flügel	mit Flügel	mit Flügel	mit Flügel u. Reserve.
Kraftstoff im Rumpf - gr.Behälter 650 l	540	540	-	-		540	540	-	-
kl.Behälter 470 l	-	-	390	390		-	-	390	390
Notbehälter 170 l	-	-	-	140		-	-	-	140
Kraftstoff im Flügel 280 l	-	232	232	232	kg	-	232	232	232
Kraftstoff gesamt	540	772	622	762		540	772	622	762
Munition	58	58	58	58		58	58	58	58
Rollgewicht	2657	2889	2772	2886		2634	2866	2749	2850
S-Lage in %									
Fahrwerk ausgefahren	19.9	23.0	23.8	23.0		19.7	22.6	23.5	22.6
Fahrwerk eingefahren	22.1	25.1	26.0	25.1		22.0	24.7	25.7	24.7

Loading specifications:

The centre of gravity should lie between 19.7 and 26 % relative to centre of wing chord. The following loadings are permissible.

	A-1 Armament 2 MK 108, Rounds 2 x 50					A-2 Armament 2 MK 151, Rounds 2 X 120			
	large fuselage tank		small fuselage tank			large fuselage tank		small fuselage tank	
	without wing tank	with wing tank	with wing tank	with wing tank & reserve		without wing tank	with wing tank	with wing tank	with wing tank & reserve
Fuselage fuel capacity:									
large tank 650 ltr	540	540	–	–		540	540	–	–
small tank 470 ltr	–	–	390	390		–	–	390	390
emergency tank 170 ltr	–	–	–	140		–	–	–	140
Wing fuel capacity 280 ltr:	–	232	232	232	kg	–	232	232	232
Total fuel capacity:	540	772	622	762		540	772	622	762
Ammunition:	58	58	58	58		58	58	58	58
Taxi weight:	2657	2889	2772	2886		2634	2866	2749	2850
C/G in %									
undercarriage extended:	19.9	23.0	23.8	23.0		19.7	22.6	23.5	22.6
undercarriage retracted:	22.1	25.1	26	25.1		22.0	24.7	25.7	24.7

Beanspruchungs - und Verwendungsgruppe.

Verwendungsgruppe H

Beanspruchungsgruppe 4, später 5

Sicheres Lastvielfaches beim Abfangen n_{si} = 4, später 6.5 bei G= 2400 kg

Höchstzulässige Geschwindigkeiten:

V_a = 700 km/h, bezogen auf Bodenluftdichte (entsprechend 750 km/h, Gerät zeigt ca 10% zu wenig an).

V_a = 700 km/h in 1 km Höhe

Flug mit ausgefahrenem Fahrwerk, sowie beim Ein-und Ausfahren 350 km/h

Flug mit ausgefahrenen Klappen - Landestellung max. 300 km/h, Startstellung max. 500 km/h.

Geschwindigkeitsbegrenzung :

V_a = 700 km/h bis H = 5000 m
V_a = 600 km/h von H = 5000 m - 7000 m
V_a = 500 km/h von H = 7000 m - 9000 m
V_a = 400 km/h von H = 9000 m -11000 m

Bei grossem Rumpfbehälter mit weniger als 350 Liter Kraftstoff ergibt sich extreme Schwerpunktlage und bei hohen Geschwindigkeiten Abnahme der Stabilität. In diesem Falle soll V_a 100 km/h weniger als die Marke am Fahrtmesser angibt, eingehalten werden.

bis 5000 m V_a = 700 - 100 = 600 km/h
5000 - 7000 m V_a = 600 - 100 = 500 km/h
7000 - 9000 m V_a = 500 - 100 = 400 km/h
9000 - 11000 m V_a = 400 - 100 = 300 km/h

Stress and Application Groups:

Application group H

Stress group 4, later 5

Safety load factor at recovery n_{si} = 4, later 6.5 at G = 2,400 kg

Maximum permissible speeds:

V_a = 700 km/h, relative to atmospheric density at ground level (corresponding to 750 km/h, ASI indicates approx. 10% below actual).

V_a = 700 km/h at 1 km altitude.

Speed with undercarriage lowered, and while lowering and retracting 350 km/h.

Speed with flaps extended: while landing max. 300 km/h, at take-off max. 500 km/h.

Speed limitations:

V_a = 700 km/h up to H = 5,000 m
V_a = 600 km/h from H = 5,000 m to 7,000 m
V_a = 500 km/h from H = 7,000 m to 9,000 m
V_a = 400 km/h from H = 9,000 m to 11,000m

Less than 350 litres of fuel in large fuselage fuel tank results in extreme centre of gravity and reduction of stability at high speeds. In this case V_a must be kept 100 km/h lower than speed shown on ASI:

up to 5,000 m V_a = 700 – 100 = 600 km/h
5,000 m – 7,000 m V_a = 600 – 100 = 500 km/h
7,000 m – 9,000 m V_a = 500 – 100 = 400 km/h
9,000 m – 11,000 m V_a = 400 – 100 = 300 kim/h

<u>Behälterinhalte:</u>	<u>Betriebsstoffe:</u>
1. Kraftstoff: ein Rumpfbehälter, gr. 650 Lt. oder kl. 470 " und ein Rumpf-Reserve-behälter 170 " ein Flügelbehälter kl. 280 " mt. 700 "	-J 2, statt J 2 kann jeder Flugkraftstoff plus 5% Öl genommen werden.
2. Kraftstoff für Triebwerk ein Behälterraum in Tragflügel 30 "	-Fl-Anlass-Kraftstoff
3. Kraftstoff für Riedelanlasser: ein Behälter im Triebwerk 2 Lt	-Benzin-Öl-Gemisch 20 : 1, bei Temp. unter 10°C Gl-Anlass-kraftstoff
4. Schmierstoff: (Füllung 16 l) ein Behälter am Triebwerk 25 Lt.	-18 l U 1, solange dieser nicht beschaffbar ist, Mischung aus 50% Flugöl S 3 u. 50% Fl-Drucköl.
5. Drucköl: ein Behälter im Fahrwerksraum 5 "	-Fl-Drucköl
6. Spindelöl: drei Stossdämpfer ca. 2,5 Lt.	-Spindelöl, grün.

<u>Verbräuche in Liter/h.</u>

	bei 500 km/h	bei 800 km/h
in Bodennähe	1400	1670
in 6 km Höhe	850	1000
in 11 km Höhe	420 420	540

Tank capacities:	**Fuels:**
1. Aviation fuel: one fuselage tank, large 650 ltr ,or small 470 ltr, plus one fuselage reserve tank 170 ltr one wing tank, small 280 ltr medium 700 ltr	J 2; in place of J 2 any aviation fuel plus 5% oil may be used
2. Fuel for power plant: one tank in wing 30 ltr	Aviation starter fuel
3. Fuel for Riedel starter motor: one tank above power plant 2 ltr	Petrol-oil mixture 20 : 1; at temps. below 10°C aviation starter fuel
4. Lubricating oil (fill to 16 ltr): one tank on power plant 25 ltr	18 ltr U 1; if this not available, mix of 50% aviation oil S 3 and 50% hydraulic oil
5. Hydraulic oil: one tank I undercarriage well 5 ltr	Aviation hydraulic oil
6. Spindle oil: three shock absorbers approx. 2.5 ltr.	Spindle oil, green

Consumption in litres/h

	at 500 km/h	at 800 km/h
at ground level	1,400	1,670
at 6 km altitude	850	1,000
at 11 km altitude	420	540

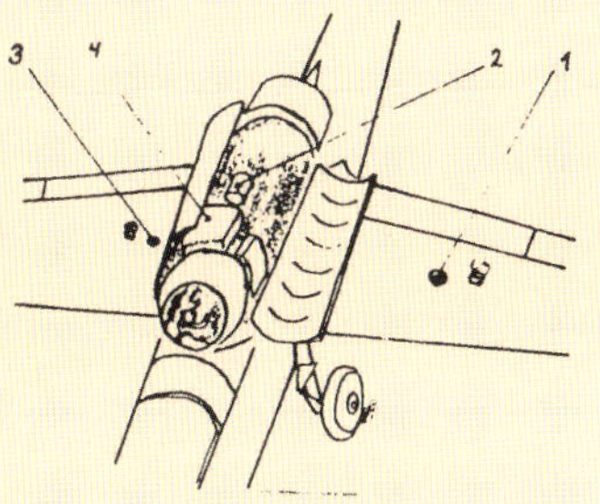

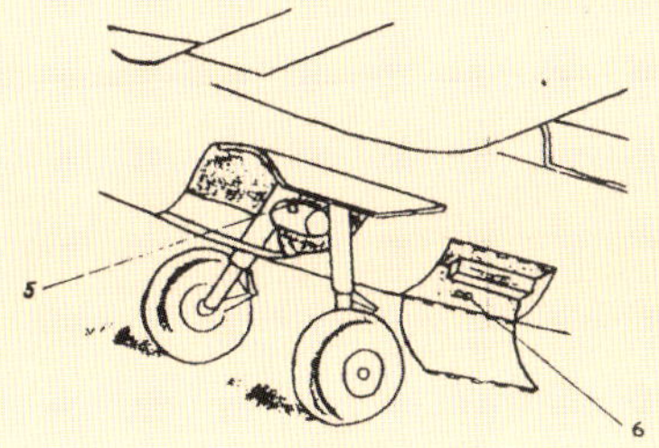

Betankung :

1. **Kraftstoff : J 2**
   Behälter im Rumpf und Tragflügel
   Einfüllverschraubung auf Tragflügeloberseite links.
2. **Kraftstoff für Riedel-Anlasser**
   Behälter vorn oben am Triebwerk, Inhalt 2 Liter,
   Einfüllverschraubung oben am Behälter.
3. **Anlaßkraftstoff für Triebwerk**
   Behälter im Tragflügel, Inhalt 25 Liter,
   Einfüllverschraubung auf Tragflügeloberseite rechts.
4. **Schmierstoff**
   Behälter am Triebwerk, Inhalt 25 Liter,
   nur 16 Liter betanken !
   Einfüllverschraubung oben am Behälter.
5. Drucköl
   Behälter im Fahrwerksraum hinter Spant 11
   Inhalt 5 Liter, Füllung 3.8 Liter.
   Einfüllverschraubung oben am Behälter.
6. Sauerstoff für Höhenatmeranlage
   150 kg/cm^2. Aussenbordanschluss im rechten Waffenraum
   hinter Spant 5.

Fuelling:

1. Fuel J 2
   Tanks in fuselage and wings
   Filler cap on upper surface left wing.
2. Fuel for Riedel starter motor
   Tank above power plant, capacity 2 ltr.
   Filler cap on top of tank.
3. Starter fuel for power plant
   Tank in wing, capacity 25 ltr.
   Filler cap on upper surface right wing.
4. Lubricating oil
   Tank on power plant, capacity 25 ltr., fill only to 16 ltr!
   Filler cap on top of tank
5. Hydraulic oil:
   Tank in undercarriage well behind Frame 11, capacity 5 ltr., fill to 3.8 ltr.
   Filler cap on top of tank.
6. Oxygen for high-altitude breathing apparatus
   150 kg/cm^2. External connection in right weapons bay behind Frame 5

II. Vorbereitungen zum Start.

1. Flugzeug gegen den Wind stellen, Bremsklötze vor die Laufräder legen, Handfeuerlöscher bereitstellen.
2. Verschlussdeckel von der Eintrittshaube des Triebwerkes abnehmen.
3. Flugzeugführersitz.

   und

   Seitensteuerpedale, nur am Boden einstellbar.
4. Zündkabel (Abreisstecker) für Starthilfe noch nicht einstecken.
5. Fallschirm in den Flugzeugführersitz legen.
6. Einsteigen, Kabinendach schliessen <u>und</u> verriegeln.
7. FT-Haube aufsetzen und anschliessen.
8. Schnappschalterhebel nach vorn auf Stellung "Umlauf".
9. Leistungshebel auf Stellung "Stop".
10. Brandhahnhebel auf Stellung "Zu".
11. Fallschirm anlegen.
12. Atemmaske aufsetzen, Dichtheit prüfen.
13. Fallschirmvorratsanzeiger "Voll".
14. Karabinerhaken der Selbsttrennstelle links in die Ringöse am Leistungshebelkasten einhaken.
15. Langen Fallschirmschlauch mit Atemmaske verbinden.
16. Kurzen Fallschirmschlauch mit Bordanlage kuppeln.
17. Sauerstoffanlage prüfen: Absperrventil öffnen, Sauerstoffanzeiger "Voll".
18. Durch Maske atmen, Lippen des Sauerstoffanzeigers bewegen sich.
19. Anschnallen, Kopfhaube anschliessen !

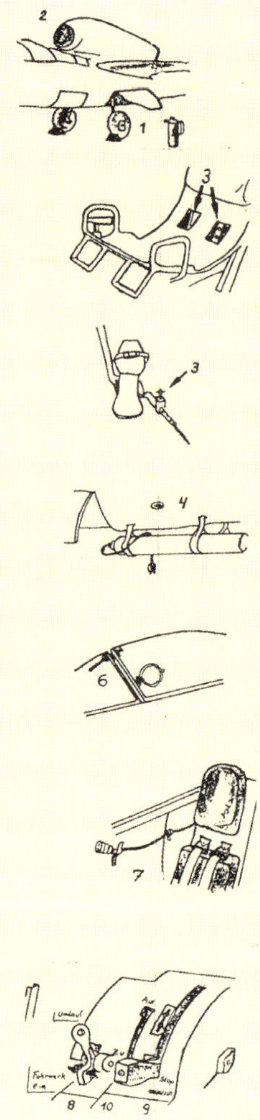

II. Preparations for Take-Off:

1. Park aircraft against the wind, place chocks in front of mainwheels, have manual fire extinguisher ready.
2. Remove engine intake cover.
3. Pilot's seat and rudder pedals adjustable only on ground.
4. Do not insert firing cable (break-plug) of take-off assistance rockets yet.
5. Place parachute pack in pilot's seat.
6. Board aircraft, close <u>and</u> lock cockpit canopy.
7. Put on helmet and plug in R/T lead.
8. Quick cut-out switch forward to 'Rotation' position.
9. Throttle lever to 'Stop' position.
10. Fuel cock lever to 'Closed' position.
11. Fasten parachute.
12. Put on oxygen mask, check air-tightness.
13. Reserve parachute indicator 'Full'.
14. Hook spring-hook of automatic disconnect into eyelet on throttle quadrant.
15. Connect long parachute tube to oxygen mask.
16. Connect short parachute tube to on-board oxygen supply.
17. Check oxygen supply: open top valve, oxygen contents indicator 'Full'.
18. Breathe through mask, membranes of indicator move.
19. Fasten harness/seat belt, connect helmet lead!

III. Anlassen.

a) Handanlassen

1. Selbstschalter für
   Bordsammler
   Schubdüse,Messanlage
   Kraftstoffpumpe e i n !

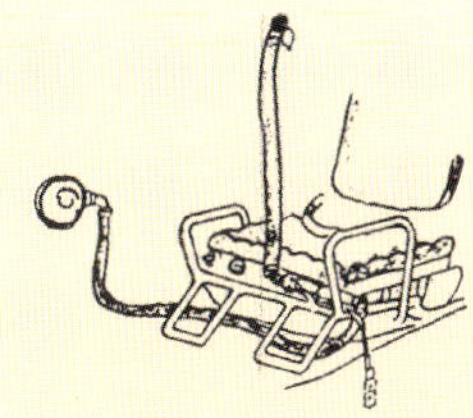

2. Schubdüsenschalter auf "S"

   Sofern Halbautomatik noch nicht eingebaut ist,muss auf Stellung "A" angelassen und erst nach ordnungsgemässem Zünden und gleichmässigem Turbinenlauf auf "S" geschaltet werden.

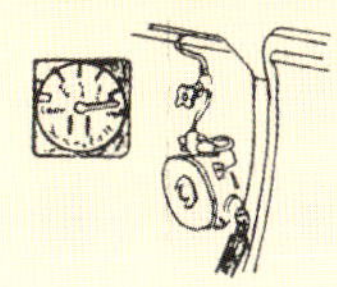

3. Anlasskippschalter etwa 2 sec (bei warmem Anlasser nur 1 sec., bei Kälte 2 x 3 sec.) nach vorn auf "Tupfen" drücken.

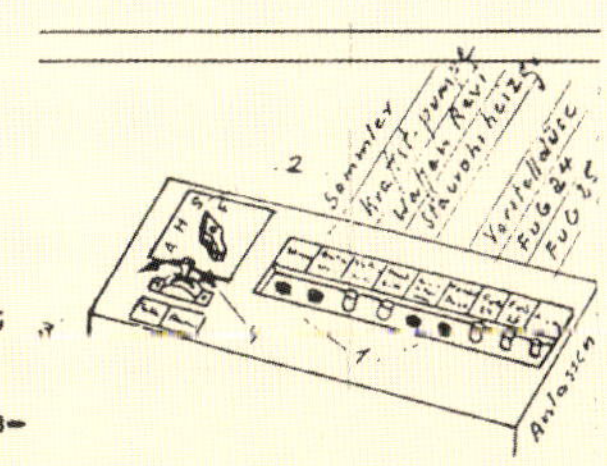

4. Anlasskippschalter nach hinten auf "Anlassen",gleichzeitig zieht der Wart das Anwerfseil rasch aufeinanderfolgend.Kleine innere Drehzahlskala gilt,solange Anlasskippschalter hinten.

5. Nach Anspringen des Riedel-Anlassers Brandhahnhebel "Auf".

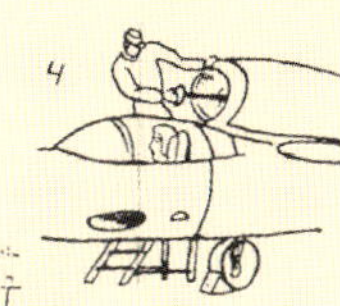

6. Bei 900 - 1100 U/min (kleine innere Drehzahlskala) Druckknopf im Leistungshebel drücken,2-3 sec. später Leistungshebel von "Stop" auf "Bodenleerlauf" vorschieben, bis Drehzahl aufholt. 1400 U/min leistet der Riedel allein.Aufholen über 1400 U/min ist Zeichen für erfolgte Zündung des Triebwerkes.Erfolgt dies nicht innerhalb 10 sec.,abstellen und Zündung und Anlasseinspritzung prüfen lassen.

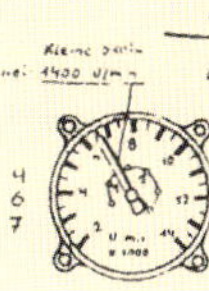

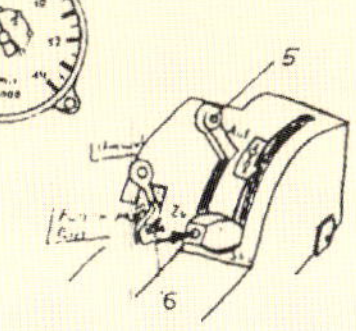

III. Starting:

a) Manual Start

1. Automatic switches for
   on-board battery
   jet nozzle, ignition/calibration
   fuel pump on!
2. Jet nozzle control switch to 'S'
   If semi-automatic setting device not yet installed, setting 'A' must be used for start and switched to 'S' only after successful ignition and simultaneous turbine start.
3. Push starter toggle switch forward to 'Ready' for approx. 2 secs. (if starter warm only 1 sec., if starter cold 2 x 3 secs.)
4. Pull starter toggle switch backward to 'Start', at same time mechanic pulls briskly on Riedel starter cable several times in quick succession. Small inner scale on rev. counter valid while starter toggle switch in rear position.
5. When Riedel starter motor catches, fuel cock lever to 'On'.
6. At 900 – 1,100 rpm (small inner scale) press button on throttle lever for 2 – 3 secs., then push throttle lever forward from 'Stop' to 'Ground idle' until revs begin to build up. Riedel starter alone produces 1,400 rpm. Build-up above 1,400 rpm indication of successful engine ignition. Should this not occur within 10 secs., switch off and have ignition and primer pump checked.

7. Bei 1800-2000 U/min Anlasskippschalter in Mittelstellung vorspringen lassen. Von jetzt ab gilt äussere Drehzahlskala. Triebwerk stellt sich auf Bodenleerlaufdrehzahl (3300 ± 200) ein.

8. Nach 2 - 3 Minuten abbremsen.

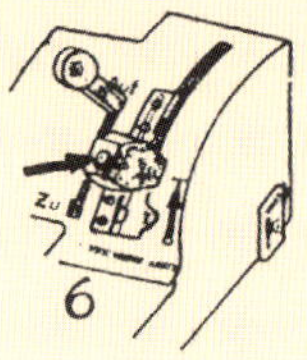

b) Anlassen mit Aussenbordstromquelle:

1. Stecker der Aussenbordstromquelle in den Aussenbordanschluss stecken und Aussenbordstromquelle einschalten.
2. Selbstschalter wie beim Handanlassen jedoch Sammler aus ! Anlasser ein !
3. Verstelldüse und Anlasskippschalter wie beim Handanlassen bedienen.
4. Riedel-Anlasser wird auf "Anlassen" elektrisch angeworfen. Nach dem Anspringen alles weitere wie beim Handanlassen.
5. Aussenbordstromquelle ausschalten, Stecker von Aussenbordanschluss abziehen
6. Selbstschalter für Sammler " e i n ".

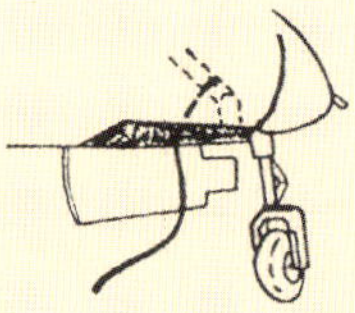

c) Anlassen mit Bordsammler.

Alle Vorgänge wie mit Aussenbordstromquelle, jedoch von Anfang an Sammler " e i n ".

Die Abgastemperatur darf beim Anlassen 750° nicht überschreiten, sonst Überhitzung im Turbinenteil. Triebwerk abstellen. Beim Triebwerksbrummen Leistungshebel auf Bodenleerlaufraste zurücknehmen.
Riedelanlasser innerhalb 15 Min. höchstens 60 sec. betätigen.
Anlassvorgang dauert 20-30 sec.
Anlasseinspritzpumpe darf höchstens 5 Min. ununterbrochen laufen.

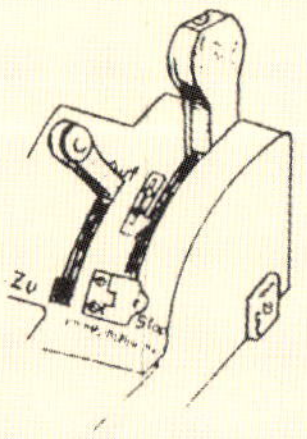

7. At 1,800 – 2,000 rpm allow starter toggle switch to jump forward into middle setting. Henceforth outer scale of rev. counter is valid. Engine accelerates under own power to ground idle (3,300 + 200 rpm).
8. After 2 – 3 minutes brake and check.

b) Starting with External Power Source

1. Insert plug of external power source into external power source socket and switch on.
2. Automatic switches as for manual start above, but Battery off! Starter motor on!
3. Operate jet nozzle control and starter toggle switch as for manual start.
4. Riedel starter motor switches to 'Start' electrically. After motor catches, continue as for manual start.
5. Switch off external power source, remove plug from external power source socket.
6. Automatic switch for battery 'On'.

c) Starting with on-board Battery

Proceed as for external power source start, but with battery switched to 'On' from the outset.

Exhaust temperatures at start must not exceed 750°, otherwise turbine overheats. Switch off engine. When engine noise reduced to just a rumble, pull throttle lever back to ground idle position.

Activate Riedel starter motor within 15 minutes for duration 60 secs. at most.

Start-up process lasts 20 – 30 secs.

Start-up primer pump must not run continuously for more than 5 minutes at most.

IV. A b b r e m s e n .

1. Sammler "aus". Kraftstoffbehälter-anzeige fällt auf 0 zurück.
2. Leistungshebel von Bodenleerlauf bis 6500 U/min zügig vorschieben,Behälter-anzeige spricht zwischen 4500 - 5000 U/min (Generatorzuschaltung) an.
3. Bei 6500 U/min Schubdüsenschalter in Stellung "S",Leistungshebel in Vollgas-Stellung. Übergang von Leerlauf auf Vollgasdrehzahl nicht unter 10 sec., zu plötzliche Beschleunigung der Drehzahl unzulässig.
4. Triebwerküberwachungsgeräte ablesen :

Drehzahl	9500 ± 100	U/min
bei kaltem Triebwerk kurzzeitig	9800	
Abgast mperatur max.	620°	C
Kraftstoffdruck bei 9500 U/min etwa	50	kg/cm^2
Schmierstoffdruck	6 - 7	kg/cm"
Generatorzuschaltung zwischen 4500 -	5000	U/min

IV. Braking and Checking:

1. Battery 'Off'. Fuel contents gauge drops back to 0.
2. Push throttle lever smoothly forward from ground idle to 6,500 rpm, gauge indicates between 4,500 – 5,000 rpm (generator hook-up).
3. At 6,500 rpm jet nozzle switch to 'S', throttle lever to full power. Transition from idle to full revs in not less than 10 secs., too sudden an increase in revolutions not permissible.
4. Check power plant control gauges:

Revolutions	9,500 ± 100 rpm
if power plant cold, briefly	9,800 rpm
Jet pipe temperature max.	620°C
Fuel pressure at 9,500 rpm approx.	50 kg/cm^2
Oil pressure	6 – 7 kg/cm^2
Generator hook-up between	4,500 – 5,000 rpm.

V. Start.

Allgemeines :

Ruder-Freigängigkeit prüfen.
Höhenflossentrimmung auf – 1°

Bordfunkanlage :

1. Selbstschalter für FuG 24 und FuG 25 eindrücken. Beide Geräte nach 1 min. betriebsbereit.
2. Bei grosser Luftfeuchtigkeit und Temperatur unter 0°C Selbstschalter für Staurohrheizung eindrücken. Sichtzeichen beobachten.

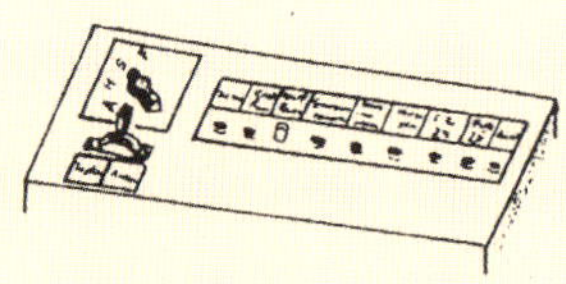

Geräte :

Fein-Grobhöhenanzeiger auf qfe bezw.qff.
Höhenatmer prüfen. Sauerstoff-Absperrventil zwei volle Umdrehungen öffnen.

Flugeigenschaften des Flugzeuges :

Keine Ausbrechneigung.Landung mit Bugfahrwerk in gleicher Weise wie bei Flugzeugen mit Spornfahrwerk einzuleiten. Ruderkräfte und Ruderwirkungen aufeinander abgestimmt,letztere für alle Flugzustände ausreichend.Sämtliche durch Fahrwerk,Landeklappen oder Gashebelbetätigung entstehenden Lastigkeitsänderungen sind beherrschbar. Überziehverhalten bei an-und zurückgestellten Landeklappen harmlos,bei vollständigem Überziehen Sackflug. Gleitwinkel bei der Landung mit voll angestellten Landeklappen und V_a= 200 km/h 1:4.

V. Take-Off:

General:

Check rudder for freedom of movement
Elevator trimming to – 1°

Radio Equipment:

1. Press in automatic switches for FuG 24 and FuG 25. Both sets ready for use after 1 min.
2. At high atmospheric humidity and temperatures below O°C press in automatic switch for pitot heating. Watch visual indicator.

High-altitude Equipment

Set fine-coarse altimeters to qfe and qff resp.
Check high-altitude breathing apparatus. Open oxygen cut-off valve two full turns.

Flying Characteristics of Aircraft

No torque. Landing approach with nosewheel to be carried out in same way as for aircraft with tailwheel. Rudder forces and rudder effects coordinated, latter sufficient for all flight conditions. All changes in trim resulting from undercarriage, flap or throttle movements are controllable. Signs of overload behaviour during extension/retraction of landing flaps harmless, total overloading will result in aircraft sinking. Angle of approach for landing with flaps fully extended and V_a = 200 km/h 1:4.

Achtung : Gleitwinkel im Sackflug steiler, Abfangen nicht mehr möglich, Folge : Bruch !

Abflug :

Landeklappen in "Startstellung" anstellen (etwa 7 Pumpenhübe). Wenn diese Anstellung erreicht ist (vergl. weisse Strichmarkierung), Handpumpengriff durch Drehen nach rechts arretieren.

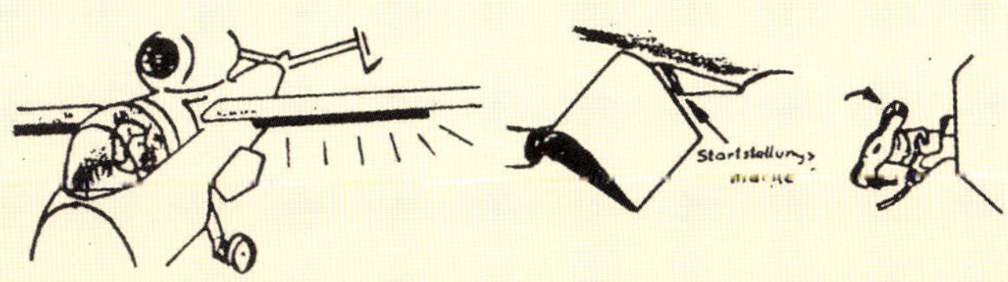

Warning: Angle of approach is steeper if aircraft sinking, recovery no longer possible, result: Crash!

Prior to Take-Off:

Set landing flaps to 'Take-off position' (approx. 7 strokes of pump). Once this position has been reached (check against white line marking), lock handle of flap manual control pump by turning to right.

Start :

1. Schubdüsenschalter auf "S".
2. Drehzahl max.9800 U/min,nach 2 min. 9500 ± 100 U/min.
3. Flugzeug in Startrichtung rollen, Bremsen betätigen.
4. Rollstrecke bei Windstille auf Betonbahn ca.650 m,auf Grasnarbe etwa 10 % mehr.Für kurzen Start kann Höhensteuer ab V_a = 180 km/h stark gezogen werden.
5. Abhebegeschwindigkeit normal 190 km/h.
6. Nach dem Abheben Fahrwerk einfahren, Schnappschalterhebel nach hinten in Stellung "Fahrwerk ein". Hebel springt selbsttätig in Stellung "Umlauf" zurück.
7. Beim Einfahren V_a= 350 km/h nicht überschreiten.
8. Landeklappen zurückstellen,hierzu Handpumpengriff in tiefste Stellung drücken und nach links drehen. Bei alter Bauausführung Drehsinn umgekehrt.

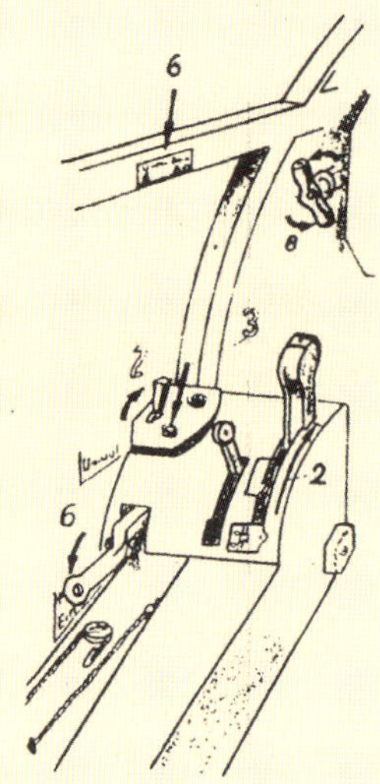

Mit Starthilfe :

1. Zeichen "fertig",Wart schliesst Zündkabel an.
2. Beim Anrollen Kippschalter auf dem Auslöseschaltkasten auf "Ein".Schaltzeichen zeigt weisses Feld.
3. Bei 100 bis 150 km/h Druckknopf drücken. Brenndauer 6 sec.bei 500 kg Schub je Gerät.

   Lastigkeit des Starthilfenschuhes erleichtert das Abheben.
4. Nach dem Abbrennen Geräte durch Ziehen des Seilzuges (hinter dem linken Bedientisch) abwerfen.
5. Nach dem Abwerfen Kippschalter auf dem Auslöseschaltkasten auf "Aus",Schaltzeichen schwarz.

Take-Off:

1. Jet nozzle switch to 'S'.
2. Revs max. 9,800 rpm, after 2 mins. 9,500 + 100 rpm.
3. Taxi aircraft into direction of take-off, apply brakes.
4. Length of take-off run on concrete runway with no wind approx. 650 m, on grass surfaces about 10% more. For short take-offs elevators can be fully employed from V_a = 180 km/h.
5. Normal lift-off speed 190 km/h.
6. After lift-off retract undercarriage, move snap-switch lever backward into 'Gear Up' position, lever automatically jumps back into 'Rotation' position.
7. During gear retraction do not exceed V_a = 350 km/h.
8. Retract flaps by pushing manual control pump into lowest position and turning to left. In early variants, direction reversed.

With Rocket Take-Off Assistance:

1. Hand signal 'Ready', mechanic connects ignition cable.
2. While taxiing, toggle switch on firing panel to 'On'. Indicator shows white.
3. At 100 to 150 km/h press firing button. Burning period 6 secs. at 500 kg thrust per rocket. Trim of rocket shoe assists lift-off.
4. After burn-out jettison rockets by pulling cable (behind left console).
5. After jettisoning, toggle switch on firing panel to 'Off', indicator black.

VI. S t e i g f l u g .

Schubdüsenschalter bis 8 km Höhe auf "S".
über 8 km Höhe auf "H" schalten.
Drehzahl hierbei 9500 ± U/min.
Volleistungs-Geschwindigkeit des besten Steigens um
V_a = 380 km/h.

VII. Reise-und Schnellflug.

1. Schubdüsenstellungen :

H = normal über 8 km Höhe.
S = normal unter 8 km Höhe.
F = Schnellflug von 0 bis 4 km
Höhe bis V_a > 650 km/h.
Bei eingebauter Halbautomatik entfällt die Stellung "S" durch direkte Kupplung mit dem Leistungshebel.
Achtung: wenn V_a = 650 km/h unterschritten wird, Schubdüse wieder zurückschalten auf "S".

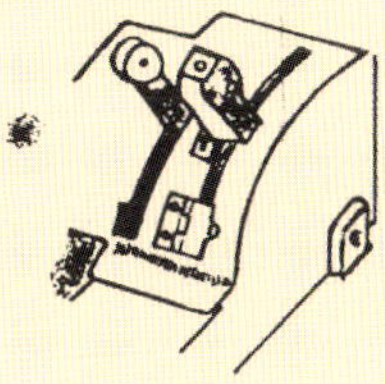

2. Betriebsdrehzahl normal 9500 U/min, Veränderung des Schubes durch Drehzahländerung. Drehzahl nicht unter 6500 U/min zurücknehmen, da Triebwerk sonst ausgeht.

3. Triebwerksüberwachungsgeräte beobachten :

Kraftstoffdruck in Bodennähe bei 9500 U/min	50 kg/cm^2
Abgastemperatur	400 – 600° C

Steigt Temperatur über 600°C, Bedienungshebel zurücknehmen. Bei trotzdem weiter steigender Temperatur weiter drosseln und evtl. Triebwerk abstellen, besonders wenn Kraftstoff steigt und Drehzahl sinkt. Störung am Triebwerk.

VI. Climbing:

Jet nozzle switch:	up to 8 km altitude on 'S'.
	above 8 km altitude switch to 'H'.
Revs during climb:	9,500 + 100 rpm.

Full-power speed for best rate of climb about V_a = 380 km/h.

VII. Cruise and High-Speed Flight:

1. **Jet nozzle settings:**
   'H' = normal above 8 km altitude.
   'S' = normal below 8 km altitude.
   'F' = high-speed flight from 0 to 4 km altitude up to max. V_a = 650 km/h.
   If semi-automatic system installed, the 'S' setting is discarded and replaced by a direct link to the throttle lever.
   Warning: if speed falls below V_a = 650 km/h, return jet nozzle setting to 'S'.
2. **Operating revolutions** normal 9,500 rpm, alterations in revs affect thrust. Do not reduce revs to below 6,500 rpm, otherwise engine goes out.
3. **Watch engine monitoring instruments:**

Fuel pressure at ground level at 9,500 rpm	50 kg/cm^2
Exhaust temperature	400 – 600°C

If temperature rises above 600°C, ease off throttle. If temperature still continues to rise, throttle back even more and if necessary switch off engine, particularly if fuel pressure rising and revs falling. Engine defect.

4. Behälterzuschaltung:

Einspritzpumpe des Triebwerks erhält durch eine Behälterpumpe den Kraftstoff aus dem Rumpfbehälter zugeführt. Kraftstoff aus dem Tragflügel fliesst in den Rumpfbehälter nach. Inhaltskontrolle des Rumpfbehälters: Vorratsanzeiger an der Flugzeugführergerätetafel. Flugzeiten überwachen,da Anzeige ungenau sein kann.

5. Durch Drosseln des Triebwerks wird an Reichweite wenig,an Flugzeit viel gewonnen.

Bordfunkanlage FuG 24

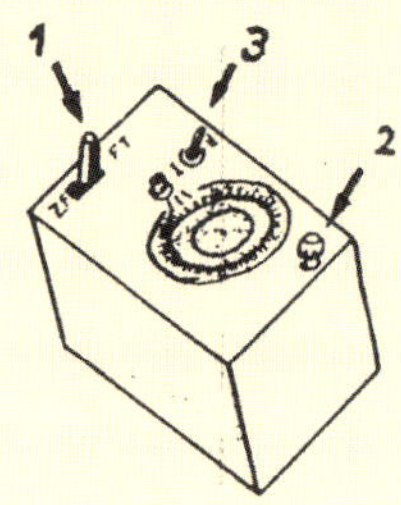

A. Sprechverkehr (FT -Betrieb):

1. Schalter am Empfänger auf "FT".
2. Empfangbetrieb nach Abstimmen auf markierte Frequenz.Hierbei Knopf für Skalenbeleuchtung auf schmalen oder breiten Leuchtsektor drehen.
3. Am Empfänger Sendefrequenz "I" (Betriebsfrequenz) oder "II" Ausweichfrequenz) wählen.
4. Zum Senden Sprechknopf vorn am Steuerknüppel drücken.

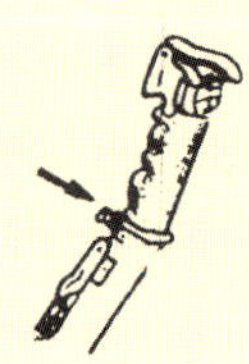

4. Fuel system:

Fuel from the fuselage tank is fed by pump to the fuel injection pump of the engine. The fuselage tank is replenished from the wing tanks.

Contents control of fuselage tank:

Amount of fuel in fuselage tank indicated by fuel contents gauge on instrument panel. Monitor flying times as gauge can be inaccurate.

5. Throttling back the engine offers little increase in range, but adds considerably to flying time.

FuG 24 on-board radio

A. Communications (R/T Traffic):

1. Turn receiver switch to 'FT'.
2. Communications received via pre-set frequency. Select dial illumination by turning knob to narrow or broad light sector.
3. On receiver box select transmission frequency 'I' (operating frequency) or 'II' (alternative frequency).
4. To transmit press button on front of control column.

B. Zielflug (ZF-Betrieb):

1. Abstimmen des Empfängers auf markierte Frequenz.

2. FT-Sprechverkehr mit Bodenstelle aufnehmen und Funkfeuer oder Dauerton anfordern. Bodenstelle schaltet daraufhin Funkfeuer ein

3. Schalter am Empfänger auf "ZF".Zeiger am AFN 2 (Anzeigegerät für Funknavigation) schlägt bei Kurzabweichung aus (in der Kopfhaube schwingender ton hörbar). Steht Kurzzeiger rechts, steht Flugzeug rechts vom Kurs und umgekehrt.

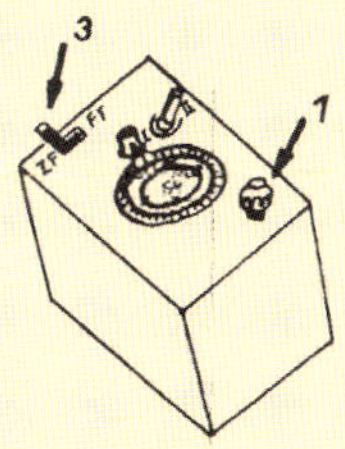

4. Kurs berichtigen,bis Kurzzeiger in Mittelstellung.

5. Seitenbestimmung: kurze Kursänderung rechts ergibt Rechtsausschlag am Gerät.Achtung: Ergibt Kursänderung rechts (links) einen Zeigerausschlag links (rechts),so erfolgt Abflug vom Sender! Das AFN 2 ist ein Anzeige-und kein Kommando-Gerät.

6. In Stellung "ZF" ist Empfang über Peilrahmen nur auf 2/3 Reichweite gegenüber Stellung "FT" möglich.
   In Stellung "ZF" arbeitet bei gedrücktem Sprechknopf der Sender jedoch mit voller Reichweite über die Leitwerksantenne.

B. Homing (ZF Traffic):

1. Set receiver to marked frequency.
2. Contact ground control via R/T and request radio beacon or continuous radio signal. Ground control switches on beacon.
3. Turn receiver switch to 'ZF'. Indicator on AFN 2 (radio-navigation indicator) signals any deviation from course (oscillating tone audible in earphones). If indicator points to right, aircraft is to right of correct course, and vice versa.
4. Adjust course until indicator in central position.
5. Determining course: a brief alteration of course to the right results in the indicator showing right. Warning: If a course alteration to the right (or left) sends the indicator to the left (or right), then the aircraft is on a reciprocal course and flying away from the transmitter! The AFN 2 is an indicator and not a command instrument.
6. At setting 'ZF' receiving range via the loop antenna is only two-thirds of that when set to 'FT'.

   However, if the transmit button on the control column is pressed while at setting 'ZF', the transmitter is effective at full range via the tail antenna.

FuG 25 a

1. Am Bediengerät BG 25 a befohlene Schlüsselkennung 1 oder 2 wählen.

2. In Schalterstellungen 1 und 2 leuchtet nach Erfassung durch Funkmessgerät Kontrollampe im Takt der abgestrahlten Kennung auf.

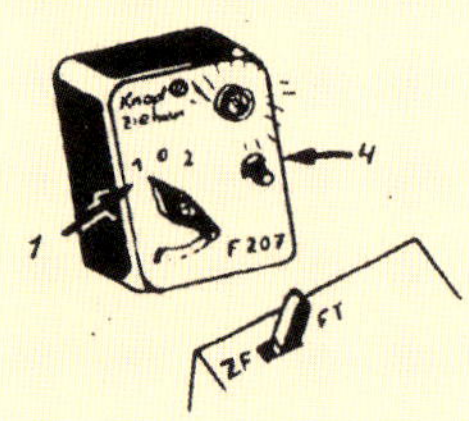

3. In Mittelstellung "0" wird bei Erfassung keine Kennung abgestrahlt.

4. Bei Drücken des Prüfknopfes leuchtet Kontrollampe im Tackte der abgestrahlten Kennung auf. (Prüfknopf nur beim FuG 25 a rote Serie in Betrieb. Funkwart fragen !).

5. Die Durchführung des erforderlichen Sprechverkehrs erfolgt über FuG 24. Sonderbefehle beachten !

FuG 25a

1. On the BG 25a control box set identification key to 1 or 2 as ordered.
2. When switched to positions 1 or 2, control lamp illuminates upon detection by ground radar and flashes in time to the signals radiated.
3. If aircraft detected while control box set to middle position 'O', no signal radiated.
4. Pressing the test button causes the control lamp to illuminate in time to the signals radiated. (Test button fitted only to red series FuG 25a. Ask radio mechanic!).
5. Any necessary R/T exchanges made via FuG 24. Listen out for special orders!

Schusswaffenanlage A- 1.

Munition : Je Waffe 50 Schuss,reicht für 6 Feuerstösse von etwa 1 sec.Dauer. Waffen sind durchgeladen.

1. Selbstschalter "Waffe" eindrücken.
2. Schiesshebel nach vorn umlegen.
3. Zum Schiessen A-Knopf drücken.
4. Bei Ausfall der Waffen durchladen, 2 sec.B-Knopf drücken.
5. Von neuem schiessen.

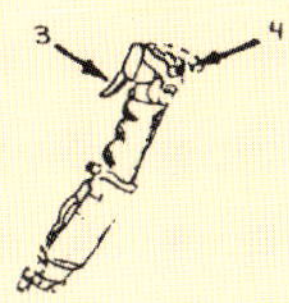

Schusswaffenanlage A - 2

Munition : Je Waffe 120 Schuss,reicht für 10 Feuerstösse von etwa 1 sec.Dauer.

1. Selbstschalter "Waffe" eindrücken,Waffen laden durch, Schauzeichen leuchten auf.
2. Schiesshebel nach vorn umlegen.
3. A-Knopf (Schiesshebel) drücken.
4. Bei Ausfall der Waffen Schiesshebel loslassen.Waffen laden, dann automatisch durch.
5. Von neuem schiessen.

Weapons System A-1.

Ammunition: 50 rounds per gun, sufficient for 6 bursts of fire each of approx. 1 sec. duration. Weapons are charged.

1. Press automatic switch 'Weapons'.
2. Push firing lever forward.
3. Press trigger (A-Knopf) to fire.
4. If weapons jam, recharge by pressing gun charging button (*B-Knopf*) for 2 secs.
5. Open fire again.

Weapons System A-2.

Ammunition: 120 rounds per gun, sufficient for 10 bursts of fire each of approx. 1 sec. duration.

1. Press automatic switch 'Weapons', weapons are charged, indicator lamps illuminate.
2. Push firing lever forward.
3. Press A-Knopf (trigger) to fire.
4. If weapons jam, release trigger. Weapons will recharge automatically.
5. Open fire again.

VIII. Höhenflug.

1. Sauerstoff-Absperrventil öffnen.
2. Spätestens ab 4000 m Flughöhe Atemmaske aufsetzen. Maske und Kleiderklammer müssen festsitzen. Zuführungsschläuche am Sitzfallschirm nicht abquetschen ! Schnelltrennstellen auf festen Sitz prüfen.
3. O_2-Wächter beobachten. Anzeige im Rythmus der Atmung.
4. Bei erhöhtem Atemwiderstand Druckknopf am Höhenatmer einige Male kurzzeitig drücken ("Sauerstoffdusche").
5. Über 8 km Höhe Schubdüse auf "H",
6. Bei einem Sauerstoffrestdruck zwischen 1/4 und Leer Höhen unter 4000 m aufsuchen. Atemmaske bei vorübergehendem Aufenthalt in geringeren Höhen nicht absetzen, sie friert sonst ein und ist nicht mehr verwendungsfähig.
7. Nach Beendigung der Sauerstoffatmung Absperrventil schliessen.

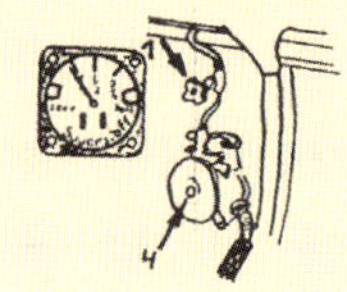

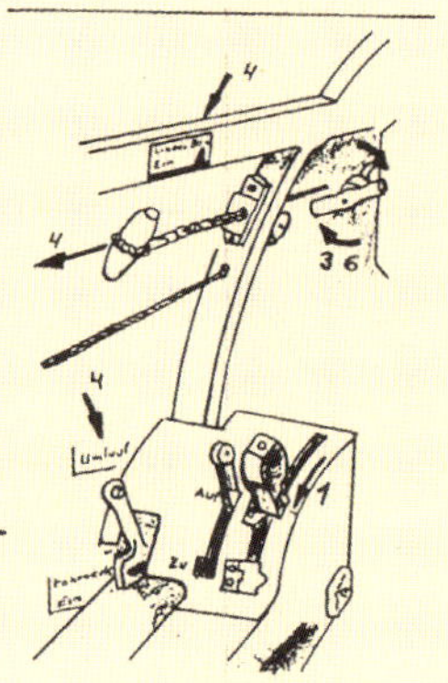

IX. Gleitflug u. Landung.

1. Zum Gleitflug Leistungshebel an Flugleerlaufraste (6500 U/min) zurückstellen. Erst beim Anschweben zur Landung unter 1 km darf auf Bodenleerlauf (3500 U/min) zurückgegangen werden.
2. Schubdüsenschalter in Stellung "S".
3. Landeklappen in "Startstellung" bei 250 bis 300 km/h anstellen. Ist Startstellung erreicht, Handpumpengriff durch Rechts drehen arretieren.
4. Fahrwerk ausfahren unter 350 km/h. Hierzu Fahrwerksentrastungsgriff ziehen. Schnappschalterhebel muss auf "Umlauf" stehen.

VIII. High-Altitude Flight:

1. Open oxygen cut-off valve.
2. Put on oxygen mask at 4,000 m altitude at latest. Mask and clip must fit securely. Make sure seat parachute does not squeeze oxygen supply tube! Test quick-release snaps for secure fit.
3. Check oxygen supply monitor. Indicator in rhythm with breathing.
4. If increased resistance to breathing experienced, briefly press button on oxygen supply a few times ('Oxygen shower').
5. Above 8 km altitude jet nozzle setting to 'H'.
6. If oxygen gauge shows between one quarter and empty, descend to altitude of less than 4,000 m. Do not remove oxygen mask during temporary flight at lower altitudes as it will freeze up and be no longer usable.
7. When oxygen no longer required close cut-off valve.

IX. Gliding and Landing:

1. To glide pull throttle lever back to flight idling position (6,500 rpm). Ground idling (3,500 rpm) may only be selected when approaching to land at a height of less then 1 km.
2. Jet nozzle setting to 'S'.
3. Lower flaps to 'Take-off position' at 250 to 300 km/h. Once selected, turn handle of manual control pump to right to lock.
4. Lower undercarriage when speed less than 350 km/h by pulling unlocking handle. Snap-action switch must be at 'Rotation'.

5. Anfliegen mit etwa V_a = 250 km/h, Landeklappen noch in Startstellung.
6. Nach Eindrehen in Landerichtung Landeklappen bei 200 km/h in "Landestellung" anstellen. Nach erreichter Anstellung Handpumpengriff durch Drehen nach rechts arretieren.
7. Lastigkeitsänderungen durch Trimmung ausgleichen, Höhenflossentrimmung etwa -0.5°.
8. Vor dem Abfangen bei laufendem Triebwerk V_a= 190 km/h, bei stehendem Triebwerk V_a= 200 km/h nicht unterschreiten.

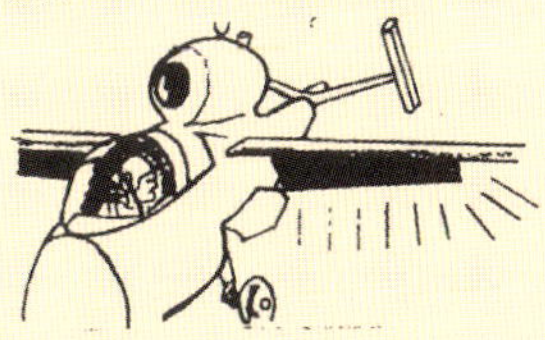

9. Flugzeug muss beim Aufsetzen voll abgefangen sein. Aufsetzen erfolgt nur auf dem Hauptfahrwerk.
10. Nach dem Aufsetzen möglichst lange mit angehobenem Bugrad ausrollen.
11. Bremsen erst nach Aufsetzen des Bugrades. Nicht mehr bremsen, als nötig.
    Achtung: Längsneigung steuern, damit Rumpfende nicht aufschlägt !

12. Schiesshebel in Ruhestellung.
13. Landeklappen nach dem Ausrollen einfahren.
14. FT - Geräte bleiben bis zum Ausrollen eingeschaltet.

5. Approach at approx. V_a = 250 km/h, flaps still in take-off position.
6. After turning onto final approach for landing reset flaps to 'Landing position' at 200 km/h. Once selected, turn handle of manual control pump to right again to relock.
7. Use trim to compensate for changes in flight attitude, elevator trimming tabs approx. -0.5°.
8. Prior to flattening out do not let speed fall below V_a = 190 km/h with engine running, or V_a = 200 km/h with engine stopped.
9. Aircraft must be fully flattened out upon touchdown. Touchdown to be made on mainwheels only.
10. After touchdown continue to roll for as long as possible with nosewheel raised.
11. Brake only after nosewheel is on the ground. Do not brake more than necessary.
12. Firing lever off.
13. Retract flaps when taxiing completed.
14. R/T remains on while taxiing.

X. Abstellen. (J 2 – Betrieb)

1. Triebwerk auf über 6000 U/min beschleunigen.
2. Leistungshebel in Stellung "Stop".
3. Brandhahnhebel "Zu".
4. Bordsammler und eingedrückte Selbstschalter ausschalten.

XI . Verhalten in Sonderfällen .

A. Anlassen im Fluge. Nur unter 4 km Höhe möglich.

1. Leistungshebel in Stellung "Stop".
2. Schleppdrehzahl des Triebwerks herabsetzen (1500 bis 2000 U/min., entspr. V_a = 300 bis 400 km/h).
3. Selbstschalter für Bordsammler, Kraftstoffpumpe, Schubdüse und Messanlage eingedrückt, alle anderen ausschalten.
4. Schubdüsenschalter in Stellung "A", bei Halbautomatik auf Stellung "S".
5. Brandhahnhebel "Auf".
6. Druckknopf in Leistungshebel drücken und nach etwa 3 sec. Leistungshebel je nach Flughöhe auf Bodenleerlauf 3500 U/min oder Flugleerlauf 6500 U/min verschieben.
7. Nach dem Anspringen des Triebwerkes Knopf am Leistungshebel loslassen.
8. Leistungshebel auf 6500 U/min bezw. so einstellen, dass Abgastemperatur 750°C nicht übersohreitet.
9. Nach dem Erreichen gleichförmiger Drehzahl Schubdüsenschalter auf "S" schalten.

B. Durchstarten :

1. Schubdüsenschalter muss auf "S" stehen.
2. Zügig Volleistung geben.
3. Fahrwerk kann eingefahren bleiben.
4. Wieder normal anfliegen und zur Landung ansetzen.

X. Switching Off (J 2 Operation):

1. Run engine up to more than 6,500 rpm.
2. Throttle lever to 'Stop' position.
3. Fuel cock lever 'Closed'.
4. Switch off battery and all automatic switches.

XI. Procedures in Special Circumstances:

A. Restarting the Engine in Flight. Only possible at altitudes of less than 4 km.

1. Throttle lever to 'Stop' position.
2. Reduce drag revolutions of engine (1,500 to 2,000 rpm, equivalent to V_a = 300 to 400 km/h).
3. Press automatic switches for battery, fuel pump, jet nozzle and ignition calibration, switch all others off.
4. Jet nozzle switch to position 'A', if semi-automatic to position 'S'.
5. Fuel cock lever to 'Open'.
6. Press button on throttle lever and, depending upon altitude, after approx. 3 secs. push throttle lever forward either to ground-idling 3,500 rpm or flight-idling 6,500 rpm.
7. After engine has fired release button on throttle lever.
8. Throttle lever to 6,500 rpm or to a setting that does not raise exhaust temperature above 750°C.
9. After reaching uniform revolutions set jet nozzle switch to 'S'.

B. Overshooting:

1. Jet nozzle switch must be on 'S'.
2. Quickly and smoothly to full power.
3. Undercarriage can remain retracted.
4. Resume normal approach and come in to land.

C. Notlandung :

1. Gut festschnallen.
2. Vor allem Landeklappen anstellen.
3. Fahrwerk nur ausfahren, wenn Bodenverhältnisse des Notlandeplatzes zuverlässig eine bruchfreie Landung versprechen. Sonst Bauchlandung.
4. Brandhahnhebel auf "Zu".
5. Leistungshebel auf "Stop".
6. Selbstschalter für Sammler ausschalten.
7. Glashaube aufklappen, jedoch nur bei wahrscheinlicher Bruchlandung.
8. Radlandung normal ansetzen. Bei Bruchlandung tadellos schiebefrei aufsetzen und Flugzeug möglichst lange geradeaus und horizontal halten ! Keine Sackfluglandung ! Bodenwellen im Ausschweben ausfliegen.
9. Bei Bruchgefahr nach dem Aufsetzen Füsse auf Steigbügel.
10. Erst nach Stillstand losschnallen und aussteigen.

D. Fallschirmabsprung.

1. Fluggeschwindigkeit nach Möglichkeit durch Hochziehen verringern.
2. Mikrophon-Trennstelle am Halse lösen.
3. Brechkupplung trennen.
4. Füsse auf Steigbügel stellen !
5. Kabinendach wie beim normalen Ausstieg aufklappen.
6. Sicherungshebel am Sitz auf der rechten Seite nach vorne umlegen.
7. Beide Hände auf Stützbügel des Sitzes stützen und Kopf am Polster anlegen. Ellbogen gegen den Körper drücken. Atemmaske über 4000 m aufbehalten.

C. Emergency Landing:

1. Tighten harness.
2. Above all, deploy flaps.
3. Lower undercarriage only if terrain of intended emergency landing site promises a crash-free landing. Otherwise belly landing.
4. Fuel cock lever to 'Closed'.
5. Throttle lever to 'Stop'.
6. Switch off battery automatic switch.
7. Open canopy, but only if crash landing likely.
8. For wheels-down landing approach as normal. If crash landing, set down without sideslipping and hold aircraft horizontal and in straight line for as long as possible! Avoid landing heavily! Avoid uneven ground by gliding.
9. If danger of crash after touchdown, place feet on stirrups.
10. Do not unfasten harness and exit cockpit until aircraft stationary.

D. Bailing Out (Ejecting):

1. If possible reduce airspeed by climbing.
2. Disconnect throat microphone at separation point.
3. Separate break-connection.
4. Place feet on stirrups!
5. Open canopy as for normal exit.
6. Push forward safety lever on right-hand side of seat.
7. Place both hands firmly on seat support handles and press head against headrest. Press elbows tightly into sides. Keep oxygen mask on if above 4,000 m.

8. Mit den Fingern der rechten Hand Abzug-
griff an den Stützbügel heranziehen.
9. Nach erfolgter Katapultierung losschnallen und
Sitz fortschleudern.
10. Fallschirm öffnen.
11. Atemmaske unter 4000 m abnehmen.

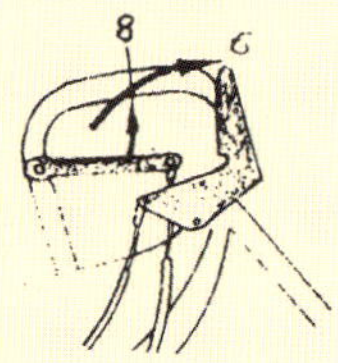

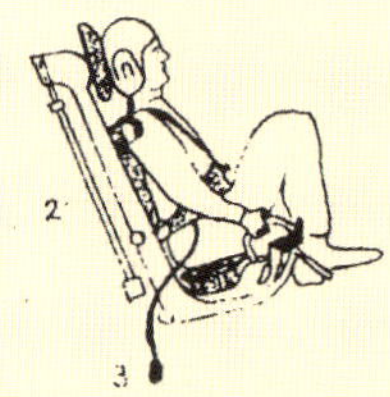

XII. Werkstattflug.

A. Wenn Flugzeug hängt :
Im Fluge bei losgelassenem Steuer Steuerknüppelausschlag und Hängen in Kugelbreiten feststellen.
Am Boden bügeln ! 1 Kugelbreite entspricht etwa 1 mm an der Hinterkante beider Querruderbügelkanten.

B. Höhenruder-Bügelkanten auf Mitte stellen. Flossentrimmung soll bei V_a = 500 km/h in etwa 1000 m Höhe zwischen + 1° und + 2° stehen. 1 Trimmteilstück entspricht 1° Flossenwinkel.

C. Wenn Flugzeug dreht, Seitentrimmung im Fluge nachstellen und feststellen. Marke braucht nicht auf Mitte zu stehen. Reicht Trimmbereich nicht aus, Federkörper im Rumpfende nachstellen lassen.
Bügelkanten an Seitenrudern nur dann bügeln, wenn Steuerkräfte einseitig. Bügelkanten nach links, Kräfte nach links werden grösser.

8. With the fingers of the right hand pull ejection trigger on seat support handle.
9. After successful ejection unfasten harness and push seat away.
10. Open parachute.
11. Remove oxygen mask below 4,000 m.

XII. Works Test Flight:

A. If aircraft rolls:
Take hands off control column in flight to determine amount of play in stick and movement of ball in turn-and-bank indicator.
Adjust trim on ground! The width of one ball corresponds to approx. 1 mm on rear edge of both aileron trimming tabs.

B. Centralize rudder trimming tabs. At V_a = 500 km/h at height of approx. 1,000 m fin trim should be between +1° and +2°. 1 trimming part strip corresponds to 1° fin angle.

C. If aircraft pitches: determine and adjust side trim in flight. Indicator need not be centralized. If trim range alone is insufficient, have spring mechanism in tail cone adjusted on ground.
Adjust rudder trimming tabs only if trim is asymmetrical. Trimming tab to left, forces to left become greater.

Appendix 2 Heinkel He 162A-2

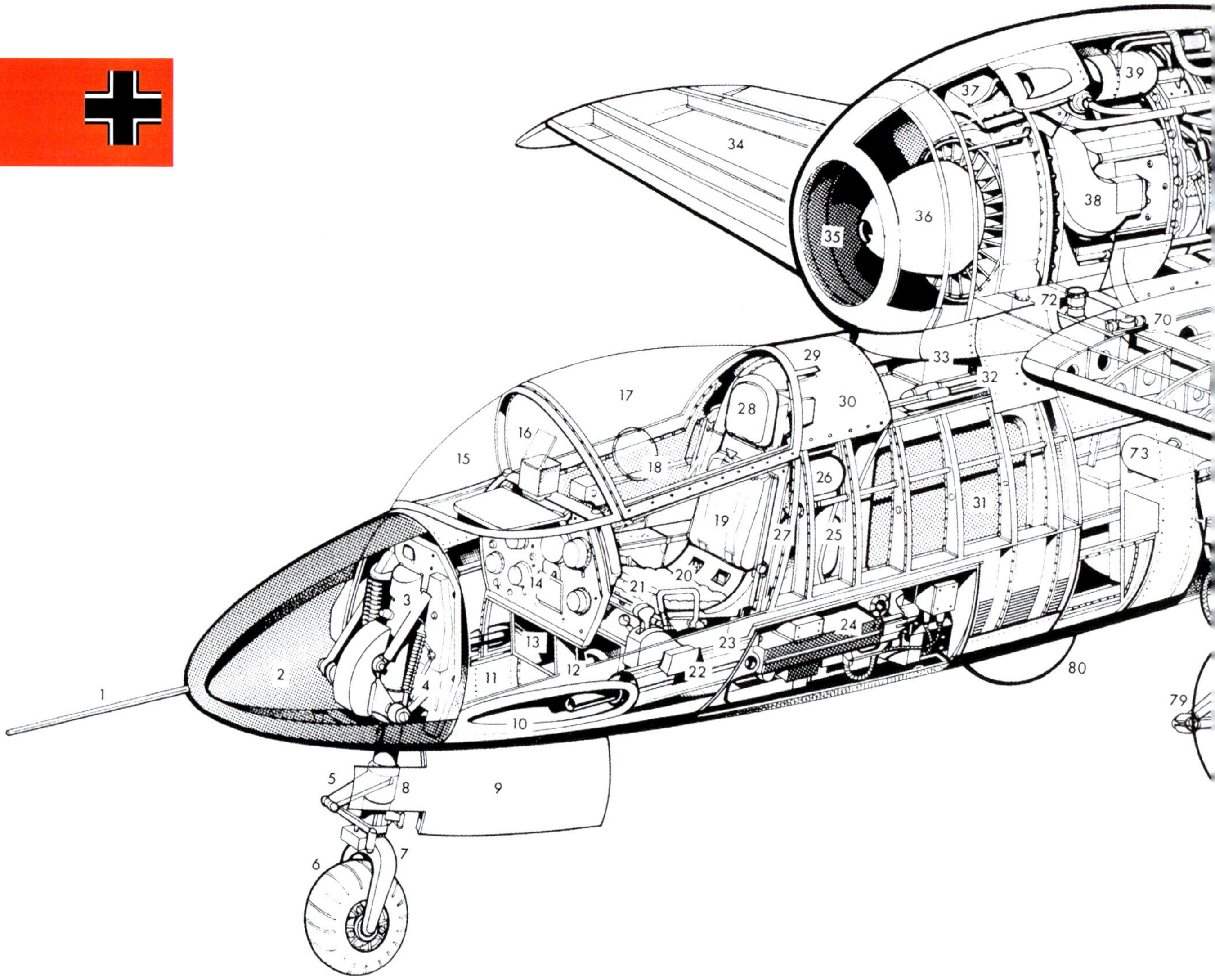

Heinkel He 162A-2

1 Pitot tube
2 Moulded plywood nose cap
3 Nosewheel retraction mechanism
4 Spring-loaded nosewheel extension assembly
5 Shock absorber scissor
6 Nosewheel
7 Nosewheel fork
8 Nosewheel leg
9 Nosewheel door
10 Gun trough
11 Nosewheel well
12 Rudder pedal
13 Window panel (visual nosewheel retraction check)
14 Wooden instrument panel
15 One-piece moulded windscreen
16 Revi 16G gunsight (interchangeable with the Revi 16B)
17 Jettisonable hinged clear-vision canopy
18 Ventilation disc
19 Heinkel cartridge-operated ejection seat
20 Ejection seat handle grip
21 Throttle control quadrant
22 Retractable entry step
23 Gun barrel shroud in cockpit wall
24 Port 20-mm MG 151 cannon
25 Ammunition chute
26 Main oxygen supply bottle (2 litre/3.5 pint capacity)
27 Explosive charge ejector rail
28 Pilot's headrest
29 Canopy hinge
30 Ammunition box behind cockpit (120 rounds per gun)
31 Flexible main tank (695 litre/153 Imp gal capacity)
32 Fuel lines
33 FuG 25a IFF radio compartment
34 Beech plywood wing skinning
35 Jet intake
36 Riedel two-stroke starter motor bullet

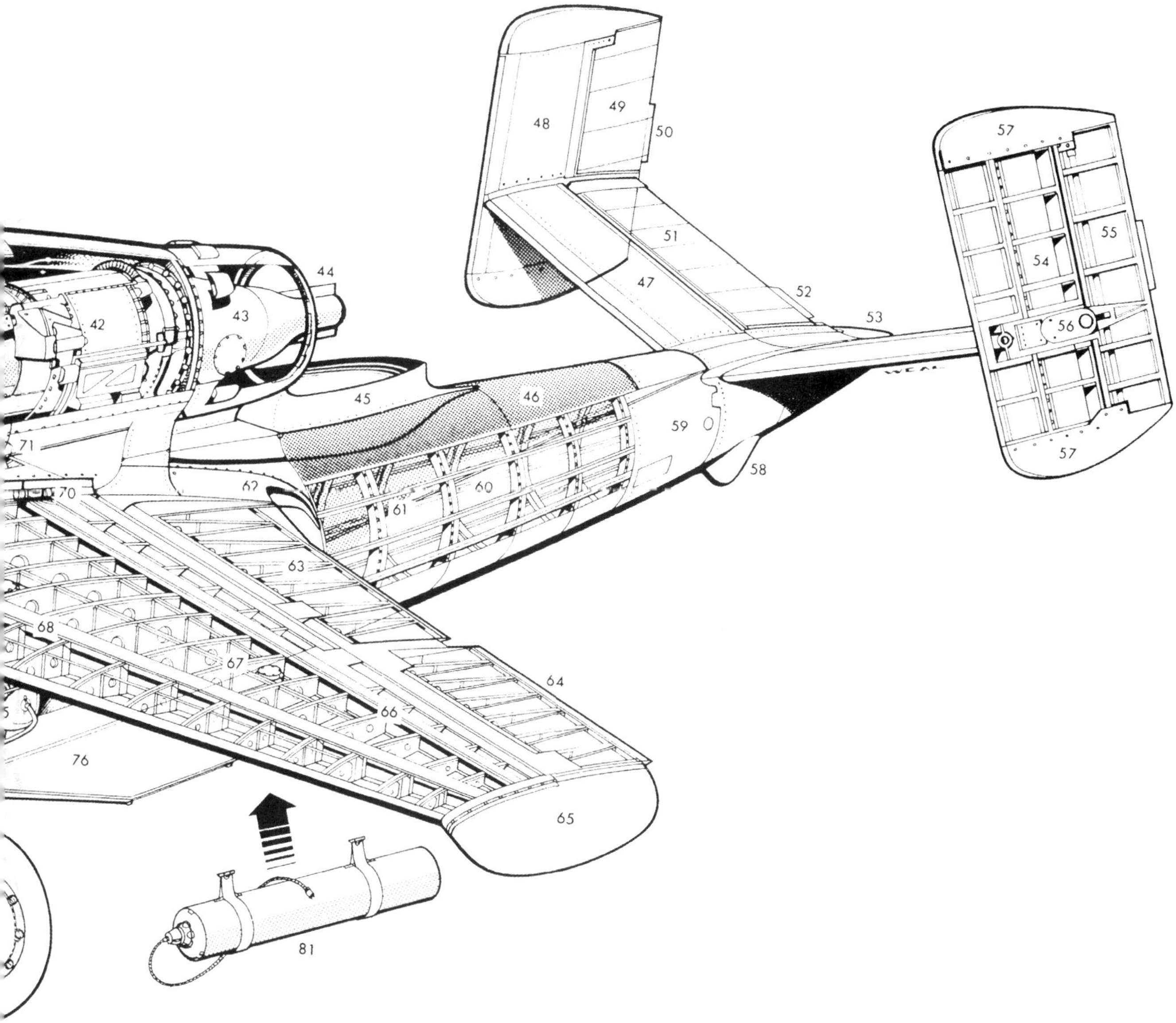

37 Oil tank
38 BMW 003E-1 Sturm axial-flow turbojet
39 Riedel starter fuel tank
40 Seven-stage axial compressor casing
41 FuG 24 R/T homing loop
42 Annular combustion chamber
43 Exhaust centre body
44 Exhaust outlet
45 Jet efflux fairing
46 Heat-resistant aft dorsal decking
47 Light metal tailplane
48 Starboard fin housing R/T receiver aerial
49 Starboard rudder
50 Rudder tab
51 Elevator
52 Elevator tab
53 Tailcone (movable through +3° to -2°)
54 Port tailfin structure
55 Rudder structure
56 Tailplane/tailfin attachment
57 Port tailfin upper and lower plates (housing R/T transmitter and IFF aerials)
58 Tailskid
59 Dural fuselage skinning
60 Monocoque fuselage construction
61 Control cables
62 Downswept wing root fillet
63 Hydraulically-operated flaps
64 Port aileron
65 Detachable downswept aluminium wingtip
66 Wooden T-section rear spar
67 Wooden wing structure
68 Wooden T-section forward mainspar
69 Impregnated integral wing tank (180 litre/39.6 Imp gal capacity)
70 Vertical wing/fuselage attachment bolts (four stations)
71 Single rear horizontal engine mounting/attachment bolt
72 Two forward vertical engine mounting/attachment bolts
73 Pressure-fed oil tank
74 Mainwheel hydraulic retraction jack
75 Mainwheel extension spring
76 Wooden mainwheel door
77 Mainwheel leg
78 Mainwheel tyre (660 mm 3 190mm)
79 Shock absorber scissor
80 Narrow-track main undercarriage assembly
81 Assisted take-off rocker unit (attached to fuselage immediately aft of mainwheel well)

Appendix 3 Captured Machines and Museum Exhibits

Above: An He 162, Werknummer 120 086, on display in England after the war. The machine still carries German markings.

Seen post-war in French markings, this is Werknummer 120 093, formerly 'White 2' of I./JG 1.

'Red 2', Werknummer 120 227, was also taken to England. It can be seen today on display at the RAF Museum in Hendon, London.

'Red 1' went to America and is pictured here wearing spurious German crosses.

In America 'Red 1', Werknummer 120 077, was coded T-2489. This photo shows US test pilot Bob Hoover landing at Muroc Air Force Base, California.

During the war 'Red 1' was flown by Leutnant Gerhard Hanf. After thorough tests in the USA it was restored and is today exhibited in the Planes of Fame Museum in Chino.

Kommodore Ihlefeld's 'White 23' originally had the Werknummer 120 230. After its tail was damaged, it was given the tail unit of the cannibalised 'White 7' and henceforth carried Werknummer 120 222.

Still bearing the Werknummer 120 222 of 'White 7', 'White 23' now resides in America's Smithsonian National Air and Space Museum (NASM) in Washington DC.

He 162A-1 'Yellow 5', Werknummer 310 003, wears all three of I./JG 1's Staffel badges. This is another of the five machines that went to France.

The Russians captured no complete examples of the He 162, but were able to reconstruct several machines out of the individual components that fell into their hands.

Above: 'Yellow 4', Werknummer 120 076, has a chequered history behind it. It was first ferried from Leck to England, then taken to the National Aviation Museum in Rockcliffe, Canada. Brought back to England, it was restored by Aero Vintage in Sussex and today stands in the Deutsches Technik Museum in Berlin.

A picture of the cockpit of 'Yellow 4' taken during restoration.

The pristine 'Yellow 4' is now at home in the Deutsches Technik Museum in Berlin.

Above: The Deutsches Technik Museum in Berlin also houses an Me 110 of the 'Dackelstaffel'. Standing in front of the machine are, from left to right, Hauptmann (retd.) Peter Spoden, Oberst (retd.) Hajo Herrmann and Oberstleutnant (retd.) Karl-Fritz Schlossstein.

A view of Berlin from one of the exhibition halls. A visit to the Technik Museum is well worth while!

Appendix 4 Heinkel He 162 Projects

The He 162c was a further development of the He 162A-2 featuring completely redesigned wing and tail surfaces. The end of the war prevented its being built.

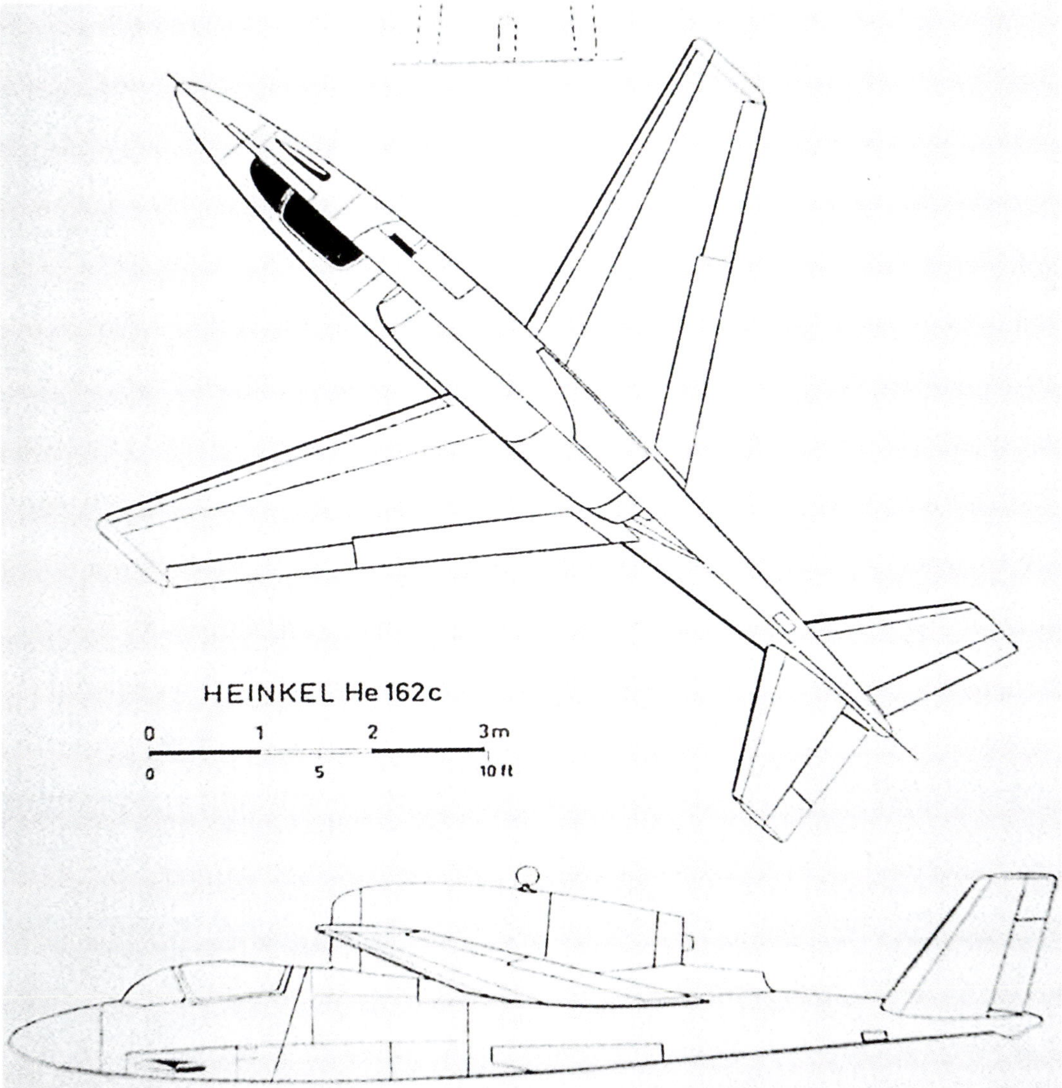

The swept-wing He 162d did not progress beyond the project stage either.

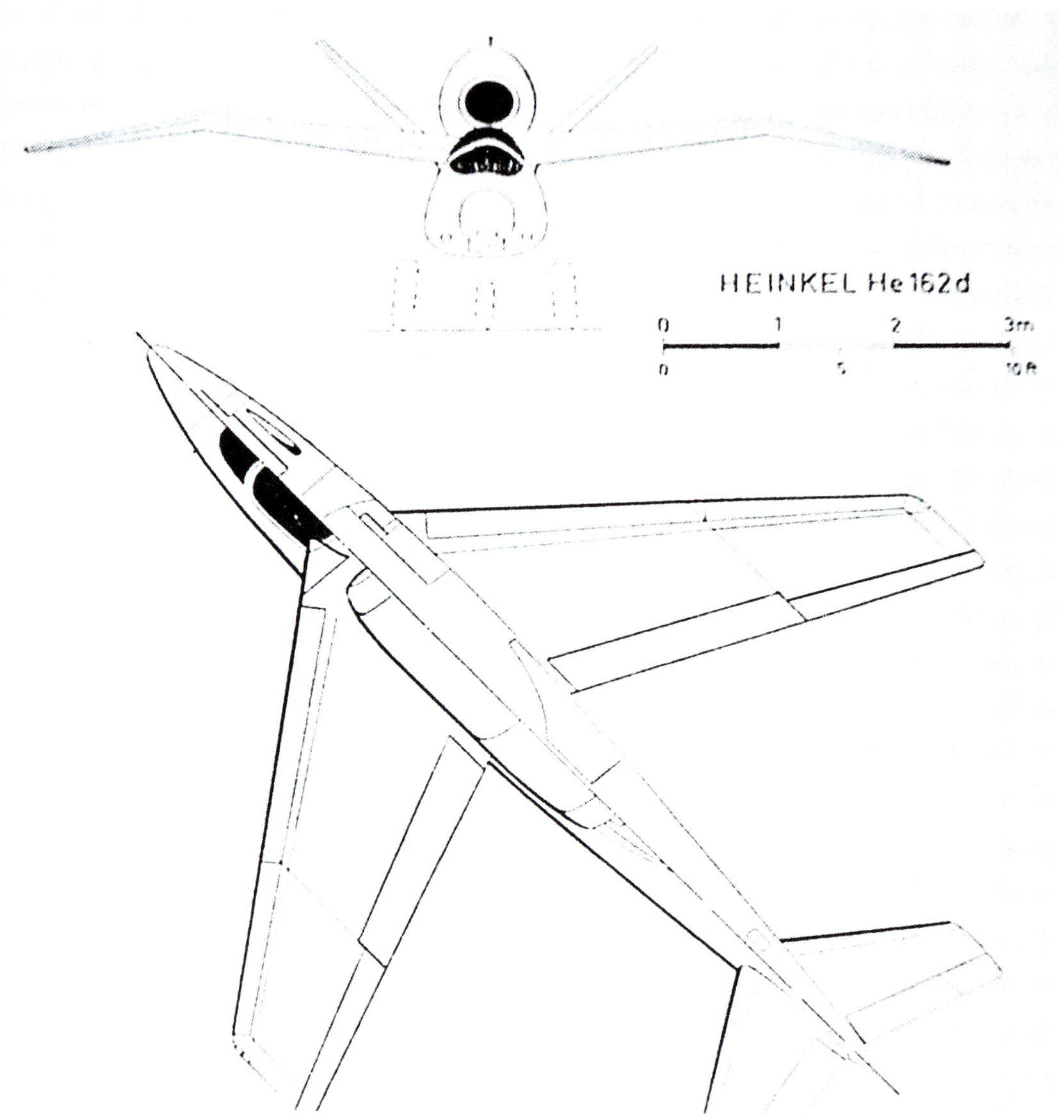

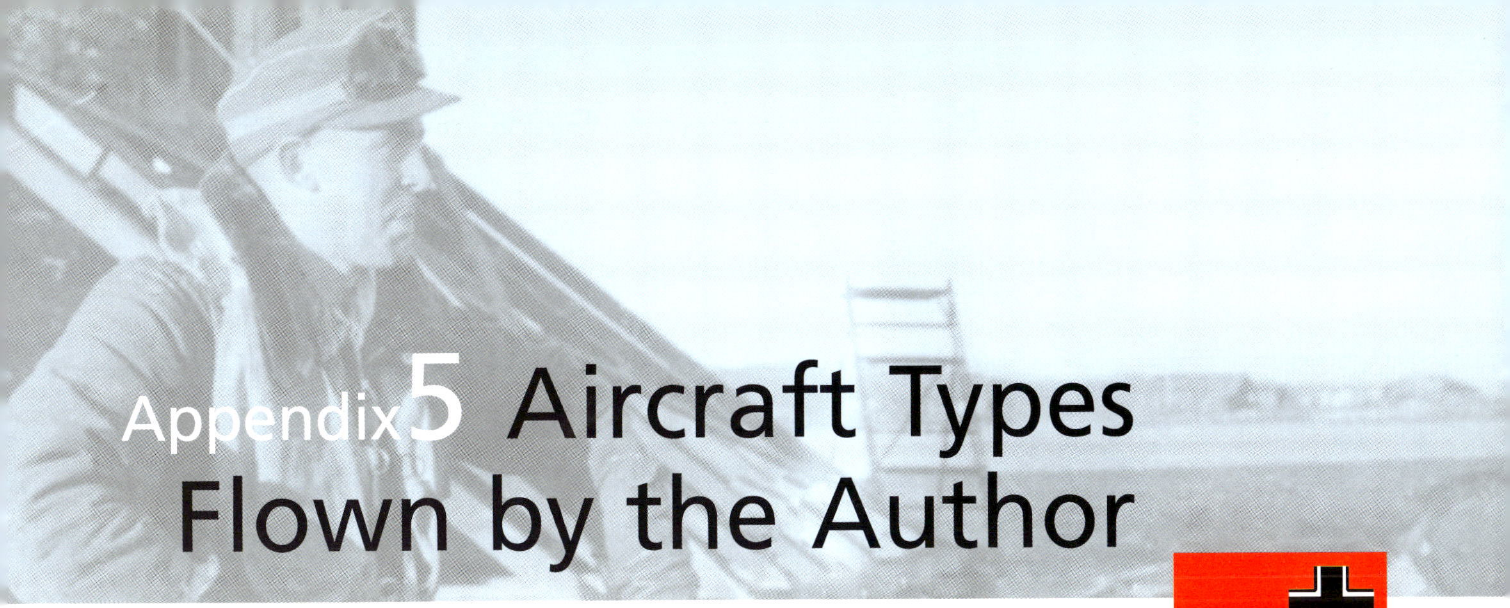

Appendix 5 Aircraft Types Flown by the Author

Arado Ar 66 and Arado Ar 96B-7

Bücker Bü 131 Jungmann

Caudron C 445

DFS Habicht and Kranich

Dornier Do 17

Fieseler Fi 156 Storch

Focke-Wulf Fw 44 Stieglitz, Fw 56 Stösser, Fw 58 Weihe, Fw 190A-6 and A-8

Gotha Go 145

Grunau Baby IIb

Heinkel He 51, He 70 Blitz, He 72 Kadett, He 111, He 162A-1 and A-2 Salamander

Junkers W 33, Ju 86, Ju 88

Messerschmitt Bf 108 Taifun, Me 110E, F and G.

Sources and Picture Credits

Sources

Bob, Hans-Ekkehard and Kube, Horst *JG 54 Grünherzjäger. Die Geschichte eines berühmten Geschwaders* (Helios-Verlag, Aachen, 2009)

Ethell, Jeffrey L. *Messerschmitt Komet* (Motorbuch Verlag, Stuttgart)

Mombeek, Eric *'Reichsverteidigung'. Die Geschichte des Jagdgeschwaders 1* (Brussels, 1993)

Schuck, Walter and Kube, Horst *Abschuss!* (Helios-Verlag, Aachen, 2007)

'Unsere Eismeer-Dackelstaffel 13. (ZS) JG 5' (Privately published)

Ziegler, Mano *Raketenjäger Me 163* (Motorbuch Verlag, Stuttgart)

Picture credits

Aero Vintage, Sussex; Archiv AK Junkers und Fliegerhorst Bernburg; Archiv Gemeinschaft der Flieger deutscher Streitkräfte, Archive Richard L. Reid, Fayetteville NC; Bernd Bredow; Deutsches Technik Museum Berlin; E.C.O. Arrivée, France; Manfred Griehl; Horst Kube; Memorial Flight Association; Musée d'Espace, France; Museum Flugsicherheit und Rettung, Baden-Airpark; Peter Petrick; Simon Schatz; Karl-Fritz Schlossstein.

Units